The Political Economy of Fiscal Reform in Central-Eastern Europe

The Political Economy of Fiscal Reform in Central-Eastern Europe

Hungary, Poland and the Czech Republic from 1989 to EU Accession

Frank Bönker

European University Viadrina, Frankfurt (Oder), Germany

Edward Elgar
Cheltenham, UK • Northampton, MA, USA

Published by
Edward Elgar Publishing Limited
Glensanda House
Montpellier Parade
Cheltenham
Glos GL50 1UA
UK

Edward Elgar Publishing, Inc.
136 West Street
Suite 202
Northampton
Massachusetts 01060
USA

A catalogue record for this book
is available from the British Library

ISBN-13: 978 1 84064 419 7
ISBN-10: 1 84064 419 2

Printed and bound in Great Britain by MPG Books Ltd, Bodmin, Cornwall

Contents

Tables

Abbreviations

AWS	Akcja Wyborcza Solidarność (Electoral Action Solidarity)
CASE	Center Analiz Społeczno-Ekonomicznych (Center for Economic and Social Research), Warsaw
CEPR	Center for Economic Policy Research, London
CERGE	Center for Economic Research and Graduate Education, Prague
CMEA	Council of Mutual Economic Assistance
CPI	Consumer price index
ČSSD	Česká Strana Sociální Demokracie (Czech Social Democratic Party)
CZK	Czech crowns
DCs	Developing countries
EBRD	European Bank for Reconstruction and Development
EU	European Union
Fidesz-MPP	Fiatal Demokraták Szövetsége Magyar Polgári Párt (Alliance of Young Democrats-Hungarian Civic Party)
FKGP	Független Kiszgazdapárt (Independent Smallholders Party)
GDP	Gross Domestic Product
GDR	German Democratic Republic
IMF	International Monetary Fund
KDNP	Kereszténydemokrata Néppárt (Christian Democratic People's Party)
KDU-ČSL	Křest'anská a demokratická unie – Československá strana lidová (Czech Christian-Democratic Party)
KLD	Kongres Liberalno-Demokratyczny (Liberal-Democratic Congress)
MDF	Magyar Demokrata Fórum (Hungarian Democratic Forum)
MSZP	Magyar Szocialista Párt (Hungarian Socialist Party)
NBER	National Bureau of Economic Research, Cambridge, Mass.
NBH	National Bank of Hungary
ODS	Občanská demokratická strana (Civic Democratic Party)
OECD	Organisation for Economic Co-operation and Development
PEPR	Political Economy of Policy Reform

PSL	Polskie Stronnictwo Ludowe (Polish Peasant Party)
RFE/RL	Radio Free Europe/Radio Liberty
SITE	Stockholm Institute for Transition Economics
SLD	Sojusz Lewicy Demokratycznej (Democratic Left Alliance)
SZDSZ	Szabad Demokraták Szövetsége (Alliance of Free Democrats)
UD	Unia Demokratyczna (Democratic Union)
UP	Unia Pracy (Labour Union)
US-DEU	Unie Svobody-Demokratická Unie (Union of Freedom-Democratic Union)
UW	Unia Wolności (Freedom Union)
VAT	Value Added Tax
WERI	World Economy Research Institute
WIIW	Wiener Institut für Internationale Wirtschaftsvergleiche (Vienna Institute for International Economic Studies)
WZB	Wissenschaftszentrum Berlin (Science Center Berlin)

Acknowledgements

This book has had a long gestation. I started thinking about fiscal reform in Eastern Europe in 1992 while working on a research project entitled 'Constitutional Politics and Economic Transformation in Post-communist Countries: A Comparative Analysis of Bulgaria, Czechoslovakia, and Hungary,' directed by Jon Elster, Claus Offe and Ulrich K. Preuß and based at the Center for European Law and Policy (ZERP) in Bremen. Back then, a dissertation on post-communist fiscal reform seemed the logical way of combining my long-standing interest in public finance and political economy with my new focus on Eastern Europe.

I brought some initial ideas for a dissertation with me to a position offered by Hans-Jürgen Wagener in the Department of Economics at the newly established European University Viadrina in Frankfurt (Oder) in 1994. My work on the political economy of fiscal reform in Eastern Europe then began to gain momentum. Due to other projects and rival obligations, however, it took me until May 1999 to complete my dissertation. Torn between economics and political science since my early student days, I eventually decided to declare my opus a dissertation in political science and to submit it to the Institute of Social Sciences at Humboldt University in Berlin. Thus, this book is based on a dissertation which originated at an institute for legal studies, was written in an economics department, and resulted in a Ph.D. in political science.

Unfortunately, other projects delayed the publication of my dissertation. In retrospect, however, this delay may have been a blessing in disguise. It has allowed me to update the analysis and to incorporate part of the findings of my post-dissertation research on post-communist fiscal reform.

On my journey, I have accumulated many debts. In Bremen, the members of the 'Bremen project' – Jon Elster, Ulrike Götting, Claus Offe, Ulrich K. Preuß, Friedbert W. Rüb – did their very best to smooth my way into academia. So did my colleagues at ZERP and at the Center for Social Policy Research (ZeS). At Viadrina, congenially located on the German-Polish border, students and colleagues alike have served as a much-appreciated source of inspiration. This particularly applies to my colleagues at the Frankfurt Institute for Transformation Studies (F.I.T.).

Over the years, I had the opportunity to present the results of my dissertation at seminars and conferences in Berlin, Frankfurt (Oder), Groningen, London, Lubniewice, Prague and Vienna. The feedback that I received on these occasions greatly helped me strengthen and refine my arguments. I would like to thank all seminar participants for their comments. In addition, I have benefited from various research trips to Hungary, Poland, and the Czech Republic and a stay in the United States in the autumn of 1996. These trips allowed me to gather additional material and to conduct numerous interviews with experts at the national ministries, the international financial institutions and at various universities and research institutes. I learned a lot from these interviews and would like to express my gratitude to all those who shared their knowledge and their time with me. Special thanks go to Michael Marrese, Jon Elster, Clemens Schütte and László Csaba who helped arrange longer stays at the IMF, at Columbia University, in Prague and in Budapest, respectively.

I owe a great deal to Claus Offe and Hans-Jürgen Wagener, my two supervisors. Both have tolerated my wandering between economics and political science and have provided valuable comments and a sense of direction at various stages of the process. A number of other people deserve mentioning. Wladimir Andreff, Bruno Dallago and three anonymous referees read the manuscript for the publisher, provided helpful suggestions and made the publication possible. At Elgar, Francine O'Sullivan and Jo Betteridge proved to be highly cooperative, efficient and patient editors. Judd Stitziel and Katherine Moran put the final touches on my English. Over the years, various student assistants helped me to collect material, make calculations and prepare tables and manuscripts. By far the most heavily involved have been Marcin Kowalewski and Karl Dang. László Csaba, Kristof Dascher, Jörg Jacobs, Kristine Kern, Katharina Müller, Klaus Müller, Friedbert W. Rüb and Andreas Ryll read and commented upon various parts of the manuscript. Klaus Deutsch and Ulrike Götting processed the most pages and served as important sources of moral support during the inevitable temporary lows. With the usual disclaimer, I would like to thank all these people for making this book possible.

1. Introduction: fiscal reform, post-communist transformation and the political economy of policy reform

> (W)e must remember that any radical reforms will be doomed to failure unless our financial policy is successful ... (Lenin, Report to the All-Russia Congress of Representatives of Financial Departments of Soviets, 18 May 1918) (Lenin 1965, p. 383).
>
> (P)ublic finance reform is a social transformation of much larger proportion than the political systemic changes of 1989 ... (it) is a profound and comprehensive social revolution requiring the redefinition of social values, individual behavior, and internalized motivations of everyday life (Bokros 1998, p. 539).
>
> (F)iscal policy became the epicenter of the transformation process (Kiss and Szapáry 2000, p. 233).

We live in an age of reform. In the last 25 years a 'global stampede' (Bergsten and Williamson 1994, p. 3) of market-oriented reforms has swept the world. Rich and poor, industrialized and developing, capitalist and formerly socialist countries alike have embarked upon far-reaching economic reforms. As part of a massive 'policy extinction' (Hood 1994), many countries have replaced economic policies that dominated the post-war scene. Fiscal reform has represented a major building block of these reforms. Governments around the world have engaged in consolidating budgets, reforming taxes and trimming government spending. The very fact that fiscal discipline comprises the first commandment of what John Williamson once dubbed the 'Washington consensus' (Williamson 1990, 1994, pp. 26-8) nicely illustrates the key role of fiscal reform in the overall drive to reform. Also indicative of this situation is the famous saying that the acronym of the IMF, one of the leading forces in world-wide economic reform, stands for 'It's Mainly Fiscal.'

This book deals with fiscal reform in post-communist Eastern Europe.[1] It does so from the perspective of the Political Economy of Policy Reform (PEPR), one of the newest branches of political economy. Pioneered by scholars such as Robert Bates, Stephan Haggard, Anne O. Krueger, Joan

Nelson and Dani Rodrik, PEPR has focused on the economic and political conditions for the initiation and consolidation of policy reforms. The rise of PEPR has been related intimately to the rush toward reform. Consequently, PEPR initially concentrated on economic reform in the developing countries and, to a lesser extent, in the OECD countries. Since the end of 1989 researchers from the PEPR camp increasingly have turned their gaze toward the East and have begun to cover the post-communist countries in transition as well.

From the perspective of PEPR, several features have made the East European transitions fascinating. By leaving almost no sphere of society untouched, reforms have amounted to ambitious attempts at designing whole societies from scratch and thus come close to the most comprehensive case of policy reform that one can imagine. The great transformation in the East has increased the number of new democracies embarking upon economic reform ('simultaneous reformers'), a class of countries that have attracted particular attention within PEPR (Haggard and Kaufman 1995). The parallel start of reforms in a sample of two dozen countries with a shared communist past has also offered unique opportunities for comparative empirical research into determinants, dynamics and problems of reform.

Fiscal reform ranks among the most interesting fields of post-communist economic reform and transformation for several reasons.[2] For starters, fiscal reform has been a crucial element of the overall reform package. Ever since the start of reforms, the utmost importance of fiscal reform for the success of economic transformation has been acknowledged almost universally. While fiscal restraint has played a key role in achieving and maintaining macroeconomic stability, comprehensive tax and expenditure reforms have represented major ingredients of the overhaul of the communist institutional framework.

A second interesting feature of post-communist fiscal reform has been its continuing relevance. Although its agenda has shifted over time, fiscal reform has remained a key reform issue, making it a fascinating site for studying how the economic and political conditions for the adoption of reforms have changed during the transformation.

Third, fiscal reform has featured prominently in overall economic reform in the West, the South and the East alike. This distinguishes fiscal reform from other, more specific components of post-communist economic reform, such as privatization, and makes it a good starting point for cross-regional comparisons and for examining the peculiarities of the post-communist context and their implications for the fate of reforms.

Finally, the broad consensus on the strategy of fiscal reform is noteworthy. Compared to other fields of economic reform, fiscal reform has been characterized by limited controversies over the outline of reforms. Some debates notwithstanding, the large majority of reformers, advisers and outside observers have agreed upon a fairly broad range of measures. This consensus has made the existing national differences in fiscal performance puzzling. At the same time, it has facilitated the identification of those factors that have governed the political feasibility of reforms. By reducing differences in preferences, the far-reaching professional consensus on the direction of reforms has made it easier to concentrate on the impact of political constraints on the design and the results of reform.

While fiscal reform thus looks particularly suited for studying the political economy of post-communist economic reform, there have been few attempts at analysing post-communist fiscal reform from a PEPR perspective. This is where this book comes in. It features a comparative analysis of the political constraints on fiscal reform in Hungary, Poland and the Czech Republic from the start of the post-communist transition to EU accession. Given this particular focus, this book builds on, and aims to contribute to, three major bodies of research: PEPR, transformation research and the literature on post-communist fiscal reform.

The political economy of policy reform

PEPR has emerged as a distinct field of political economy over the last 15 to 20 years. It has brought together different disciplines, most notably economics and political science, and has featured 'hard' formal modelling as well as 'soft' informal reasoning, case studies as well as econometric analyses. What has held the field together has been a shared interest in the economic and political conditions for the successful initiation and consolidation of policy reforms.[3] This focus has rested on the assumption that reforms normally face endemic obstacles which render their adoption politically difficult and unlikely.

Several trends in the social sciences have favoured the consolidation of this new field and have been conducive to its broad interdisciplinary orientation. On the most general level, economists' renewed interest in political-economic interactions has converged with political scientists' increasing insistence on the political determinants of economic performance. Within economics the Public Choice school, New Development Economics and New Political Macroeconomics have propagated positive theories of economic policy-making that have ended the reign of welfare economics' benevolent dictator by bringing politics back into economics (Drazen 2000; Persson and Tabellini 2000, 2004). Within political science a powerful comparative political economy has emerged since the late 1970s which has likewise dwelt upon the impact of political variables on the choices and the outcomes of economic policy (Hall 1997). Along with the general rediscovery of institutions and the spread of the rational choice approach within political science, this double renaissance of political economy has paved the way for interdisciplinary collaboration and mutual cross-fertilization.

The rise of PEPR has been closely linked to the wave of economic reforms that have shaken the world since the early 1980s. Early empirical analyses largely focused on economic adjustment and reform in developing countries in the aftermath of the debt crisis of the early 1980s (Bates and Krueger (eds) 1993a; Haggard and Kaufmann (eds) 1992; Nelson et al. 1989; Nelson (ed.), 1990; Krueger 1993). Reforming OECD countries have been included only gradually and selectively. Coverage has been more or less confined to the new democracies of Southern Europe, with an occasional glance at New Zealand and Australia (see Haggard and Webb (eds) 1994; Bresser Pereira et al. 1993; Williamson (ed.) 1994). Although authors from the PEPR camp have drawn on findings for OECD countries, for instance those on corporatism, they so far have largely 'respected' the traditional domains of comparative public policy and comparative political economy and have refrained from systematically including the experience of a broader set of OECD countries. Post-communist countries, however, have been embraced more quickly. Since the mid-1990s, a number of authors have started to address post-communist economic reform from the perspective of PEPR (Bartlett 1997; Greskovits 1998, 1999, 2000, 2001; Haggard et al. 2001; Nelson 1993, 1997, 2001; Müller 1999, 2003; Orenstein 2000).[4] Some have used the post-communist case to launch strong attacks against part of the conventional PEPR wisdom (Hellman 1998; EBRD 1999, Chapter 5; Stark and Bruszt 1998, pp. 109-201; Treisman 1998; Shleifer and Treisman 2000; Schamis 2002).

This book builds upon the burgeoning PEPR literature and utilizes insights from PEPR for understanding post-communist fiscal reform. Simultaneously, it seeks to contribute to PEPR by bringing to bear evidence from new cases and unexamined fields. Testing the 'portability' of PEPR concepts and hypotheses, it investigates the extent to which the post-communist experience confirms, refutes or qualifies standard findings on the economic and political conditions necessary for a successful initiation and consolidation of reforms.

Transformation research

Fiscal reform has represented but one building block of the great overall transition to capitalism and democracy. This transition has transformed communist into post-communist studies and has given birth to a new field of research that is now widely known as transformation research (King 2000). Given its PEPR perspective, this book takes a specific position within this booming field of research.

At the very heart of the post-communist transformation is a political project of large-scale economic and political change (Offe 1991; Wagener 1997; Wiesenthal 1997; Roland 2000). Consequently, transformation research focuses on the dynamics, problems and consequences of comprehensive institutional reforms. Roughly speaking there are two classes of characteristic transformation problems. A first set of issues clusters around the conditions for the passage of reforms and the introduction of a new set of formal institutions. Seen from this angle, typical transformation problems include issues such as the solution of collective action problems, the exploitation of political windows of opportunity, the design and sequencing of reforms, the establishment and maintenance of political support and credibility, the avoidance of hyperrationality traps, the handling of rationality limits and dilemmas of simultaneity.

A second set of problems is associated with the transplantation of formal institutions in a new and different context. Given different cultural patterns and traditions,[5] imported institutions often do not produce the same outcomes achieved in the West but instead generate unintended and unexpected results. Hence, a second class of typical transformation problems comprises issues such as the transfer of institutions, local adjustments of formal institutions, the co-evolution of formal and informal institutions, the moral infrastructure of institutions and the gradual diffusion of new behavioural patterns.

Post-communist fiscal reform can be analysed from both angles. It can be conceived either as an exercise in overcoming political resistance to unpopular tax and expenditure reforms or as an attempt to make a 'new' tax system work in societies still characterized by a bundle of 'old' administrative traditions, attitudes towards the state and notions of justice. It goes without saying that both perspectives complement each other and are perfectly legitimate. With its PEPR approach, however, this book subscribes to the first perspective and concentrates on the political dynamics of fiscal reform.[6]

This book also differs from some of the literature on post-communist transformations in that it puts East European economic reform into a comparative perspective. The investigation emphasizes the commonalities of fiscal reform in the First, Second and Third World and regards the uniqueness of the East European transition as an open question rather than as a given. All too often, the belabouring of the exceptional and unprecedented character of the East European transitions, as well as ritualized complaints about the missing theory of transformation, have tended to separate research on Eastern Europe from the general social science literature. In many cases, the resulting ghettoized research failed to exploit available knowledge on economic and political reform and has prevented observers from drawing the general lessons that the East might have to tell (Schmitter and Karl 1994; Karl and Schmitter 1995).

Against this background, this book's contribution to our understanding of post-communist transformations is twofold. By examining the economic and political factors that have governed the likelihood and the course of fiscal reform, the analysis adds to the growing body of literature on the determinants of post-communist economic reform. Prompted by the striking national differences in patterns and outcomes of post-communist economic transformation, various authors have sought to identify those economic and political factors that explain why, despite apparently similar starting conditions, reform trajectories have differed so greatly (Åslund et al. 1996; Fish 1998; Hellman 1998; EBRD 1999: Chapter 5; Kitschelt 2001, 2003, 2004). On a more general level, this book also sheds some light on the peculiarities of the transition countries. It asks to what extent the economic and political conditions for the initiation and consolidation of reform that have prevailed in the East have differed from those in the South and the West and, moreover, how these differences in the context of reforms have influenced the patterns and outcomes of reform. Hence, this is also a study about the 'normalcy' and the 'normalization' of post-communist fiscal reform.

Post-communist fiscal reform

Post-communist fiscal reform cannot seriously be called a neglected issue. Quite to the contrary, it has attracted considerable attention right from the beginning of the transformation. Unlike so many other difficulties and complications, the fiscal problems that have surfaced since 1989 have been, by and large, anticipated problems. From early on observers have voiced warnings that a fatal combination of 'downward' trends in revenue and 'upward' trends in expenditures might result in a severe fiscal crisis. Renowned economists such as János Kornai (1990, 1992a), Ronald McKinnon (1993) and Vito Tanzi (1991a, 1991b, 1993a, 1993b, 1994, 1996, 1997, 1998, 2001; Tanzi and Tsibouris 2000, 2001) have dealt with post-communist fiscal reform. International organizations, in particular the IMF and the EBRD, have addressed it broadly. Leading international research institutes and networks such as CASE, CEPR, the Institute for EastWest

Studies or the International Center for Economic Growth have organized major comparative research projects.[7] Besides economists, sociologists (Campbell 1992, 1994, 1995a, 1995b, 1996, 2001; Jessop 1993) and, with some delay, political scientists (Dimitrov 2006, Brusis and Dimitrov 2001; Haggard et al. 2001; Hallerberg et al. 2002a, 2002b) have addressed the issue.

This impressive body of literature notwithstanding, some blind spots can easily be identified. The single most prominent is the selective coverage of political constraints. Although the available literature on the OECD and developing countries consistently notes the crucial role of political constraints in shaping the record of fiscal reform, there are still only a few in-depth analyses of post-communist fiscal reform from a political economy perspective. Moreover, the available studies focus on particular countries, most notably Hungary and Russia (Haggard et al. 2001; Shleifer and Treisman 2000), or concentrate on specific aspects such as the role of elections (Hallerberg et al. 2002a, 2002b) or the importance of budgetary institutions (Gleich 2003; Brusis and Dimitrov 2001; Dimitrov 2006).

This book aims at complementing the existing analyses of fiscal reform in Eastern Europe by systematically reconstructing the impact of temporal changes and national differences in the political feasibility of reforms on the design and the outcomes of post-1989 fiscal reform in Hungary, Poland and the Czech Republic, three front runners of economic transformation.

Methodological approach and country sample

In order to tackle these issues, I have used an approach which Gustav Ranis and Syed Akhtar Mahmood (1992, p. 213) once slightly ironically dubbed 'comparative analytical economic history.' The empirical part of the analysis fashions case studies of post-communist fiscal reform in Hungary, Poland and the Czech Republic.[8] It goes without saying that such a qualitative approach causes some problems and makes it difficult to subject hypotheses to a rigorous testing.[9] In view of this book's topic, however, two considerations have tipped the balance in favour of case studies and against a quantitative approach.

For one thing, the small number of observations, the intricate problems of controlling for collinearity in a situation of transition and the bad quality of the data, especially for the first years of transformation, have severely limited the scope for serious econometric studies (Kitschelt 2001). Thus, it is not surprising that only a handful of authors have dared to present quantitative studies of the determinants of fiscal deficits in the transition countries so far (Abed and Davoudi 2000, pp. 24-30; Pirttilä 2001; Gleich 2003; Hallerberg et al. 2002a).

A second rationale for a qualitative research design stems from the fact that many of the variables on which this book focuses are complex and multidimensional and, therefore, difficult to quantify. This applies to the dependent as well as to the independent variables. As for the dependent variable, quantitative indicators such as the size of the deficit or revenue and expenditure shares are often not sufficient to fully characterize the state of fiscal reform. Difficulties are even bigger in the case of the independent variables. While plenty of literature on quantitative indicators of government strength or political stability exists (Wagschal 1996, pp. 39-72; Sierman 1998, pp. 27-47), it seems fair to say that the empirical specification of these concepts remains a big problem. Political systems are complex institutional configurations, highly contextual and shaped by myriad institutional devices. Moreover, political outcomes are more indeterminate and path-dependent than economic ones (Pierson 2000). This is why it is so difficult to capture the functioning of political institutions by a limited number of quantitative indicators and why these indicators more often than not look crude, ad hoc and arbitrary. Such crudeness may not be a significant problem in a huge sample of stable political systems. Yet it is bound to become one in the case of small samples of new democracies which still suffer from a lack of institutional consolidation.

Various considerations have been made in the choice of the particular country sample upon which this book rests. To start with, Hungary, Poland and the Czech Republic are among the transition countries that are best-suited for studying the role of political constraints at various stages of the transformation. The three countries have belonged to the front runners of economic and political reform ever since the demise of communism. This is evidenced by all country rankings and it is also borne out by the fact that Hungary, Poland and the Czech Republic are among the first wave of EU members from the East. Hence, the country sample chosen allows an investigation of how the conditions for the initiation and consolidation of reform have shifted since 1989 and how 'normal' political constraints have become in the course of the transformation.

Second, the country sample is characterized by a combination of similarities and differences which makes it possible to hold constant some background variables and to concentrate on the impact of a handful of variables that feature prominently in PEPR.[10] To start with similarities, Hungary, Poland and the Czech Republic have shared a number of important features:

- The basic commitment to economic reform and transformation has been uncontroversial. Anti-Communist forces won the first parliamentary elections and the former communist parties have either been marginalized (Czech Republic) or transformed (Hungary, Poland).[11] Ever since 1989, Hungary, Poland and the Czech Republic have been among the most advanced transition countries.

- The countries belonged to the 'outer' empire of the Soviet Union and were independent states before 1989. Hence, they did not face the problems of state-building that haunted many successor states of the former Soviet Union or the former Yugoslavia.
- None of the three countries has been confronted with civil war or Russian-style regional disintegration. They have all maintained a functioning state apparatus. The numerous problems with patronage and corruption notwithstanding, the 'privatization' of the state has been limited (Bönker 2003a).
- The three countries have shared a far-reaching orientation towards the EU. Due to history, geography and reform commitment, they have been regarded as prospective EU members right from the beginning of the transformation. This has made the EU an important 'external anchor' for the transformation (Berglöf and Roland 1997; Bönker 2006a).

Owing to these similarities, the broad context of fiscal reform in Hungary, Poland and the Czech Republic has been similar. At the same time, other conditions that are likely to influence the feasibility of reforms have varied across the three countries. Due to distinct modes of extrication from communism, the new democratic governments enjoyed different reform mandates and 'honeymoons.' The economic and fiscal situation during early transformation was more critical in Poland than in Hungary and Czechoslovakia. Moreover, the three countries have differed with regard to political stability, executive authority and the position of reformers within government. It is this peculiar mixture of similarities and differences which allows for a 'most similar systems' design and makes this study's country sample suited to comparative research into the economic and political conditions for the initiation and consolidation of reforms.

The third reason behind this study's country sample is that Hungary, Poland and the Czech Republic have all witnessed important changes in key explanatory variables over time. As regards to the economic situation, all countries have experienced both periods of economic recession and periods of economic growth. Political conditions have likewise been subject to changes. This applies to the popular support for reforms, executive authority and the position of reformers within the government. These shifts make it possible to complement cross-sectional comparisons with analyses of the impact of changing conditions in individual countries. Such 'within-case' (or 'internal') comparisons alleviate the problems of over-determination and lack of discrimination which haunt small-N studies with their characteristic combination of few cases and many variables.

Plan of attack

I continue in Chapter 2 with a survey of previous findings on the political economy of fiscal reform in the OECD countries and the developing countries. This overview recalls why fiscal reform is a politically difficult and unlikely project and elaborates upon those economic and political conditions that facilitate the initiation and consolidation of reforms. In doing so, Chapter 2 also identifies the key variables to be analysed and the guiding hypotheses to be examined in the empirical parts of the study.

Chapter 3 sketches the peculiarities of post-communist fiscal reform. It highlights the salience of fiscal reform by providing a stylized description of the communist fiscal system and by outlining some important relationships between fiscal reform and other elements of post-communist economic transformation. In addition, it summarizes the debate over the strategy of post-communist fiscal reform and demonstrates that the latter has been a relatively uncontroversial element of economic transformation. Finally, Chapter 3 contrasts starting points, agendas and contexts of fiscal reform in OECD, developing and transition countries in order to introduce the specific conditions for post-communist fiscal reform.

The next three chapters feature in-depth analyses of different stages of post-1989 fiscal reform in Hungary, Poland and the Czech Republic. Chapter 4 looks at the initiation of fiscal reform at the outset of the transformation; Chapter 5 deals with the continuation of fiscal reform during the post-communist fiscal crisis; and Chapter 6 covers fiscal reform from the end of the post-communist fiscal crisis to EU accession. Each of the chapters reconstructs how the prevailing economic and political conditions have shaped fiscal reform and to what extent political constraints can account for common and/or divergent national trajectories.

Chapter 7 concludes the analysis by putting the different pieces together and by relating the empirical findings to the issues raised in this introduction and in Chapters 2 and 3. More specifically the chapter asks what post-communist fiscal reform in Hungary, Poland and the Czech Republic reveals about the sources of national differences in fiscal performance, about the factors that make the initiation and consolidation of reforms likely and about the peculiarities that set the transition countries apart from other countries.

NOTES

1. The terms 'Eastern Europe' and 'Central-Eastern Europe' are used quite differently in the literature. This book takes 'Eastern Europe' as a generic term for all post-communist countries in Europe and on the territory of the former Soviet Union. It thus regards Central-Eastern Europe as part of Eastern Europe.
2. For the general case on why public finances are a good starting point for addressing broader social and political issues, see Schumpeter 1918.
3. For surveys of PEPR, see Haggard and Webb 1993; Haggard et al. 1995; Rodrik 1993, 1996, Tommasi and Velasco 1996 and, more recently, Haggard 2000. Some early classics are collected in Sturzenegger and Tommasi (eds) 1998.
4. For my own earlier attempts at analysing post-communist economic and fiscal reform from a PEPR perspective, see Bönker 1995, 2001a, 2001b.
5. A shorthand for informal institutions, social capital, culture, knowledge, social norms, human capital, capabilities, trust, skills etc.
6. The second perspective has, for instance, been taken by the interesting research project on cultural determinants of Russian tax policy and taxation by Jakob Fruchtmann and Heiko Pleines (Fruchtmann and Pleines 2002).
7. CASE: Dąbrowski 1997, 2000; Dąbrowski et al. 2005; CEPR: Newbery (ed.) 1995; Ambrus-Lakatos and Schaffer (eds) 1997; Cracôw Academy of Economics: Campbell and Owsiak (eds) 1994; Institute for EastWest Studies: Mizsei (ed.) 1994; International Center for Economic Growth: McLure et al. 1995.
8. From the perspective of this study, Czechoslovakia and the Czech Republic can be treated as a single case since the key economic reformers remained the same and economic policy exhibited a high degree of continuity before and after the dissolution of Czechoslovakia at the end of 1992.
9. This is not the place to engage in debates on the general merits and drawbacks of qualitative and quantitative research designs. For overviews, see Collier 1993; King et al. 1994; Hall 2003; Brady and Collier (eds) 2004.
10. For a systematic comparison of Hungary, Poland and the Czech Republic, see also Offe 1996, pp. 134-44.
11. As Fish (1998) has shown, there was a strong correlation between the outcome of the founding elections and the state of post-communist economic reform in the mid-1990s. For the underlying mechanisms, see also Bunce 1998, pp. 199-205 and Kitschelt 2003.

2. The political economy of fiscal reform in the OECD countries and the developing countries

2.1 INTRODUCTION

Fiscal reform has been a key element of the wave of economic reforms that have swamped the world in the last two decades. In both the OECD and developing countries, governments have sought to reduce budget deficits, to contain spending and to overhaul taxes.[1] This global move toward fiscal reform has provided plenty of material for studying the conditions for the successful initiation and consolidation of policy reform. Against this backdrop, this chapter takes stock of our knowledge about the political economy of fiscal reform. Drawing on findings from economics and political science, as well as on the experience of both the OECD countries and the developing countries, it brings together different strands of the literature, with a view to identifying key variables and guiding hypotheses for the subsequent analysis of post-communist fiscal reform.

Section 2.2 outlines a number of endemic obstacles that make fiscal reform a politically costly and 'courageous' project. With these notorious problems and impediments in mind, the chapter goes on to elaborate upon those economic and political conditions that may help render fiscal reform nevertheless feasible. Variables discussed include crises and mandates (Section 2.3), the position of reformers within government (Section 2.4), the government's executive authority (Section 2.5), the consolidation of democracy (Section 2.6), government ideology (Section 2.7), reform design (Section 2.8) and international organizations (Section 2.9). Section 2.10 concludes by discussing the relationships among these variables.

2.2   MISSION IMPOSSIBLE: WHY FISCAL REFORM IS UNLIKELY

Despite ubiquitous talk of reform, policy reforms are in fact rare and unlikely events. If initiated at all, reforms are normally delayed, watered down or only partly implemented. Drawing on the theoretical literature, the basic obstacles and barriers which make policy reforms politically difficult can be placed under three headings: collective action problems, distributional conflicts and investment problems.[2] The snag with fiscal reform is that it is regularly fraught with a combination of all three types of impediments. The cumulation of these obstacles renders fiscal reform a politically difficult and, in effect, unlikely undertaking. Under 'normal' economic and political conditions, fiscal reform tends to be unpopular and to draw fierce resistance from all kinds of interest groups. This is why the advocates of reform are normally isolated within government, why governments, as a rule, tend to shy away from reforms and why, as a consequence, fiscal reform so rarely occurs.[3]

Collective action problems

Many policy reforms are collective goods in that the benefits they bring about are non-exclusive and almost universal (Geddes 1994, pp. 24-42). Yet if everyone gains from a reform, regardless of one's own contribution to its success, rational actors will not invest effort in a reform and instead will wait for others to act. As a result of such free riding, common interests can easily remain latent. Such collective action problems constitute one endemic obstacle to the adoption of reforms.

Fiscal reform often shows some features of a collective good. Virtually everybody benefits if the tightening of the fiscal stance brings down inflation, if fiscal restraint helps to prevent an overheating of the economy or if tax reform improves efficiency by reducing the dead-weight losses of taxation. Yet it is precisely this common interest in fiscal reform which makes it so difficult to find volunteers in the battles against budget deficits and for tax reform. Everyone will seek instead to protect his or her pet expenditures and tax concessions and hope that the others will make sacrifices and concessions.

Distributional conflicts

Collective action problems occur in the case of homogeneous interests. A second set of problems arises from heterogeneous interests and distributional struggles. Most policy reforms produce some losers. Since compensation is often unfeasible and/or not credible (Dixit 1996), these losers will turn against reforms and may succeed in blocking changes, even if they represent only a tiny minority of the population. As a small group, losers normally benefit from the notorious asymmetries of collective action that privilege small groups facing concentrated costs over large groups confronted with diffuse benefits (Olson 1965). The more concentrated the costs or benefits are and the higher the awareness of an issue is, the stronger the incentives are to get engaged and the easier it is to overcome problems associated with collective action. In addition, institutional arrangements may bestow losers with veto positions, thereby giving them a disproportionate say in the political process.

Three mechanisms further complicate these distributional conflicts. First, prospect theory suggests that, contrary to the standard notion of expected utility maximization, losses are regularly felt more strongly than gains. This 'negativity bias' further strengthens the losers' chances of successfully blocking reforms (Pierson 1994, p. 18). Secondly, uncertainty can hamper the adoption of reforms. Ex ante uncertainty regarding the identities of winners and losers can lead to the ex ante rejection of reforms that would be supported by a majority ex post, even if individuals are risk-neutral and maximize their expected utility (Fernandez and Rodrik 1991). Likewise, uncertainty about other groups' willingness to pay for reforms can heighten distributional conflicts and result in a 'war of attrition' (Alesina and Drazen 1991; Bulow and Klemperer 1999).[4] Third, distributional conflicts can lead to unstable coalitions. In the case of zero-sum distribution problems, majority voting does not result in stable majorities because losers can bribe part of the majority coalition (Tullock 1959).

In the case of fiscal reform, distributional conflicts loom large. The general gains resulting from fiscal reform are often diffuse and not sufficient to compensate those hurt by cuts in expenditures or a broadening of the tax base. Moreover the burden of fiscal adjustment can be distributed in different ways. This degree of freedom invites struggles over the distribution of adjustment costs which can prevent the passage of reforms or lead to problematic compromises.

Investment problems

Further impediments to reform can arise from what might be called investment problems. Policy reforms frequently take the form of investments, with costs accruing up front and preceding benefits. Moreover, while costs are regularly well known ex ante, benefits tend to be uncertain and often can be learned only ex post. Such a j-curve payoff structure entails a genuine temporal problem. If benefits materialize only after a substantial delay, 'impatience,' as caused by risk aversion and short time-horizons, can bedevil policy reforms by tipping the balance in favour of the status quo.

As a matter of fact, fiscal reform also tends to raise severe investment problems. According to conventional wisdom, a consolidation of the budget and a tightening of the fiscal stance go hand in hand with substantial transitory social costs.[5] According to this interpretation, which is based on Keynesian and structuralist thinking, macroeconomic stabilization typically implies recession and unemployment in the short run. As a consequence, fiscal reformers normally are faced with the politically risky challenge of having to lead the electorate through a 'valley of tears' before things get better and benefits start to materialize.

2.3   CRISES AND MANDATES

Even though reforms are unlikely, they nevertheless occur. PEPR has identified a number of mechanisms that can help start and sustain fiscal reform. Among the most prominent are crises and mandates (Keeler 1993). Anne O. Krueger (1993, p. 124) has summarized the conventional wisdom:

> Most reforms seem to take place in one of two circumstances: Either a new government comes to power or a perceived economic crisis prompts action. To be sure, these two events are not mutually inconsistent: A new government is more likely to result when performance is perceived to be unsatisfactory; and that perception is more probable when an economic crisis takes place.

Crises and mandates share a common characteristic: Both can help overcome obstacles to reform by granting reformers 'a temporary autonomy from the push and pull of short-term political pressures' (Rodrik 1994, p. 212). By weakening resistance to reforms in the short-run and by temporarily strengthening the position of reformers, crises and mandates can open up reform windows and give rise to what Leszek Balcerowicz (1994a, pp. 176-7, 1994b, pp. 84-7) has called 'periods of extra-ordinary politics.'

Crises often serve as 'focusing events' (Kingdon 1995, p. 94; Birkland 1997) and wake-up calls.[6] Apart from increasing the costs of non-reform, they may also signal the non-sustainability of the current policies. In effect, they tend to stimulate collective learning processes and to discredit entrenched governments and policy packages. Crises activate macro-political concerns about the legitimacy and the survival of the government (Grindle and Thomas 1991, pp. 104-7). The widespread feeling that 'something must be done,' joined by a sense of urgency and fear, increases the readiness to grant greater autonomy to reformers and to forgo short-term advantages. For all these reasons, crises can serve as catalysts, 'shocking countries out of traditional policy patterns' (Williamson and Haggard 1994, p. 562).[7]

Plausible as the 'crisis hypothesis' may sound, its problems and weaknesses are also well-known.[8] First, its ability to predict is limited. For starters, it is difficult, if not outright impossible, 'to determine what is, and what is not, a crisis' (Krueger 1993, p. 124). A deterioration of the economic situation can be interpreted rather differently by the various actors and observers. The political fallout resulting from economic problems strongly depends on whether they are perceived as exogenous or endogenous, temporary or long-lasting. There also is the possibility of pre-emptive reforms, that is, reforms triggered by anticipated crises. Moreover, while crises may favour certain responses, they do not determine fully the timing and the content of reforms.[9] The bottom line of all this is that it is quite difficult to subject the crisis hypothesis to empirical testing and nearly impossible to draw clearly the implications of a worsening economic situation for the intensity and the direction of reforms.

A second problem with the 'crisis hypothesis' is that crises also can inhibit reforms, whether by withdrawing resources or by intensifying political pressures on the government. For instance, while ballooning budget deficits may stimulate attempts at macroeconomic stabilization, they also deprive the government of much-needed resources to sweeten reforms and to compensate losers. Generally speaking, crises put a premium on those reform measures that can be adopted relatively quickly, but have an ambivalent effect on more complex structural reforms. Cases in point are tax and social security reforms that may benefit from the momentum generated by economic and fiscal crises but which may need simultaneously time and money in order not to fall victim to short-term political and fiscal manoeuvring. This ambiguity is at the heart of the long-standing debate in the literature on tax reform as to whether 'fiscal health' or 'fiscal stress' is more conducive to tax reform.

Against this background, it is not surprising that the empirical evidence for the 'crisis hypothesis' is mixed. On the one hand, the available research basically confirms the broad connection between economic problems and policy responses. Economic reform in the developing countries over the past 25 years has been stimulated by the failure of economic populism and by the economic difficulties in the wake of the debt crisis. This is suggested by the fact that many publications on economic reform in the developing countries, in one way or another, combine the words 'crisis' and 'reform' (or 'adjustment') in their titles.[10] More importantly, a number of quantitative analyses for different samples of developing countries find that severe growth and inflation crises are in fact associated with greater reform efforts (Bruno and Easterly 1996; Drazen and Easterly 2001; Pitlik and Wirth 2003).

In a way, however, these findings may not be more surprising than observing smoke following a fire (Rodrik 1996, p. 27). If crises indicate non-sustainability, one would expect eventually a kind of policy correction almost by definition. In fact, closer examination of the 'crisis hypothesis' suggests caveats and qualifications (Corrales 1998). While crises often have played a critical role in stimulating reforms, they are 'clearly neither a necessary nor a sufficient condition' (Williamson and Haggard 1994, p. 565). One can recall plenty of cases of crisis without reform and, more importantly, reform without crisis, including Australia in 1983, Colombia in 1989 and Portugal in 1985. Moreover, the nexus between crisis and reform remains vague, as most available studies do not reveal a clear relationship between the nature of crises, on the one hand, and the timing and the character of the policy responses, on the other (Nelson 1990, pp. 325-6). Given the broad spectrum of conceivable responses to a deteriorating economic and fiscal situation, neither universal thresholds and trigger points nor general patterns of reaction to crises have been identified so far.

The experience with tax reform is not very conclusive either. Although Thirsk, in his survey of tax reform in the developing countries, arrives at the conclusion that 'the most important stimulus to tax reform in many countries has been the presence of large and persistent fiscal deficits' (Thirsk 1993, p. 178), a number of cases of reform despite weak macroeconomic pressure (for example, Colombia 1986/88, Indonesia 1983/86) and cases of pressure without reform can be identified (Burgess and Stern 1993, pp. 805-11). Eduardo Lora, in his econometric analysis of the determinants of structural reform in 20 Latin American countries between 1985 and 1995, also does not find a positive correlation between the size of fiscal deficits and the extent of tax reform either (Lora 2000).

Crises are related closely to mandates because a deteriorating economy often leads to changes in government. According to the mandate hypothesis, such changes favour the initiation of reforms, particularly if they are associated with huge 'swings' and strong majorities for the new government. Mandates can help get reforms started and implemented in different ways (Keeler 1993, pp. 437-9): Public authorization strengthens the position of the government vis-à-vis both its supporters and the new opposition. More often than not, electoral defeat throws the new opposition into disarray. New governments also may benefit from 'promised land' and 'honeymoon effects' (Rodrik 1994). To start with the former, if the incoming government legitimately can claim to articulate a broadly shared vision, it more easily can count on the population's patience. In contrast, 'honeymoon effects' are associated with a new government's opportunities to claim the 'benefit of the doubt' and a grace period and to lay the blame for unwelcome developments and social hardships on its predecessor and the chaos left behind. Especially when they have been excluded from power for a long time, new governments are not burdened with a track record of non-reform and thus do not face a lack of credibility stemming from earlier failures. Finally, newly elected governments, almost by definition, simply have more time until the next elections and can thus 'afford' to be marginally more unpopular. For all these reasons, new governments are normally endowed with a particular stock of 'political capital' (Remmer 1993) which can be invested in reforms.[11]

In fact, there is strong empirical evidence from both developing and OECD countries that new governments, whether democratic or authoritarian, right-wing or left-wing, are more likely to successfully engage in fiscal reform than are incumbent governments (Boltho 1994, pp. 86-7; Burgess and Stern 1993, p. 818; Little et al. 1993, pp. 369-70; Remmer 1993; Weyland 1998a; Dollar and Svensson 2000). Almost all successful Latin American stabilizations since the mid-1980s have been initiated by new governments. In many OECD countries, the fiscal consolidation in the 1980s also was preceded by changes in government. By contrast, one of the most prominent cases of delayed fiscal reform, namely Italy, combined a steady increase in public debt with political continuity.

Although support for the 'mandate hypothesis' initially seems strong, some important deviant cases easily can be identified. Again in a 'surprising number of cases' (Williamson and Haggard 1994, p. 571) either new governments have not embarked upon economic reform or incumbents have done precisely that. Moreover in several cases, including Spain and Mexico, new governments have launched reforms only with considerable delay, thus raising doubts about the salience of the mandate effect. Finally a striking number of reform episodes have taken place under new governments that had not campaigned on a platform of reform. The most spectacular examples of such post-election U-turns may be President Menem's stabilization in Argentina after 1989, President Fujimori's neo-liberal turn in Peru in 1990 and the economic reforms under Prime Minister Gonzalez in Spain. While such cases of 'neoliberalism by surprise' (Stokes 2001) certainly can be reconciled with a broad version of the mandate hypothesis, they are not compatible with a narrow reading that demands a well-defined authorization of the government through elections.[12]

2.4   CHANGE TEAMS

Crises and mandates can only temporarily open windows for reform. In order to seize the resulting opportunities and initiate and consolidate reforms, additional conditions are needed. For starters, there must be a strong team of reformers who are determined to embark upon reforms, able to respond quickly to both the deteriorating economic situation and the associated political opportunities and capable of designing and implementing a coherent program. As evidence from both the OECD countries and the developing countries suggests, the strength required of reformers has a personal and an institutional dimension. For one thing, reformers must be competent, determined and capable of building political support. For another, the recent reform drive provides strong evidence that the successful initiation and consolidation of reforms are not only shaped by the (non-)availability of a 'handful of heroes' (Harberger 1993), a 'doughty champion' (Sandford 1993, p. 199) or 'vigorous political leadership' (Sachs 1994, p. 503), but also depend on a number of less contingent and more amenable institutional factors.

Strong change teams are important because the problems that complicate policy reforms are also likely to resurface within government. Costs and benefits of economic and fiscal reform tend to be asymmetrically distributed among the 'generalists' within government, most notably the prime minister and the finance minister on the one hand, and the spending ministers on the other (Alesina and Perotti 1999; von Hagen and Harden 1996; Milesi-Ferretti 1997; Velasco 1999, 2000). With government revenues representing a kind of common property, spending ministers reap the full benefits of spending but bear only part of the economic and political costs associated with the financing of expenditures. Conversely, expenditure constraint and fiscal consolidation does not boost the reputations of the spending ministers but rather those of the prime minister and the minister of finance. Due to this incomplete internalization of the costs of spending, a bias toward overspending and deficits and against fiscal reform is likely to exist. Its size strongly hinges upon the fragmentation of fiscal policy-making and the position of reformers within the government.

The PEPR literature testifies to the importance of the reformers' institutional position (Nelson 1993, p. 436; Williamson and Haggard 1994, pp. 578-9; Maravall 1997, pp. 33-4). A recurrent theme within this literature is the critical importance of strong and coherent 'change teams' (Waterbury 1992, pp. 191-2), which are held together by shared convictions and outlooks, bestowed with broad powers and shielded against political pressures both within and external to the government. Such teams have centred either around the head of government itself (Salinas in Mexico, Cardoso in Brazil after 1994, Özal in Turkey after 1984) or around a strong minister of finance (Özal in Turkey from 1980 to 1982, Cavallo in Argentina, Boyer and Solchaga in Spain, Cardoso in Brazil from 1993 to 1994). In almost all cases, the position of reformers was strengthened through the weakening, if not abolishment, of rival ministries, the creation of specialized economic cabinets and the granting of far-reaching staffing powers which allowed reformers to 'conquer' the state apparatus. If change teams centred around finance ministers, these ministers were often 'superministers' and enjoyed a special relationship with the prime minister or president. Moreover, some of the leaders of successful change teams were 'technopols' who combined economic expertise with political skills, responsibilities and resources.[13]

These observations on the importance of strong change teams are confirmed by the recent wave of empirical research on the fiscal impact of different budgetary institutions. Pioneered by Jürgen von Hagen and Mark Hallerberg, this research consistently notes a strong correlation between the centralization of the budget process and the commitment to fiscal discipline. These analyses show that a strong position of the finance minister in government, binding spending targets for each ministry, narrow limits on parliamentary amendments to the budget and a transparent budgetary process are normally associated with superior fiscal performance. By contrast, a higher fragmentation of fiscal policy making is likely to lead to higher deficits.[14]

2.5   EXECUTIVE AUTHORITY

In addition to the institutional position of reformers within government, the overall executive authority of government matters for the likelihood of reforms. Regardless of its high degree of determination and insulation from interest group pressures, a strong change team can compensate only partially and temporarily for unfavourable political-institutional 'fundamentals.' Both the initiation and, to an even greater extent, the consolidation of reform presuppose a government capable of imposing losses and able to formulate and implement coherent reform programs even in the face of widespread opposition. The literature has focussed largely on three potential determinants of this capacity: the degree of stateness and administrative capacity, the type of political regime and the particular constellation of institutions and actors.

Stateness and administrative capacity

The first and most fundamental dimension of executive authority is the degree of stateness and administrative capacity. As destatization can be accomplished only by the state (Kahler 1990; World Bank 1997), economic reform presupposes a state capable of formulating and implementing reforms. Without uncontested public authority over the whole territory and a functioning public administration, reforms are unlikely to succeed. This insight is the major reason for the international organizations' new interest in 'good governance' and the quality of institutions (Bönker et al. 2002). Moreover, it explains why issues of tax administration and public expenditure management have featured so prominently on the agenda of fiscal reform.

Type of political regime

A second dimension of executive authority which has attracted considerable attention in the literature refers to the political regime. Given the absence of electoral pressures and the repression of interest groups, authoritarian regimes are often held to be in a better position to carry out unpopular reforms. In fact, some of the most spectacular cases of economic reform in the last decades, including Chile and several East Asian high performers, have taken place under authoritarian auspices. However, the overall empirical evidence is more ambiguous. As with economic growth (Barro 1996; Przeworski and Limongi 1993), no clear-cut relationship between regime-type on the one hand and fiscal performance or economic reform on the other can be identified (Lindenberg and Devarajan 1993; Remmer 1990; Siermann 1998, pp. 101-10; Biglaiser 2002). For every authoritarian high-performer there is a low-performing authoritarian regime or a high-performing democracy. Hence, most literature now agrees that the overall message from the available empirical studies is that the alleged authoritarian advantage is simply a myth and that regime type as such does not influence the likelihood or success of economic reform.[15]

The 'disappointing' reform record of many authoritarian governments can be explained differently. For one thing, they often simply lack the willingness to engage in reforms. For another, one may doubt that authoritarian governments are in fact 'strong' governments and enjoy a higher reform capacity than democratic governments. While it is true that rulers in authoritarian systems can rely on repression and do not face electoral and constitutional constraints, they still have to fear coups. That is why political instability can be higher under authoritarian than under democratic regimes. Authoritarian governments also suffer from a lack of legitimation and an endemic inability to bind themselves. Given the lack of checks and balances, they cannot credibly commit themselves to a certain policy, so that reforms often suffer from time-inconsistency. Seen from this angle, authoritarian regimes often turn out to be rather 'weak' governments.

Political institutions and actor constellations

On a third level, the likelihood of fiscal reform is shaped by the particular architecture of political institutions and the prevailing constellations of actors. Both of them can differ substantially across countries with the same type of political regime. As for democratic regimes, theory and evidence suggest that the initiation and consolidation of fiscal reform is most likely to be shaped by three closely related factors: the electoral cycle, the number of veto players and the degree of political stability.

Elections

It is a commonplace that unpopular reforms are more likely to be adopted after an election than before one.[16] Upcoming elections tend to shorten the time-horizons of governments. As elections draw nearer, both the concern with popularity and the temptation to put off reforms that might alienate voters increase. This intuition, backed by abundant anecdotal evidence and enjoying great popularity in the literature on politico-economic cycles, is supported by a number of quantitative analyses. Min Shi and Jakob Svensson (2002a, 2002b), in a comprehensive analysis of a panel of 91 countries over the period from 1975 to 1995, find that the fiscal stance deteriorates substantially in election years, especially, but not exclusively in developing countries. These results are in line with older quantitative studies on different groups of developing and OECD countries.[17]

Veto players

According to conventional wisdom, policy reforms are also more likely to be initiated and consolidated the less fragmented the political system is and the smaller the number of veto players inside and outside government are (Tsebelis 2002). A large number of actors and institutions involved in decision-making gives opponents more chances to block reforms and makes it more difficult for the government to agree upon, to push through and to stick to reforms. On a general level, this is simply to say that an unconstrained democratic government seems to be in a better position to launch reforms than a government constrained by a plethora of checks and balances. Other things being equal, one thus would expect that majoritarian democracies are more conducive to reform than consensus democracies, that reforms are more likely in unicameral than in bicameral parliamentary systems and that one-party governments score better than multi-party governments.

However these standard assumptions, which dominate the literature in political science and, to an even greater extent, economics, need to be qualified. To begin with, a small number of veto players may well be a double-edged sword. As Paul Pierson has argued in his analysis of welfare state retrenchment in the United Kingdom and the United States, concentration of authority goes hand in hand with concentration of accountability (Pierson 1994, pp. 32-6). To put it differently, a 'stronger' government, while in a better position to push through reforms, also runs a higher risk of being held responsible for unpopular measures and thus may refrain from reforming. Conversely broad-based coalition governments, weak as they may look at first sight, may benefit from being able to spread out the blame more broadly and thus may be more likely to embark on reform at the end of the day.

A second problem with unconstrained authority is that it may undermine policy coherence (Bresser Pereira et al. 1993, pp. 208-12; Stark and Bruszt 1998, pp. 188-207). Missing checks and balances can result in technically inferior laws and regulations, as a government able to impose measures unilaterally may be tempted to ignore criticism and rush through half-baked measures. If the appropriate policy choices are controversial, unconstrained executive authority also favours erratic policy swings and stop-and-go patterns which may be harmful in the longer run. Finally, an unconstrained democratic government, like an authoritarian one, faces problems associated with an inability to bind itself.

The available empirical research on executive authority and fiscal performance has been shaped largely by two seminal articles by Nouriel Roubini and Jeffrey Sachs (1989a, 1989b). In these articles, the two authors uncover strong empirical evidence for a correlation between the size of post-1973 fiscal adjustment in the OECD countries and the dispersion of power. More specifically, their results show higher fiscal deficits under minority governments, presidential systems with divided government and multiparty coalitions in parliamentary systems.[18] They interpret this as confirmation of the assumption that weaker and more fragmented governments will find it more difficult to react to negative shocks and to initiate fiscal adjustment.

These findings by Roubini and Sachs, which have found their way into the textbooks, have stirred a still ongoing debate. While some authors have arrived at similar results,[19] others have questioned the robustness of the findings. According to Per-Anders Edin and Henry Ohlsson (1991), the political-institutional effects found by Roubini and Sachs can be attributed almost exclusively to the inferior fiscal performance of minority governments. Sung Deuk Hahm (1996) argues that the alleged fiscal effects of power dispersion holds true only for unstable parliamentary systems, but not for presidential systems and stable parliamentary regimes. Jakob de Haan and co-authors (de Haan and Sturm 1994, 1997; de Haan et al. 1997), as well as Uwe Wagschal (1996, Chapter 5) and Clemens Siermann (1998, pp. 123-5), report no significant impact of government strength on fiscal performance for a number of different specifications and different samples of OECD and EU countries.

More recently a number of contributions have begun to address the impact of veto players on tax reform. Mark Hallerberg and Scott Basinger (1998, 1999) and Uwe Wagschal (1999a, 1999b) have presented some evidence that reductions in corporate income tax rates in the course of the 1980s were greater in those OECD countries in which the executive authority was less constrained by multi-party coalitions, divided government and other limits on government authority. In line with the conventional wisdom and the findings by Roubini and Sachs, these analyses suggest that fragmented executive authority complicates the adjustment of the tax system to global pressures. As with Roubini and Sachs, however, the robustness of the empirical results has remained controversial (Ganghof 1999).

Comparable quantitative analyses for developing countries unfortunately do not exist.[20] However, the available case studies basically confirm the conventional wisdom on the detrimental effects of institutional fragmentation (Haggard and Webb 1993, pp. 150-51). More specifically, Haggard and Kaufman's comparative analysis of economic reform in 12 new democracies suggests that the fragmentation and polarization of the party system is the single most crucial institutional variable (Haggard and Kaufman 1995). In line with Roubini and Sachs, they find that countries with two-party or dominant-party systems have been more capable of managing the economy and initiating reform than countries with more fragmented party systems. They report, however, no systematic differences between presidential and parliamentary systems.

Political stability
A third and closely related aspect of executive authority that has featured prominently in the literature is the degree of political stability. According to a widely held view, political instability, as indicated by frequent changes in government and low average tenure, is inimical to fiscal performance and the launching of fiscal reform (Borrelli and Royed 1995, p. 234; Wagschal 1996, pp. 233-4).[21] Frequent changes in government not only cause friction due to changes in personnel and the like. More importantly, the perception of instability, fuelled by a history of frequent turnover, may lead governments and coalition partners within government to adopt a short-term perspective and to use a high public debt as a device to constrain the choices of prospective successors (Alesina and Tabellini 1990; Alesina and Perotti 1995b, pp. 12-15).

Obviously, political stability is related closely to the frequency of elections and the strength of executive authority. At least in the case of democratic regimes, changes in government normally coincide with elections. Likewise, broad coalition governments and governments constrained by a plethora of checks and balances tend to be more prone to instability. It is for these reasons that concepts such as government strength, executive authority and political stability are often used interchangeably in the literature. Noting the lower average durability of coalition governments, Roubini and Sachs (1989a, 1989b), for example, treat power dispersion and political instability almost as synonyms.[22]

There are a few empirical analyses of fiscal performance that explicitly control for political stability. For the OECD countries, Vittorio Grilli et al. (1991), in a frequently cited article, find some evidence for political instability going hand in hand with weaker fiscal performance. So does Wagschal (1996, Chapter 5) in his more comprehensive analysis. For the developing countries, the cross-sectional analyses by Sebastian Edwards and Guido Tabellini (1991a, 1991b), Nouriel Roubini (1991), Clemens Siermann (1998, pp. 116-18) and, albeit less strongly, Clemens Siermann and Jakob de Haan (1993) likewise hint at a tiny negative impact of political instability on the fiscal stance.

2.6   ARE NEW DEMOCRACIES DIFFERENT?

Together with the waves of democratization that have swept the world in the last 25 years, the growing awareness that differences within authoritarian and democratic regimes may be more important than differences between the two categories has increased interest in the fate of new democracies. This has made the comparative performance of new democracies one of the recurring and most controversial issues in the literature on policy reform (Haggard and Kaufman 1989, 1995, pp. 149-306; Diamond 1995).

Optimists have pointed to the mandates writ large, enjoyed by the new democratic governments, arguing that these governments can trade economic costs against political gains and, hence, should be in an even better position than newly elected governments in established democracies to benefit from the whole arsenal of 'honeymoon' and 'promised land effects.' However, these assets need to be balanced against a number of possible liabilities. First, since the transition to democracy typically goes hand in hand with an increased level of political mobilisation, new democratic leaders are likely to face previously repressed demands, heightened social and economic expectations and strong pressures to reward supporters and allies. Pre-occupied with consolidating both democracy and their position within it, these leaders may also be prone to compromise on economic issues and to sacrifice economic for political goals, especially if the forces of the old regime are still strong and have not yet accepted the new rules of the game. Finally, one would expect a transition to democracy to be accompanied by high turnover in key economic positions. In this case, the resulting frictions and the incumbents' feelings of uncertainty threaten to undermine the capacity of governments to embark on reforms.

By and large the available empirical analyses lend themselves to the less optimistic interpretation. This applies to Haggard and Kaufman's (1989) pioneering study of 25 Latin American, African and Asian countries between 1978 and 1986, Marc Lindenberg and Shantayanan Devarajan's (1993) statistical analysis of economic performance in 89 developing countries from 1982 to 1988 and to some extent Karen Remmer's (1990) analysis of economic trends in 11 Latin American countries in the wake of the debt crisis.[23] These studies converge in suggesting that new democracies generally display a weaker fiscal performance than both old democracies and authoritarian regimes. Furthermore, they find transitions to democracies to be associated with a deterioration in economic indicators and a loosening of economic policy from a diachronic perspective.

The economic and fiscal repercussions of democratic transitions have been most pronounced in those countries in which changes in regime have occurred amidst economic crisis and have gone hand in hand with massive economic challenges (Haggard and Kaufman 1995, pp. 149-306). In countries such as Argentina, Bolivia, Brazil or Peru, the transition to democracy in the course of the 1980s initially was accompanied by heterodox experiments and worsening fiscal and economic performance. Economic stabilization and fiscal reform typically took place not under the first, but under the second democratically elected government (Morales 1996). New democracies carrying out economic reforms that already had been initiated under authoritarian rule – as in Chile, Turkey, Thailand or Korea – have been characterized by a rather high degree of continuity in economic and fiscal policy.

Evidence from the OECD countries also suggests that democratization comes with an economic price. In Greece, Portugal and Spain, the three new democracies of Southern Europe, economic reform had a slow start (Ethier 1997; Maravall 1993). Fearing that social unrest might put the new democracy at risk, reformers in these countries postponed unpopular economic reforms. In order to avoid endangering the consolidation of democracy, social demands were accommodated by softening fiscal policy. Although it achieved success in political terms, the economic price of this 'democracy first'- strategy was a substantial deterioration in the economic and fiscal situation in the first years after the transition to democracy. It took until the early 1980s for these problems to be addressed by sweeping economic reforms, including tax reform and subsidy cuts.[24]

2.7   GOVERNMENT IDEOLOGY

One of the basic issues in political economy is the extent to which the ideological complexion of governments leaves an imprint on policy outcomes. On a general level, debates have focused on whether politicians are merely opportunistic office-seekers or are committed to particular ideologies and constituencies. The juxtaposition of 'partisan' and 'opportunistic' models has featured prominently in the literature on political business cycles and politico-economic interactions. Within comparative public policy, the impact of parties has remained an evergreen. Hence, it is no surprise that the role of partisan orientation in fiscal reform has attracted some attention. Most research has started with the assumption that leftist governments – whether due to their more Keynesian leanings or because of their greater tolerance for inflation – care less about deficits than governments of the right.

The bulk of the existing studies of partisan effects on fiscal policy focus on the OECD countries. Despite differences in methods, variables and data, they consistently show that, contrary to expectations, leftist governments do not run higher fiscal deficits. Most of the available analyses report no systematic impact of partisan orientation on the size of fiscal deficits and the extent of fiscal adjustment whatsoever (Alesina et al. 1997, pp. 201-7, 240-42; de Haan and Sturm 1994; Hahm 1996; Hahm et al. 1996; Hallerberg and von Hagen 1999; Peters 1991, pp. 115-26; Siermann 1998, pp. 124-5; Annett 2002; Pamp 2004). Moreover, the few studies that discover a significant correlation between fiscal reform and partisan orientation surprisingly find leftist governments to be more effective at containing fiscal deficits and at curbing government expenditures (Alesina and Perotti 1995a, pp. 232-5; Borelli and Royed 1995; Wagschal 1996, pp. 209-24; Ross 1997).[25]

The partisan hypothesis has featured less prominently in analyses of developing countries. Most analysts believe that the familiar left-right distinction is not appropriate for developing countries (Haggard and Webb 1993, p. 149). Williamson and Haggard (1994, pp. 568-71) discuss but ultimately refute the hypothesis that right-wing governments might be more inclined toward economic reform. As a matter of fact, one can point to dozens of cases where fiscal reform has been accomplished by 'unlikely' governments with leftist or populist credentials – the most famous instances being Argentina under President Menem and Peru under President Fujimori.

In sum, it seems that differences in partisan orientation have played only a minor role in shaping fiscal adjustment. There is not much empirical evidence for right-wing governments being more determined about fiscal reform. Quite to the contrary, leftist governments have often taken the lead. These observations can be interpreted differently. First, it may well be that supply-siders with their emphasis on tax reductions and their strong belief in Laffer curve effects serve as a right-wing equivalent to the supporters of Keynesian deficit spending on the left. Secondly, a 'Nixon-in-China' effect may place leftist governments in a better position to preach austerity and to avoid the blame for retrenchment (Ross 1997; Tommasi and Velasco 1996, pp. 203-4; Cukierman and Tommasi 1998). Finally, one may argue that the situation results from strategic use of fiscal policy. As Alberto Alesina and Guido Tabellini (1990) and Torsten Persson and Lars E.O. Svensson (1989) have argued in famous articles, right-wing governments may find it rational to increase the public debt in order to prevent possible left-wing successors from a spending bonanza. Some elements of this calculus may be found in the Reagan deficits or in the high deficits under the Swedish right-wing government from 1976 to 1982.

2.8   REFORM DESIGN

The success of reforms also hinges upon their design. By shaping the distribution of costs and benefits among groups and over time, the particular way in which reforms are undertaken influences their credibility and sustainability. Consequently a clever design can help ease political constraints both before and after the start of reforms (Przeworski 1991, Chapter 4; Roland 2002). Design may be instrumental in forging a pro-reform coalition and in rendering the initiation of reforms feasible in the first place. Design can also help make reforms sustainable by promoting the emergence of a pro-reform constituency and by increasing the costs of reform reversal. Four design features have received particular attention in the literature, namely the sequencing of reforms, the use of compensation, the consultation of interest groups and the composition of fiscal adjustment.[26]

Sequencing of reforms

Reforms may be introduced either in phases or all at once. If they come in steps, the sequencing can take different forms. Stimulated by examples of post-communist economic reform, there is now a broad formal literature on the relative merits of different approaches. The theoretical case for gradualism has been advanced most eloquently by Mathias Dewatripont and Gérard Roland (cf. the overview in Roland 2000, Part 1). In several articles, both have shown how gradualism can help overcome political constraints, whether by alleviating ex ante uncertainty through reversal options, by splitting the opposition or by building reform constituencies through a clever exploitation of complementarities between different reforms. Other authors have sought to demonstrate the virtues of a 'big bang,' arguing that a 'radical' reform may serve as a signalling device, may help balance gains and costs through widening the agenda and may make reforms irreversible by burning bridges (Rodrik 1989; Martinelli and Tommasi 1997).

Empirically, the recent experience with policy reform clearly points in favour of a 'radical' approach (Haggard and Webb 1993, pp. 158-60). Almost all recent showcases of economic reform in the OECD and developing countries have been characterized by rather comprehensive and rapid reforms. This also holds true for fiscal reform. It is difficult to find examples of successful gradual stabilizations. There is also plenty of evidence in support of 'packaging' tax reform. Cases in point are the radical tax reforms undertaken in New Zealand and the United States in the course of the 1980s. According to most observers, the political feasibility of these reforms critically hinged on the fact that their comprehensive character helped prevent special interest groups from blocking the process (Sandford 1993, pp. 201-5).

Compensation of losers

An obvious way to overcome obstacles to reforms, particularly if reforms are associated with net gains, is to buy off resistance by compensating losers and/or opponents. However, as appealing as the idea may sound, compensation is fraught with several problems related to information and incentives which threaten to make it costly and ineffective. One intrinsic problem is associated with the notorious difficulties in identifying 'true' losers and/or opponents. Another problem typically results from the inherent inability of governments to credibly commit themselves to the continuation of compensation (Dixit 1996). For these and other problems, cases of direct, explicit compensatory payments are rare. More common, however, are various forms of indirect compensation through complementary reforms (Graham 1994; Greskovits 1998, Chapter 8).

Again, case study evidence suggests that some form of compensation may be an ingredient of successful reforms (Haggard and Webb 1993, pp. 160-62). Two frequently cited examples for the successful use of compensation are Spain under Gonzalez and Chile after Pinochet. In both cases, popular support for the initiation and consolidation of economic reform was maintained by a parallel expansion of social services. With regard to tax reform proper, the evidence is less clear (Sandford 1993, pp. 217-19). Most tax reforms in the 1980s were revenue-neutral, thus defying the conventional wisdom that the passage of tax reforms depends on compensatory tax reductions.

Consultation of interest groups

A third evergreen within the PEPR literature has been the role of consultation and social pacts in the initiation and consolidation of reforms (Bresser Perreira et al. 1993, pp. 208-12; Haggard and Kaufman 1995, pp. 340-45; Maravall 1997, pp. 35-6). As a matter of fact, prominent reform episodes, including Spain, Mexico, Ireland and Israel, have been associated with some form of social pact. In New Zealand, the seminal 1984/88 tax reform package was adopted after a long round of consultations (Sandford 1993, pp. 205-8). More recently, post-Maastricht fiscal consolidation in the EU has gone hand in hand with a revival of social pacts (Ebbinghaus and Hassel 2000). In line with these observations, Alberto Alesina and Silvia Ardagna's analysis of fiscal adjustment in 10 OECD countries in the 1980s found parallel wage agreements to be conducive to the success of fiscal adjustment (Alesina and Ardagna 1998, pp. 512-16). But the contribution of 'social pacts' to economic reform remains highly controversial. While some observers regard any search for social consensus as futile and a sure recipe for delay (Sachs 1994, pp. 505-10), others argue that consultations can help start and sustain reforms by strengthening legitimacy.

The available evidence suggests that social pacts may in fact help overcome resistance against economic reform. The evidence also demonstrates, however, that the positive contribution of social pacts is highly contingent upon a number of rather demanding conditions. One major precondition is the presence of well-organized and representative interest organizations. For social pacts to work, participants must be able to aggregate interests and to bind their constituency. This is the main reason why there have been relatively few successful social pacts in developing countries. A second essential precondition for functioning social pacts seems to be firm government leadership. Otherwise the danger of a watering down of reforms looms large. Finally the type of economic reform may matter: the case for consultation and social pacts is most convincing for structural reforms with a wide array of actors and institutions involved but less clear when reforms are of a more narrow and technical nature.

Composition of fiscal adjustment

Finally there is strong evidence that the particular composition of measures relating to expenditures and revenues matters for the success of reforms. As first maintained in a seminal article by Alberto Alesina and Roberto Perotti (1995a) and later corroborated by other analyses,[27] the sustainability of fiscal adjustment strongly depends on the particular way in which it is accomplished. Evidence for both OECD and developing countries suggests that fiscal adjustments that rely primarily on cuts in expenditures, in transfers, in social spending and in government personnel costs are more likely to induce a lasting consolidation of the budget than adjustments that are primarily based on tax increases. The importance of composition stems from different sources: Economically, expenditure-led consolidations tend to tackle fiscal problems at the source and generally are less inimical to growth; politically, they signal a stronger commitment to reform and thus may help governments to overcome credibility problems and to push through reforms.

2.9   EXTERNAL FACTORS AND INTERNATIONAL ORGANIZATIONS

Recent economic reforms have also been shaped by a host of external factors.[28] Changes in the international economic context and in the intellectual climate have been an important part of the overall move to reform. In developing countries, the drying up of capital inflows in the wake of the debt crisis increased the pressure to adjust. Likewise, the secular spread of neo-liberalism has discredited the status quo and has strengthened the position of reformers. In the EU, the deficit criteria of the Maastricht Treaty have served as powerful commitment devices (Rhodes 2002; Pitruzello 1997). This variety of external influences notwithstanding, PEPR so far has focused largely on the role of international organizations, most notably the IMF and the World Bank.

The available empirical evidence suggests that the Washington twins and external assistance have only had a limited impact on the likelihood of reform (Bird 1998; Dollar and Svensson 2000; Killick 1998; Stone 2002, Chapter 3). As the meagre record of compliance with IMF and World Bank conditionality illustrates, the leverage of these organizations is often quite overrated. Despite their reputation for omnipotence, international financial organizations lack the power to unilaterally impose or induce reforms. That is why so many IMF or World Bank programmes get off track and why so many deviations remain unsanctioned. Consequently, almost all empirical evidence indicates that neither the tightness of conditionality nor the size of external assistance have a strong independent influence on the successful initiation and consolidation of reform.

However, to reject fantasies of omnipotence is not to deny that the involvement of international organizations can make a difference in the launching of reforms if some degree of commitment to reform exists in the recipient country, that is if reforms, in World Bank jargon, are 'owned' by national governments (Johnson and Wasty 1993; Killick 1998, Chapter 4). In this case international organizations and external assistance may help put economic reforms on track and keep them there (Sachs 1994). To start with the initiation of reform, the prize of external assistance may tip the balance in favour of reform. The prospect of external assistance reduces the relative costs of reform and may allow reformers within government to capitalize on their good connections to international organizations. Agreements with the Washington twins may also help increase the credibility of reforms, as the seal of the IMF signals a certain consistency of measures and a commitment to reform. Finally, governments can use IMF conditionality to blame the Washington twins for unpopular measures by claiming that their own hands are tied.

2.10   CONCLUSION

This chapter has reviewed the factors that appear to have some bearing on the political feasibility of policy reform in general and of fiscal reform in particular. One can conclude from this discussion that the successful adoption of reforms cannot be attributed to a single factor, but depends upon a particular combination of mutually interdependent and reinforcing conditions. It also seems that key conditions for the initiation of reform differ from those for the consolidation of reform.

Concerning the initiation of reforms, the available experience from the OECD and developing countries suggests that crises, mandates and the position of reformers within government comprise the single most important variables. Some combination of crisis and mandate seems to be almost indispensable for the initiation of reform. However, the opportunities that arise must be seized, and this is where the position of reformers comes in. The successful launch of reforms depends on a strong and coherent change team, ready and willing to capitalize on the temporary weakening of reform opponents. Overall executive authority appears to be of secondary importance for the initiation of reform. In times of crisis and honeymoons, formal constraints on the government's position can be offset at least temporarily by situational factors and strong and determined reformers. The position of reformers can be strengthened by the involvement of international organizations.

The situation is likely to change after the launching of reforms when the costs of reform are materializing and the original reform mandate is evaporating. At this stage, executive authority tends to feature more prominently. In order to stay the course, governments must be able to forgo the populist temptation to retreat from or to water down reforms. This is why electoral pressures, shaky majorities, narrow constitutional constraints or political instability are likely to complicate the consolidation of reforms.

NOTES

1. A few remarks on terminology: In the following, fiscal reform has a macroeconomic and a structural dimension and covers both the adjustment of the aggregate fiscal stance and the adoption of tax and expenditure reforms. For the particular agenda of post-communist fiscal reform, see Chapter 3 below.
2. For similar expositions and related 'impossibility theorems' see Bates 1989; Haggard and Kaufman 1995, pp. 156-9; Wiesenthal 1997, pp. 93-101.

3. In the following, I simply take the existence of reformers within government for granted and do not elaborate on their motivation and preferences. In line with the standard rational choice model, I instead focus on the restrictions and constraints that reformers face.
4. For the relationship between these two types of uncertainty see Drazen 1996.
5. This view has increasingly come under fire. In a seminal article, Giavazzi and Pagano (1990) have argued that positive expectational effects associated with deficit reduction may offset the negative Keynesian effects. For empirical evidence on this issue, see Alesina and Ardagna 1998; Alesina and Perotti 1997; Alesina et al. 1998; McDermott and Wescott 1996 on the OECD countries and Adam and Bevan 2005; Easterly 1996; Gupta et al. 2004 on the developing countries. Within the PEPR literature, the 'revisionist' position has been articulated by Rodrik (1996, pp. 29-30) and Tommasi and Velasco (1996, pp. 210-12).
6. 'Crisis concentrates attention,' as Lasswell once epigrammatically put it (cf. Hirschman 1963, p. 261).
7. For a broader discussion of crises as an ingredient and as a trigger of reforms, see Bates and Krueger 1993b, pp. 452-4; Drazen 2000, pp. 444-54; Drazen and Easterly 2001; Hirschman 1963, pp. 260-64; Keeler 1993, pp. 440-42; Maravall 1997, pp. 32-3; Rodrik 1996, pp. 26-9; Tommasi 2004; Tommasi and Velasco 1996, pp. 189-201; Williamson and Haggard 1994, pp. 562-5. Drazen and Grilli (1993) and Tornell (1995) provide formal models. Weyland (1998a, b) draws on insights from prospect theory to provide 'microfoundations' for the crisis hypothesis.
8. Rodrik 1996, pp. 26-9; Tommasi and Velasco 1996, pp. 197-202; Krueger 1993, pp. 124-5; Toye 1994, p. 41; Haggard and Webb 1993, pp. 153-4.
9. Thus, it is not surprising that a major strand of comparative research focuses precisely on alternative responses to crises. See, e.g., the classic studies by Gourevitch (1986) and Scharpf (1991).
10. See, for example, the standard accounts by Bruno (1993); Edwards (1995) and Little et al. (1993).
11. These arguments can be supplemented by a psychological one. Long-standing leaders may suffer from a status-quo bias and thus be less receptive to bold changes than new leaders (Weyland 1998a, pp. 649-50).
12. Such a narrow version of the 'mandate hypothesis' ('a government may be able to introduce reforms if it campaigned on a program of reform in the preceding election') can be found in John Williamson's original paper for the Institute for International Economics's project on 'The Political Economy of Policy Reform' (Williamson 1994, p. 25). Interestingly, this hypothesis is simply ignored in the concluding chapter by Williamson and Haggard (1994).
13. The notion 'technopol', as opposed to 'technocrat', was coined by Richard Feinberg and popularized by John Williamson (1994). For a discussion, see Dominguez 1997.
14. See Alesina et al. 1996; Gavin and Hausmann 1998; Stein et al. 1999 for Latin America and Hahm et al. 1996; Hallerberg and von Hagen 1999; von Hagen and Harden 1996 and Hallerberg 2004 for the OECD countries.
15. For 'the myth of authoritarian advantage,' see Maravall 1994, as well as the summarizing remarks in Bates and Krueger 1993b, p. 459; Haggard and Webb 1993, pp. 144-7; Nelson 1993, p. 435; Williamson and Haggard 1994, pp. 568-9.
16. Obviously, the 'electoral hypothesis' overlaps with the 'mandate hypothesis' presented above. However, the latter is more specific in that it focuses on the extra leeway enjoyed by a new government or by a government re-elected with a strong majority.
17. See, in particular, Schuknecht 1996 and Gavin and Hausmann 1998, pp. 52-3 for the developing countries and Alesina et al. 1997, pp. 201-7, 240-42; Corsetti and Roubini 1992; Wagschal 1996, pp. 195-6; Clark and Hallerberg 2000 and Franzese 2002, pp. 178-82 for the OECD countries. The findings by Shi and Svensson have been questioned by Brender and Drazen (2005) who argue that political deficit cycles are confined to new democracies.

18. Roubini and Sachs measure power dispersion by a composite index that combines those three dimensions. The index runs from 0 to 3 and takes the following values (Roubini and Sachs 1989a, pp. 923-4):

    0: parliamentary systems with a one-party majority; presidential systems in which the president's party has a majority in the legislature;

    1: parliamentary systems with a majority coalition consisting of two parties; presidential systems with divided government;

    2: parliamentary systems with a majority coalition consisting of three or more parties;

    3: minority governments.

    In Roubini and Sachs 1989b (pp. 114-5), the definition of the index slightly differs. Here, the index takes the value 2 only if there are four or more coalition partners. For a critical discussion of the index, see Borrelli and Royed 1995, pp. 235-6 and Wagschal 1996, pp. 51-2.

19. See in particular Alesina and Perotti 1995a, pp. 232-4; Alesina et al. 1997, pp. 240-42; Borrelli and Royed 1995; Corsetti and Roubini 1992; Franzese 2002, pp. 175-8.

20. For a rare econometric attempt at testing the fiscal impact of government strength for a country sample which includes both OECD and developing countries, see Edwards and Tabellini 1991b, who use an index of government strength which is close to the one suggested by Roubini and Sachs. However, Edwards and Tabellini do not find any evidence for the importance of government strength.

21. Again, a similar argument looms large in the mushrooming literature on the political determinants of economic growth. For a survey, see Brunetti 1997, pp. 172-6.

22. It should be noted, however, that some authors regard political stability and executive authority strength as rival concepts denoting the unwillingness and the inability to reform, respectively (see, e.g., Edwards and Tabellini 1991b; Grilli et al. 1991).

23. These findings are also backed by the above mentioned paper by Brender and Drazen (2005) on political budget cycles in new versus established democracies. In contrast, van de Walle (1999, pp. 25-7) and Gasiorowski (2000) do not find any impact of democratization on fiscal performance.

24. The coincidence of democratic consolidation and delayed economic reform in Southern Europe has led influential observers to view the postponement of economic reforms as an important ingredient of a successful consolidation of democracy (Linz and Stepan 1996; Maravall 1993).

25. A third position is taken by Carlsen (1997), Cusack (1999) and Sakamoto (2001) who suggest that the impact of partisan orientation is contingent on the prevailing macroeconomic situation. According to their analyses, deficits tend to be more counter-cyclical under left-wing governments.

26. For additional design features, see Pierson 1994.

27. See in particular Alesina and Ardagna 1998; Alesina and Perotti 1997; McDermott and Wescott 1996; Mackenzie et al. 1997; Perotti 1996, 1998; Perotti et al. 1997.

28. For different attempts at charting the international context and the various external determinants of reform, see Bönker 1994; Schmitter 1996; Stallings 1992 and Whitehead 1996.

3. Agenda and context of post-communist fiscal reform

3.1 INTRODUCTION

Fiscal reform has represented an essential element of East European economic reform. Since the pre-1989 fiscal system was tailored closely to the mechanisms and requirements of a communist economy, the transition to capitalism has entailed a fundamental overhaul of the old fiscal system. The close links among fiscal, economic and political institutions have effectively ruled out the retention of the old fiscal system and have necessitated far-reaching reforms. This chapter sketches the agenda and the context of fiscal reform in Eastern Europe. It puts post-communist fiscal reform into a comparative perspective and provides a benchmark for assessing the progress reached.

The chapter is divided into four parts. Section 3.2 elaborates on the need for fiscal reform by providing a stylized description of the ancien régime and by outlining the relationship between fiscal reform and other components of economic transformation. While most observers agreed on the necessity of fiscal reform, there were some controversies over the strategy of reform. Section 3.3 surveys these debates and finds that, compared to other fields of reform, fiscal reform has been a rather uncontroversial element of the economic transformation. Section 3.4 compares the starting points, the agendas and the contexts of fiscal reform in the East, the West and the South with a view to identifying the major peculiarities of post-communist fiscal reform. Section 3.4 concludes and leads over to the analysis of fiscal reform in Hungary, Poland and the Czech Republic.

3.2 THE COMMUNIST FISCAL SYSTEM AND THE NEED FOR REFORM

The communist economic system was characterized by a tight coupling of the economic and the political sphere. A single elite, the *Nomenklatura*, governed both the polity and the economy. State ownership and state planning, along with the unlimited power of the ruling elite, provided for nearly complete and highly discretionary political control of the economy (Kornai 1992b). The economic reforms that were adopted in some of the communist countries since the mid-1960s did not succeed in overcoming the old mechanisms of 'bureaucratic co-ordination' (ibid. 97-100). They did result in a certain decentralization of decision-making, an extension of enterprise autonomy and a consequent change in the bargaining positions of the centre and the enterprises. But due to the maintenance of party control over the economy and the resulting persistence of soft budget constraints and discretionary interventions, neither the 'softening' of planning in the state-owned sector nor the attempts at nourishing a limited private sector showed the desired results.

The communist fiscal systems mirrored the economic systems in which they were embedded. They thus differed substantially from the fiscal systems in both the OECD countries and in those developing countries with a similar per capita income. Running parallel to developments in their overall economic systems, the communist fiscal systems underwent certain changes over time. Similar to reforms in general, however, these changes left basic characteristics of the old system untouched. Contrary to some fashionable speculations in the late 1960s (see, e.g., Musgrave 1969, pp. 61-2), communist and capitalist fiscal systems did not converge before 1989. Instead, the tax reforms that were adopted in most OECD countries in the course of the 1980s further widened the gulf between fiscal systems in the East and the West. The only communist country to see a substantial move towards a Western-style fiscal system before 1989 was Hungary where the economic reforms in the second half of the 1980s included a far-reaching tax reform.[1]

Qualitative features of the communist fiscal system[2]

Indistinct boundaries

Under communism, the boundaries of the fiscal system were indistinct. No clear demarcation line separated the state budget, state-owned enterprises and the central bank. A large portion of fiscal activities were not included in the state budget. Central banks undertook massive quasi-fiscal activities; a plethora of extra-budgetary funds existed and many social services and recreational facilities were provided off-budget directly by state-owned enterprises. The planning bureaucracy decided arbitrarily to which extent the latter had to finance their investments out of retained profits or were eligible to budgetary subsidies or credits from the central bank. In some cases, profits remained in enterprises in order to finance investment. In other cases, profits were transferred to the state budget and redirected by handing out subsidies.

Sometimes branch ministries redistributed profits among 'their' enterprises outside the budget.

Subordinate role of fiscal institutions
These unclear boundaries went hand in hand with the subordinate role of fiscal institutions. The budget and other financial plans were drafted on the basis of the physical plan. 'Planning dictated budgeting, not the other way round' (Straussman 1993, p. 81). In practice, the relation between the two types of plans was never that hierarchical, and physical and financial plans were drawn up in an interactive process. Yet physical planning remained preeminent, thus severely restricting the role of fiscal instruments. The secondary position of the fiscal system was reflected by the budget's subordinate role in governing the economy. Unlike capitalist economies, the budget did not serve as the main lever of economic policy (Premchand and Garamfalvi 1992).

The state's control over the economy allowed for a high degree of implicit taxation. Given the communist state's double role as property owner and planner, economic policy could rely heavily on non-budgetary instruments. Policymakers were able to determine tax revenues either by setting tax rates or by changing prices, freeing them from having to rely on taxes and subsidies in order to pursue their allocative and distributive goals. Alternatively, they could produce the desired results by fixing prices administratively. Instead of taxing wages, planners could directly constrain the growth of nominal wages or reduce real wages through higher retail prices. Likewise, they could alter interest rates instead of taxing savings or subsidising debtors.[3]

The economic reforms that were adopted in the communist bloc since the late 1960s increased the role of financial planning and fiscal instruments. The turn to a more parametric style of planning gave the budget more importance as a means of economic policy. Direct controls of prices, investments, and wages were replaced partly with tax-based fiscal incentives. In all communist countries, excess-wage taxes and levies on fixed capital assets were introduced from the 1960s onwards in attempts to 'economize' the use of labour and capital. However, the shift toward hands-off governance remained limited. Even in Hungary, the front runner of communist economic reform after 1968, reforms never fully abolished direct state interventions. Moreover, economic decentralization was accompanied by an increase in extra-budgetary funds and in off-budget activities by state-owned enterprises. Altogether, economic reforms thus had an ambiguous impact on the role of the budget.

High differentiation
Communist fiscal systems were highly differentiated and opaque and can be characterized as 'a hodgepodge of inconsistent levies on various activities at different rates' (McKinnon 1993, p. 122). Personal income tax rates were differentiated according to type of economic activity and employer. State-owned enterprises were subject to a number of different levies on profits which figured partly as taxes and partly as dividends. The labels attached to these levies as well as the underlying definitions of profits were arbitrary and prone to frequent changes. Turnover taxes, the single-stage product-specific sales taxes that represented the backbone of indirect taxation under communism, were set indirectly by fixing consumer and producer prices for particular goods. As a consequence, most communist countries had hundreds or even thousands of different rates which were changed frequently on an ad hoc basis.

This differentiation of the fiscal system reflected the interventionist bias and the discretionary, non-parametric character of fiscal policy. Under communism, taxation did not aim primarily at mobilizing resources for financing public spending but instead served far-reaching allocative and distributive goals. Tax systems were characterized by extensive non-neutrality, for tax rates were set with a view to privileging one activity, one sector or even one enterprise over another. In their desperate attempt to ensure plan fulfilment and to prevent disequilibria, planners engaged in short-term interventions and ad hoc measures which undermined the credibility of fiscal rules. This instrumentalization of the fiscal system went hand in hand with pervasive bargaining over taxes and subsidies between the state and state-owned enterprises. 'Soft taxation' represented a major manifestation of the notorious 'soft budget constraints' under communism (Kornai 1992b, p. 142).

Pre-1989 reforms eliminated neither the extreme differentiation of the tax system nor the discretionary character of taxation. The relaxation of central planning increased the use of taxes and subsidies for allocative and distributive purposes. While reforms made profit tax rates more uniform, they were accompanied by a further differentiation of turnover taxes. More importantly, reformers never succeeded in establishing parametric taxation and ending ex post bargaining over taxes. Quite to the contrary, the greater autonomy of enterprises in the aftermath of reforms further increased the scope for tax bargaining.

Differential treatment of private and public enterprises
A further aspect of the characteristic differentiation of the communist tax systems was the existence of different tax regimes for the private and the public enterprise sector. Under communism, the private sector was subject to

specific tax codes. Incomes from private economic activities were taxed at considerably higher rates than incomes from the socialized sector. Instead of the turnover tax, private enterprises had to pay specific sales taxes. Tax policy was used as a means to discourage, contain and control private economic activities. While taxation of the private sector was relaxed somewhat in the course of reforms, it remained high and never lost its highly discretionary character.

Strong reliance on state-owned enterprises
The communist countries raised the bulk of tax revenues from state-owned enterprises. The private sector's share in the economy was small. Personal income taxes played a minor role, if any, and were collected largely through withholdings. The same held true for social security contributions which were not 'individualized,' but calculated on the basis of the total enterprise payroll. Profit and turnover taxes were collected from state-owned enterprises. This strategic role of state-owned enterprises made tax collection under communism easy and fairly effective, 'almost idyllic' (Tanzi 1993a, p. 6). First, the small number of state-owned enterprises also implied a small number of taxpayers. Second, informational asymmetries between state-owned enterprises and tax collectors were weak, since the state determined prices and quantities and tax administrators had more or less unrestricted access to enterprise books and records. Third, since state-owned enterprises had to keep accounts with the central bank and could use only certain methods of payments, tax collection could be accomplished simply by debiting the accounts of the state-owned enterprises at the central bank. With tax collection being an integral part of the general planning process, there was no need for a separate Western-style tax administration (Casanegra de Jantscher et al. 1992).

In addition to administrative convenience, channelling the vast majority of taxes through state-owned enterprises also served ideological purposes. The official ideology distinguished between 'taxes on the population' and 'revenues from the socialized sector' (Musgrave 1969, pp. 46-7). The first category was confined primarily to personal income taxes, while the second included revenues as diverse as profit taxes, capital charges, commodity taxes and often social security contributions. In the official understanding, 'revenues from the socialized sector' did not count as taxes, but were treated as a dividend paid out of the produced surplus. The predominance of these revenue sources, in some countries even enshrined in law, was praised for confirming the superiority of the communist 'owner state' to the capitalist 'tax state.'

By implication, communist fiscal systems were characterized by nearly invisible taxation and a great deal of fiscal illusion. The explicit tax burden on the population was low, and the withholding of personal income taxes and social security contributions in the socialist sector tended to render the perceived burden even lower. As a result, 'the average citizen was never confronted by the tax system or by tax inspectors. He never had to file a return and, in most cases, was not even aware of the existence of taxes' (Tanzi 1994, p. 151). Partly because of this limited tax consciousness, there was little popular discontent with the communist tax system.

A quantitative comparison of expenditure and revenue patterns

It goes without saying that these qualitative differences render any quantitative comparison of tax and expenditure ratios in communist and capitalist countries complicated, if not dubious. These caveats notwithstanding, various attempts at comparing fiscal indicators have been undertaken.[4] Building on this literature, this section presents a comparison of expenditure and revenue patterns in the former communist countries,[5] the OECD and EU countries and a sample of 26 developing countries with a per-capita income similar to the East European countries at the end of the 1980s.[6]

Budget deficits
According to official pre-transition statistics, the communist countries regularly ran balanced budgets or even achieved budget surpluses. Between 1928/29 and 1988, the Soviet Union recorded deficits only for 1941, 1942, and 1943. It took until the late 1980s before the Soviet leadership officially admitted the existence of deficits in the Soviet Union (Birman 1990). Hungary regularly reported budget deficits, albeit diminutive ones, ever since the early 1960s, but was the only country in Central-Eastern Europe to do so. The Polish government admitted a substantial deficit for 1981 but reported a surplus already in 1982. As is now well-known, these rosy figures resulted from an intimately entwined combination of peculiar accounting standards and deliberate, discretionary falsification (Birman 1981; Cheasty 1992, pp. 38-46). For instance, only part of the high military spending was included in the official expenditure figures. At the same time, financing items such as treasury bonds or central bank loans to the government routinely were treated as above-the-line budget items and counted as revenues instead of as financing.

Recalculated figures reveal regular deficits (Table 3.1), yet suggest that, despite all manipulations, the East European countries' deficits in the late 1980s were still smaller than average deficits in both the West and the South (Åslund 2002, p. 47-8). The figures also document that the fiscal performance of the communist countries substantially worsened in the course of the 1980s. The declining fiscal performance was related to the deteriorating economic situation of the communist economies in the 1980s. It also lends support to the conjecture that the move toward reform socialism went hand in hand with increased macroeconomic tensions (Kornai 1992b, Chapter 23). Among the East European countries, Romania and the Soviet Union represented special cases. Romania accumulated substantial fiscal surpluses in the second half of the 1980s as a result of the country's radical austerity strategy, while the Soviet Union ran above-average deficits. Declining world market prices for energy and Gorbachev's *perestroika* (including the campaign against alcohol) prompted a decline in revenues which could not be compensated by cuts in expenditures (McKinnon 1993, pp. 120-61; Ofer 1989; Padovano 1991).

Table 3.1   *General government fiscal balances in East European and other countries, 1985-89 (% of GDP)*

	1985	1986	1987	1988	1989
Albania*	na	na	na	na	-8.6
Bulgaria	-0.8	-2.5	-5.2	-5.5	-1.4
Czechoslovakia	-0.6	-0.8	-0.6	-2.4	-2.8
Hungary	-1.1	-3.1	-3.6	0.0	-1.3
Poland	0.1	-0.3	-0.8	0.0	-8.0
Romania	3.0	4.6	7.3	6.0	8.4
Soviet Union	-2.4	-6.2	-8.4	-9.2	-8.5
OECD average	-5.2	-4.2	-3.5	-2.6	-2.7
EU average	-6.2	-5.0	-4.9	-3.6	-2.3
DCs' average	-3.3	-4.9	-4.1	-3.8	-3.6

Notes: * Central government

Sources: IMF Government Finance Statistics; Holzmann 1992a, p. 181, Table 1; own calculations.

The rather small communist deficits reflected institutional conditions conducive to deficit management (Campbell 1995a, pp. 767-8; Cheasty 1992, pp. 38-46). As discussed above, communist planners enjoyed far-reaching discretionary powers regarding taxes and expenditures and were in a position to react flexibly to acute or anticipated fiscal problems. Moreover, they commanded the national central banks and were able to rely on both open and disguised central bank loans. For instance, it was not unusual for planners to tell the state bank to give credits to state-owned enterprises in distress in order to enable them at least to fulfil their tax obligations. As a result, deficits remained comparatively low until the very end of communism.

Level of fiscal intermediation
Under communism, relatively small budget deficits corresponded to huge shares of government expenditures and revenues in the GDP, that is, a high level of fiscal intermediation (Tables 3.2 and 3.3). Aggregate expenditure and revenue ratios were not only about two times higher than in other middle-income countries; they also exceeded OECD and EU averages and were matched only by the European high spenders. This high level of pre-transition expenditures becomes even more drastic if one controls for differences in per capita income. Ever since Adolph Wagner put forward his famous law of the expanding scale of state activity, economists generally have assumed a positive association between per-capita income and the size of the public sector. In fact, a number of studies seem to confirm this hypothesis for cross-sections of countries at different income levels (Lindauer and Velenchik 1992; Easterly and Rebelo 1993, pp. 433-42).[7] Against this background, it is possible to contrast actual East European expenditure levels with predicted ones on the basis of regression analyses for a broader sample of countries. In this vein, Muraközy (1989, pp. 231-5) estimates that the expected expenditure ratio for a capitalist country with the Hungarian per-capita income was about half of the actual ratio in 1981. Similarly, the seminal comparative analysis of developing countries' government expenditure by Heller and Diamond (1990) suggests that total non-interest expenditure in the mid-1980s exceeded the expected level by between 40 and 80 per cent in Hungary and 25 and 45 per cent in Poland. Given this incongruity between per-capita income and spending ratios, one may speak of 'premature' levels of fiscal intermediation.

Unfortunately, no comprehensive time series of expenditure and revenue ratios in communist countries exist.[8] The available empirical evidence suggests that expenditure ratios in the East fell in the 1950s, stagnated in the first half of the 1960s and rose strongly between the late 1960s and the mid-1970s. In the last decade before 1989, expenditure trends differed sharply: In Bulgaria and Czechoslovakia, the expenditure ratio increased, in particular in the second half of the 1980s. But expenditure ratios in Poland, Hungary and the Soviet Union remained more or less constant. Again, Romania stands out with a highly volatile expenditure ratio. These striking national differences run parallel to different reform trajectories (Holzmann 1991, pp. 151-3). The orthodox governments of Bulgaria and Czechoslovakia reacted to the deteriorating economic situation by further extending subsidies and by increasing government spending. In Hungary, Poland and the Soviet Union, greater commitment to reform resulted in stagnating expenditure ratios. For one thing, reforms included cuts in consumer subsidies and a reduction in the state's role in financing state-owned enterprises. For another, greater enterprise autonomy in the course of reforms favoured a decline in revenues which in turn severely constrained the scope for expenditure increases.

Composition of revenues and expenditures
The institutional features of communist fiscal systems were associated with a peculiar composition of government revenues and expenditures which differed from both the OECD and the developing countries (Tables 3.2 and 3.3). On the revenue side, profit taxes comprised an unusually high proportion of total revenues. Reflecting the state's tight grip over state-owned enterprises, profit tax revenues in communist countries were considerably higher than those in the West and the South. In Bulgaria, Poland and the Soviet Union, profit taxes even represented the single most important source of revenue. This strong reliance on corporate income taxation coincided with a subordinate role of revenues from personal income taxes. Measured as a percentage of GDP, the latter reached a level similar to the other middle-income countries but remained far below OECD and EU averages. The quantitative weight of the remaining indirect and social security taxes, however, was not that different from the Western countries: the share of domestic taxes on goods and services was similar in all three groups of countries. The share of international trade taxes was slightly higher than in the OECD and the EU but still below the average level in the developing countries. Finally, the share of social security taxes in overall revenues was similar to the OECD average. All in all, the composition of government revenues under communism came closer to that of the West than that of the South. This is even more true if one follows Nick Stern and distinguishes three broad categories of tax revenues – domestic indirect taxes, income and social security taxes, and trade and other taxes (Burgess and Stern 1993, pp. 775-6, Hussain and Stern 1993, pp. 67-72; EBRD 1994, p. 81).

On the expenditure side, central planning and state involvement manifested themselves in rather high levels of government consumption and subsidies. The share of expenditures on goods and services in total spending, in communist countries was about twice the level found in the OECD countries and the developing countries, and the share of subsidies was even three to six times higher than in the West and the South. Taken together government consumption and subsidies accounted for about half of all government spending in most communist countries. This compares to an average of roughly one-fifth in both Western and developing countries. The high share of spending on government consumption and subsidies was compensated for by lower relative spending on wages and salaries, interest payments, social security and, in some countries, public investment. Whereas the small interest bill stemmed from low indebtedness and repressed domestic interest rates, the modest spending on wages and salaries and social security reflected the large-

Table 3.2   *Level and composition of general government revenues in East European and other countries, 1989*

	Total revenues (per cent of GDP)	Composition of revenues (per cent of total revenues)					
		Total tax Revenues	Profit taxes	Personal income taxes	Domestic indirect taxes	International trade taxes	Social security taxes
Albania	51.3	86.2	21.6	0.0	44.1	0.0	9.6
Bulgaria	64.0	80.4	37.7	6.1	17.8	1.4	16.6
CSFR	69.5	76.2	15.8	9.9	25.5	2.6	21.6
Hungary	59.6	82.5	13.6	9.0	27.0	na	23.8
Poland	40.8	93.2	23.8	1.7	21.6	4.8	18.1
Romania	52.4	27.3	0.7	0.2	0.2	0.0	22.6
SU	41.0	93.9	29.8	10.7	28.8	15.4	8.5
OECD average	41.4	87.1	8.6	24.9	25.9	1.7	18.8
EU average	43.3	89.9	6.8	22.3	27.0	1.1	26.2
DCs' average	23.6	76.2	11.1	6.5	25.9	14.0	9.9

Sources: IMF Government Finance Statistics; EBRD 1994; own calculations.

Table 3.3   *Level and composition of general government expenditures in East European and other countries, 1989*

	Total expenditures (per cent of GDP)	Composition of expenditures (per cent of total expenditures)					
		Expenditures on goods & services	Expenditures on wages & salaries	Interest payments	Subsidies	Investment	Social security transfers
Albania	56.8	17.6		na	15.3	51.6	na
Bulgaria	61.8	32.9	8.1	5.9	23.9	8.9	19.2
CSFR	72.3	24.9	10.0	0.0	34.6	1.0	18.8
Hungary	60.9	19.9	13.5	7.4	19.9	8.3	23.6
Poland	48.8	5.1	13.9	0.0	26.4	na	23.0
Romania	44.1	24.0	10.1	0.3	0.0	0.9	21.5
SU	49.5	9.1		na	17.2	14.5	na
OECD average	44.2	14.8	22.2	11.7	4.2	6.2	30.1
EU average	47.9	12.9	21.4	11.7	4.3	6.2	37.6
DCs' average	25.8	15.7	28.4	14.9	4.8	10.3	14.1

Sources: IMF Government Finance Statistics; EBRD 1994; own calculations.

scale subsidization of consumer goods and the provision of comprehensive social services by the state and by state-owned enterprises.

The relationship between fiscal reform and other elements of post-communist economic reform

Given the 'tight coupling' between the fiscal and the economic system under communism, there were strong complementarities between fiscal reform and other elements of post-communist economic reform. For one thing, the retention of the communist fiscal system would have jeopardized economic reform and economic transformation by infringing on economic restructuring and by undermining the effectiveness of other reforms. For another, the 'old' fiscal system would not have functioned under the 'new' economic circumstances. In particular, it would have lost its capacity to mobilize sufficient revenues, thereby endangering the funding of state activities and the maintenance of fiscal balance. Both types of linkages put fiscal reform high on the initial reform agenda.

To start with the first set of problems, the discretionary, distortional aspects of the old fiscal system were in particular need of reform, given the new capitalist context. The retention of the highly differentiated communist tax system would have prevented an efficient, market-driven allocation of resources. The myriad turnover tax rates would have counteracted the liberalization of prices, just as the highly differentiated profit taxation would have infringed on the liberalization of market entry. Economic incentives would have been stifled by the continued redistribution of profits from successful to ailing enterprises, while the discrimination of the private sector and confiscatory taxes on profits would have discouraged the mushrooming of the private sector.

The second set of problems has been associated with the repercussions of other economic reforms on the functioning of fiscal institutions. The main challenges to the old system have stemmed from economic liberalization and privatization, which have eroded the conditions upon which the old system was based. Tanzi (1994, pp. 149-50) has aptly summarized these changes:

> By disbanding the planning mechanism and by removing constraints to private-sector activities, the transition to a market economy (1) removes controls on quantities produced and on prices, thus reducing the information available to the government; (2) increases sharply the number of producers in the economy through the creation of private enterprises and the breaking up of state enterprises; (3) removes existing restrictions on the methods of payments by allowing enterprises to make payments in cash and to hold multiple accounts in different banks; (4) eliminates the role of the monobank in collecting revenue ...; and (5) stimulates the growth of those activities that

have been difficult to tax in market economies (small shops, services, independent contractors).

These developments radically transformed the conditions for the collection of revenues (Tanzi and Tsibouris 2000, pp. 13-15). In effect, the start of the economic transformation raised the danger of a massive decline in revenues. Given this spectre, it is no wonder that dire scenarios of a 'post-communist fiscal crisis', along with complementary calls to arms, abounded in the early days of the transformation (Campbell 1992; Kornai 1992a; McKinnon 1993; Tanzi 1991a). Unlike so many other transformation problems, the fiscal problems most transition countries experienced during the first stage of the transformation had been foretold. It is partly for this reason that there has been such broad agreement on the crucial importance of fiscal reform.

3.3   HOW TO REFORM: ISSUES AND NON-ISSUES IN THE REFORM DEBATE

While the need for fiscal reform was widely accepted right from the beginning of the transformation, the direction and the strategy of reform of course have been contested. As with other fields of reform, different ideas about how to orchestrate the transition from plan to market have been propagated. From a comparative perspective, however, it seems safe to say that the general outline of fiscal reform has remained relatively uncontroversial. Compared to other elements of post-communist economic transformation, fiscal reform has been characterized by a rather broad consensus on the design and the strategy of reform.[9] This particularly applies to the case for fiscal restraint.

The case for fiscal restraint

The consensus on fiscal restraint has partly reflected the general scepticism against demand management and deficit spending which has emerged over the last 20 years or so and has been enshrined in the famous 'Washington consensus.'[10] During the early stages of the transformation, various structural features of the post-communist economies further strengthened the case for fiscal tightness: Embryonic and shallow capital markets set narrow limits to the non-inflationary financing of budget deficits and made the crowding-out of private investment more likely. The inflationary potential associated with other reform measures, in particular price liberalization, inspired macroeconomic restraint, while the ubiquitous problems of conducting monetary policy in transition economies made fiscal policy the main lever for stabilization.

In the course of the transformation, the rationale for fiscal restraint has shifted. The combination of strong economic growth, surging capital inflows and widening current account deficits that many of the more advanced transition countries have faced since the mid-1990s has provided a new justification for fiscal discipline. Given the notorious problems with conducting monetary and exchange rate policy in the face of strong capital inflows, fiscal policy has been perceived widely as the single most important instrument of macroeconomic policy to prevent the emergence of a currency crisis (Begg et al. 2002).

Of course, the consensus on fiscal restraint has always been far from unanimous. Quarrels over the exact size of economically tolerable and politically feasible deficits have lingered. During early transformation, the greater-than-expected decline in output led many economists to warn against deflationary overshooting (Kołodko 1992; Sachs 1996, p. 130). Others pointed out the problem that overly restrictive deficit ceilings might slow the transfer of off-budget fiscal activities to the budget and retard the reallocation of labour from the state to the private sector (Tanzi 1993b; Chadha and Coricelli 1997). More recently, debates have raged over the use of fiscal restraint as a means of reducing moderate inflation and the question of the appropriate fiscal stance in the face of a temporary slowing of economic growth.

However, all these qualifications should not hide the surprisingly broad consensus on the need for fiscal rectitude. Most of the reported controversies have boiled down to debates over the operationalization of a common position. Heterodox views have appeared infrequently and have been confined largely to unreconstructed advocates of a more 'expansionist' and 'growth-oriented' fiscal policy within the reforming countries. Within the international policy community, Kazimierz Laski and the Vienna Institute have stood almost alone with their explicitly Keynesian position (Laski 1993; Laski and Bhaduri 1997; Laski and Podkaminer 1995).

It testifies to the consensus on fiscal restraint that the most important left-wing manifestos on the post-communist transitions have basically shared the commitment to fiscal discipline. In this vein, Eatwell et al. (1995, p. 182) concede that 'it is hard to challenge the wisdom of fiscal restraint during the transition.' While Przeworski et al. (1995, pp. 85-90) call for higher social spending and public investment, they equally are concerned with stabilization and suggest financing those expenditures by higher taxes. Likewise, the Agenda group (Kregel et al. 1992, pp. 109-32) and Amsden et al. (1994) are rather brief on fiscal policy and concentrate their critique on 'do-nothing microeconomic policies.' It is symptomatic that their macroeconomic recommendations do not go beyond a cautious call for 'a mildly expansive monetary and fiscal policy' (Kregel et al. 1992, p. 122).

Reforming fiscal institutions

Reform of inherited fiscal institutions has been even less controversial than the case for fiscal restraint. Given the fear of an unfolding fiscal crisis, the overhaul of the old institutional framework generally has been regarded as a high priority. Roughly speaking, reforms have consisted of three main elements: the delineation of new boundaries among the different tiers of government, central banks, social security funds and state-owned enterprises; the introduction of a Western-style tax administration; and the transformation of budgetary procedures and fiscal management (Andic 1994; Premchand and Garamfalvi 1992, pp. 282-9).

The drawing of new boundaries has included the separation of social services from state-owned enterprises, the transfer of off-budget fiscal activities to the budget, the termination of quasi-fiscal activities by the central bank, and the clarification of 'ownership rights' within the public sector through a clear assignment of fiscal competencies to central, local, state and regional governments. These measures have been widely regarded as necessary requirements for increasing the transparency of public finances and for maintaining fiscal control.

After the start of transformation, fiscal transparency has also suffered from the spread of new forms of quasi-fiscal activities. Governments have often put some pressure on banks and public utilities, especially in the energy sector, to keep struggling enterprises afloat by handing out credit, by lowering prices or by accepting non-payment (Petri et al. 2002; Lorie 2003: 10-12). Moreover, they have established special 'transformation institutions' to recapitalize bankrupt banks or to administer and to spend privatization proceeds. The limiting of such fiscal activities outside the budget has been an important element of drawing clear boundaries between the public and the private sector.

The utmost importance of a quick reform of tax administration, the second reform element, also has been uncontroversial. Given the nexus between the old fiscal institutions and the communist economic system, most have acknowledged the rapid establishment of a Western-style tax administration as a top priority. The creation of a tax administration capable of handling a 'mass' tax system with large numbers of taxpayers and able to work in a market economy under the rule of law has required sweeping organizational changes, an increase in staff, massive training activities and the introduction of new rules governing the relationship between citizens and the state (Casanegra de Jantscher et al. 1992).

A third building block of reform has been the overhaul of budgetary procedures in order to put fiscal management on a new footing and to overcome the dispersed authority over fiscal policy that had characterized communism (Allan 1994). Again, the agenda has been comprehensive, including issues as diverse as the introduction of new accounting and reporting systems, the establishment of budget offices and treasury systems (Ter-Minassian et al. 1995), the development of capacities for macro-economic analysis, the adoption of a multi-year budgeting framework, and, last but not least, the reallocation of budgetary responsibilities among the parliament, the ministry of finance and the other ministries.

Tax reform

Post-communist tax reform has been relatively uncontroversial as well. Not only was there an almost universal consensus on the need for tax reform, but until the late 1990s, most actors also broadly agreed on the strategy and design of reforms. Unlike in other fields of economic transformation and contrary to general tax reform debates, the issue of big bang versus gradualism did not feature very prominently. Moreover, most reformers and advisers were highly sceptical of 'untested' solutions and shared the conviction that post-communist tax reforms should follow standard advice and should be patterned broadly on existing Western institutions. For both reasons, controversies over tax reform in practice focused largely on mundane and 'technical' issues.[11]

The fact that the initial debate on post-communist tax reform was only rarely framed in terms of big bang vs. gradualism had different causes. On the one hand, the broad agreement on the urgent need for comprehensive reforms worked against any tinkering with incrementalism. With tax reform being treated as an emergency issue calling for immediate measures, such discussions looked all but frivolous in the East European context. On the other, most observers were aware that tax reform could not be achieved overnight. In this situation, the differences between a parallel and a staggered introduction of new tax laws appeared rather negligible, if compared to the range of options available in other fields.

During most of the 1990s, debates on the design of the new tax system were also limited. While some tax reform entrepreneurs from the West emphasized the notorious deficiencies of the current Western tax systems and the unique reform opportunities associated with the tabula rasa in the East,[12] the bulk of advisers, including those by the IMF and the EU, warned against risky experiments and argued for a more pragmatic approach. The mainstream recommendations on the design of the new tax system can be characterized as follows (Stepanyan 2003, p. 5):

- Heavy reliance on a (sic!) broadly-based sales taxes, such as VAT, preferably with a single rate and minimal exemptions, and excise taxes levied on petroleum products, alcohol, tobacco and a few items that are considered luxuries.
- No reliance on export duties, which inhibit international competition, or on small nuisance taxes, administration of which is not effective.
- Import taxation at as low levels as possible, with a limited dispersion of rates to minimize effective rates of protection.
- An administratively simple form of personal income tax, with limited deductions, a moderate top marginal rates (sic!), and (an) exemption limit large enough to exclude persons with modest incomes, and a substantial reliance on withholding.
- A corporate income tax levied at only one moderate-to-low rate aligned with the top personal income tax rates (sic!), with depreciation and other non-cash expenditure provisions uniform across sectors and minimal recourse to sector or activity-specific incentive schemes.

The tax reform debate in the transition countries took a new turn in the second decade of transformation when the idea of a flat income tax gained ground in the region. Initially derided as an idiosyncracy of some liberal Balts, the idea did not feature very prominently in post-communist tax reform debates until the late 1990s. Later on, however, it has been taken up and popularized by policy entrepreneurs in many transition countries and implemented, inter alia, in Russia (Ivanova et al. 2005) and Slovakia (Brook and Leibfritz 2005). The move to flat-rate income taxes in the region has been controversial. It has not only met the resistance of leftist forces, but has been regarded with some scepticism by the IMF, the EU and most mainstream economists as well.

Expenditure reform

Expenditure reform has represented the single most controversial field of fiscal reform. While there was some consensus on the need for deep cuts in subsidies and other forms of 'economic' spending (Chu and Holzmann 1992), the particular size, sequencing and composition of expenditure cuts during transformation was, and still is, controversial. Advocates of industrial policy have been less enthusiastic about reducing subsidies and public investments than liberal reformers. Likewise, different positions on the 'appropriate' level of social spending have prevailed, reflecting different attitudes toward the welfare state in general and the role of social policy in the context of transition in particular (Götting 1998, pp. 264-8; Nelson 1997, pp. 257-8). Since the expenditure ratios in most of the advanced transition countries are still higher than that of countries with a similar income level (Begg and Wyplosz 2000; Funck (ed.) 2002; von Hagen 2005; Bönker 2003b), these controversies over the need for expenditure reform have lingered on.

Why fiscal reform has been so uncontroversial

There are various reasons why fiscal reform has been less controversial than most other elements of economic reform. While general trends in economic thinking have certainly played the most important role, they are not the entire story. Two other closely related factors are also worth mentioning. First, since the issue of fiscal reform has not been confined to post-communist countries, reformers have been able to draw on substantial experience with fiscal reform in the West and the South. Second, fiscal reform has been set apart from other areas of economic reform by the strategic role of the IMF. The prominent role of the IMF in world-wide fiscal reform has introduced a relatively small, well-integrated 'policy-community' into the equation. Though far from monolithic, this group of policy-oriented economists inside and outside the IMF has been characterized by a high degree of internal coherence. Common socialization and experience as well as organizational imperatives have promoted the creation of a common outlook.

Conditions in other fields of reform have been less conducive to the emergence of a policy consensus. Cases in point are privatization and social policy reform. While the general case for privatization has increasingly been accepted, policy makers and economists have disagreed over the optimal strategy to achieve it. Given the unprecedented scope of post-communist privatization, experience gathered in the OECD and the Third World has not been much help (Rosenbaum et al. 2000). Moreover, before 1989 few economists had thought about how to privatize a whole economy. Nor has there been an organization as dominant as the IMF that could have 'structured' the debate. Instead, a plethora of different institutions and advisers have entered the field, promoting a wide array of different strategies for privatization. A similar story can be told about social policy (Götting 1998, pp. 84-8; Wagener 1999). The scale of social policy reform has been unprecedented and no single organization has dominated the scene. Those international organizations that have been active in the field have been committed to divergent approaches (Deacon and Hulse 1997). Even within both the IMF and the World Bank the consensus on social policy has remained fragile. This 'lack of templates' (Nelson 1997, p. 259) has made social policy reform more controversial than fiscal reform.

3.4 EAST EUROPEAN FISCAL REFORM FROM A COMPARATIVE PERSPECTIVE

In a way, the East European transitions have been part of a broader reform wave. Up to a certain point, they have shared a number of important commonalties with the economic and political reforms that have been adopted in a number of OECD and developing countries in the last 20 to 25 years. Given the prominent role of fiscal reform within the 'Washington consensus' and the pivotal role of the IMF in the South and the East, this applies especially to fiscal reform. However, these commonalties should not hide some important peculiarities of post-communist fiscal reform.

Starting point

Post-communist fiscal reform has been a by-product of the transition to capitalism. Although many factors contributed to the demise of the old regime and although some communist countries suffered from high deficits in 1989, it is fair to say that fiscal problems and discontent with the fiscal system did not feature among the main reasons for the initiation of fiscal reform. In contrast to the OECD and the developing countries, the move to fiscal reform in the East was not driven by an actual or perceived 'fiscal crisis' or by rising discontent with the old fiscal system. Deficits under the old regime were relatively low and significantly smaller than average pre-reform deficits in those developing countries that embarked on IMF-supported stabilization programmes (Bennett et al. 1995, pp. 8-10). More importantly, if they existed at all, communist deficits were seen as symptoms of the deteriorating economic situation rather than as the main causes of the prevailing economic problems, as has been the case with fiscal deficits in the West and in the South. Nor was there anything similar to the 'tax revolt' which has haunted the tax collectors of the Western welfare states ever since the mid-1970s. Quite to the contrary, the communist tax systems with their apparently low tax burden 'on the population' continued to enjoy a high degree of popularity.

Reform agenda

Despite all similarities, the agenda of post-communist fiscal reform has been more comprehensive than in both the OECD and the developing countries (Alam and Sundberg 2002, pp. 1-2). It has covered short-term and long-term measures, macroeconomic adjustment and structural reforms, expenditures and revenues, and tax policy and tax administration.

In a way, the East European agenda has combined the challenges faced by the OECD and the developing countries. Revenue reforms in post-communist countries have been similar to those in developing countries. Both sets of countries were plagued by a legacy of highly fragmented and distorted tax systems combined with weak tax administrations. Consequently, reforms in both groups of countries have meant creating a new tax system from scratch. In contrast, the large-scale tax reforms that have shattered the OECD countries since the 1980s have built on established and operating systems. Radical as they have been, they have essentially been about streamlining existing systems, not establishing new ones. On the expenditure side, however, the reform agenda in the East has been more akin to the Western one. Similar to the OECD welfare states, reforms have called for fiscal retrenchment and a reduction in the redistributive role of the state. In this regard, reforms have clearly gone beyond expenditure reforms in most developing countries where the level of fiscal intermediation at the outset of reforms was much lower.

Reform context

Fiscal reform in Eastern Europe has been part of a 'systemic' transition. Again, this contrasts with the other reform episodes. Granted, fiscal reforms in many OECD and developing countries also have gone hand in hand with other reforms, such as privatization, deregulation and, in some cases, even far-reaching political reforms. However, East European fiscal reforms certainly have been special in that these 'parallel' reforms have covered virtually the whole fabric of the society (Offe 1991; Wagener 1997). Owing to the simultaneity of numerous, equally urgent economic and political reforms, East European fiscal reform has proceeded in a much more turbulent environment, characterized by changing economic and political institutions, a severe 'transformational recession' (Kornai 1994) and a fluid economic structure. This simultaneity has aggravated the problems of sequencing and reform design and has confronted reformers with massive spill-over effects, crowded agendas and difficult decisions about the optimal allocation of their limited political resources. At the same time, it has allowed reformers to capitalize on strong mandates, to exploit the high overall uncertainty associated with the comprehensiveness of reforms and to trade economic losses against political gains. Moreover, 40 years of communism and the particular mode of transition in the East also meant that post-communist fiscal reform had taken place in a demobilized society characterized by weak interest groups, popular acquiescence and an inclination toward individual strategies.[13]

Two additional contextual peculiarities that have characterized post-communist fiscal reform can be identified. Accompanied by the dissolution of three federations (Soviet Union, Yugoslavia, Czechoslovakia), the great transformation in Eastern Europe has included an important territorial dimension (Offe 1991; Linz and Stepan 1996, Chapter 2). Needless to say, these processes have also had a fiscal side. Initially, issues of fiscal federalism featured prominently on the reform agenda (Hewitt and Mihaljek 1992). Fiscal reform was complicated by the need to accommodate regional and local interests and had to find an assignment of fiscal responsibilities capable of reconciling separatist demands and anti-centralist sentiments with the maintenance of overall fiscal control. With the eventual demise of the old federations, the agenda shifted. The newly independent states were forced to build up national fiscal systems. In doing so, some of them not only faced the challenge of creating a self-sustaining national administrative apparatus but were also confronted with the withdrawal of substantial federal transfers.

A final East European peculiarity has been the massive involvement of external actors. Especially in Central East European countries, external actors have played an unparalleled role as an external anchor for economic reform (Bönker 1994, 2006a). Out of a plethora of different actors that moved into the vacuum created by the breakdown of the CMEA and the Warsaw Pact, the two most important have been the IMF and the EU. Almost all countries in transition have been keen to negotiate agreements with the IMF and have subjected themselves to IMF conditionality (Dąbrowski 1998; Zecchini 1995). Besides the IMF and other international financial organizations, the EU has exercised strong influence, both by providing substantial (conditional) assistance and, even more importantly, by offering membership (Berglöf and Roland 1997; Bönker 2006a). The prize of EU membership has functioned as an important incentive for economic and political reform, as it did in Spain, Portugal and Greece. Needless to say, the influence of the IMF and the EU has been felt particularly strongly in the area of fiscal reform. The involvement of the IMF in Eastern Europe has increased the pressure to engage in fiscal adjustment and to subscribe to the 'Washington consensus.' Likewise, aspiration to join the EU has made EU tax regimes and even the fiscal criteria of the Maastricht Treaty focal points for the reforming countries.

3.5   CONCLUSION

This chapter has discussed the agenda and the context of post-communist fiscal reform. The analysis lends itself to a number of important conclusions. First, it has shown that the strong links between the fiscal and the economic system under communism and the resulting complementarities between fiscal reform and other elements of post-communist economic reform have made fiscal reform a crucial part of the reform agenda. Second, it has demonstrated that post-communist fiscal reform stands out as the site of a relatively broad consensus on the strategy and design of reforms. This high degree of consensus has set fiscal reform apart from other elements of post-communist economic transformation and suggests that national differences in reform trajectories have been driven by differences in political constraints rather than by different beliefs and convictions of reformers. Finally, the analysis has demonstrated that post-communist fiscal reform has been characterized by an agenda and a context substantially different from fiscal reform in the West and the South.

By reconstructing the reform 'requirements,' debates and conditions, Chapter 3 has also set the stage for the second part of this study. The following three chapters reconstruct the trajectories of post-communist fiscal reform in Hungary, Poland and the Czech Republic. They look at the implementation of the reform agenda sketched in Section 3.3 and ask how the peculiarities of post-communist fiscal reform reported in Section 3.4 have shaped the eventual fate of reforms.

NOTES

1. For the background to and details of the Hungarian 1987/88 tax reform, see Section 4.4 below.
2. Classic accounts of the communist fiscal system include Davies 1958; Holzman 1955; Musgrave 1969, pp. 45-62 and Nove 1977, Chapter 9. For more recent overviews, see Gray 1991; Haase 1980; Hutchings 1983; John 1998, Chapter 2; Maggs 1979; Newcity 1986 and Wanless 1985.
3. One might even argue that a well-planned communist economy should require hardly any form of explicit taxation (Musgrave 1991, p. 35).
4. See, for example, EBRD 1994, pp. 80-82; Fakin and de Crombrugghe 1995; Gordon 1994, pp. 38-40; Holzmann 1992a, pp. 180-81, 186-91; Hussain and Stern 1993, pp. 67-72; Kopits 1991, pp. 372-8; Kornai 1992b, pp. 134-8; Gandhi and Mihaljek 1992, pp. 143-5, as well as older contributions such as Hedtkamp 1970; Pryor 1968; Castles 1986.
5. The GDR and Yugoslavia have been excluded because of the lack of comparable data and/or national peculiarities.
6. According to the standard World Bank classification, the East European countries were (and still are) lower middle or upper middle income countries. In the following, the reference group of developing countries thus includes those middle-income countries that achieved a GNP per capita of more than US$ 1000 in 1989 and for which data are available. Listed in order of the size of national income, the sample consists of Thailand, Botswana, Cameroon, Colombia, Paraguay, Tunisia, Turkey, Peru, Jordan, Chile, Syria, Costa Rica, Mexico, Mauritius, Malaysia, Panama, Brazil, South Africa, Uruguay, Argentina, Gabon, Venezuela, Republic of Korea, Portugal, Greece and Oman.
7. But see Burgess and Stern 1993, pp. 774-5; Ram 1987, pp. 199-203. Ever since Musgrave (1969, pp. 110-19), it has been observed that cross-sections that include both industrialized and developing countries tend to support Wagner's Law, while those that include only one of these subsamples do not.
8. For estimates, see Bahry 1983; Hutchings 1983, pp. 79-97, 133-5; Muraközy 1989; Schroeder and Pitzer 1983.

9. Basic articles on the strategy of post-communist fiscal reform include Chand and Lorie 1992; Gordon 1994; Holzmann 1992a; Kopits 1991; Newbery 1995; Tanzi 1991a, 1993a, 1993b, 1994. In addition, see Hartwig and Wellesen 1991; Oberhauser 1993. The relative consensus on fiscal reform is highlighted further by the fact that most of the early classics on how to reform a communist economy stress the salience of fiscal reform, but do not pay much attention to its particular design (see, for instance, Blanchard et al. 1991; Fischer and Gelb 1991; Lipton and Sachs 1990). The main exception is Kornai's 1990 book which has a separate chapter on stabilization and tax reform (Kornai 1990).

10. It should be noted, however, that tax-smoothing theory, as pioneered by Barro (1979), would have lent itself to a far-reaching justification for transitional deficits in the transforming countries. Tax-smoothing theory starts from the assumption of a welfare-maximizing government setting tax rates given a known time path of public expenditure. In this case, social welfare is maximized if tax rates are set at the level of permanent spending and effects of temporary expenditure or revenue shocks are smoothed by tolerating temporary budget imbalances. Now, one can easily think of at least three reasons for the tendency of short-term expenditures and revenues in Eastern Europe to deviate from their permanent levels: First, the transition countries have experienced severe 'transformational recessions' (Kornai 1994). Second, the medium-term level of public expenditure is expected to be below the current one. Finally, revenues have remained below their permanent level because of transitory difficulties in establishing compliance with the new tax regime. Within the framework of tax-smoothing theory, these considerations add up to a strong case for tolerating transitional deficits. For one of the surprisingly rare references to tax-smoothing theory in the context of transformation, see Gordon 1994, p. 46.

11. Major normative contributions on tax reform in countries in transition include Gandhi and Mihaljek 1992; Holzmann 1992b; Hussain and Stern 1993; McKinnon 1993; Musgrave 1991; Owens 1991; Tanzi 1991b. See also the literature on post-communist fiscal reform in general cited in note 9 above. For the reform of particular taxes, see, for instance, Cnossen 1992; Tait 1991; 1992 on VAT and Mutén 1992 on income taxes.

12. During early transformation, the most prominent advocates of such 'revolutionary' reforms have been Charles McLure and the German KNS group. Both have propagated inflation-adjusted, consumption-oriented income taxes and have been active in a number of countries (see, for instance, McLure 1992 and Rose 1999b). The proposals of the KNS group also found their way into a comprehensive model tax code for transition countries that was commissioned by the German Federal Ministry of Finance (Lang 1993, 1999). Part of the proposals were implemented in Croatia (Wagner and Wenger 1996; Keen and King 2002).

13. For the differentiation, articulation and organization of interests in post-communist societies, see Elster et al. 1998, Chapter 1; Greskovits 1998, Chapter 5; Schmitter and Karl 1994, pp. 179-80; Wiesenthal 1997, pp. 107-11.

4. Getting started: the initiation of fiscal reform after the fall of communism

4.1 INTRODUCTION

Fiscal reform had a different start after the fall of communism. In Poland the Balcerowicz Programme brought the initiation of large-scale fiscal reform soon after the first post-communist government had been formed. The new political elites in Czechoslovakia launched similarly radical reforms in 1990/91, after some delay. In contrast the Hungarian Antall government more cautiously continued earlier reforms after the 1990 founding elections.

This chapter analyses the initiation of post-communist fiscal reform in Czechoslovakia, Hungary and Poland with a view to identifying the economic and political factors that have shaped the speed and scope of reforms and can account for the substantial national differences. The chapter starts with an analysis of the Polish case (Section 4.2). As Poland was the first East European country to break with communism, the Polish experience also shaped the developments in the two other countries. Moreover, the fact that the economic and political conditions in Poland at the outset of the transformation were extremely favourable to the initiation of reform also makes the country a good point of reference from an analytical perspective. The section on Poland is followed by sections on Czechoslovakia (Section 4.3) and Hungary (Section 4.4). The chapter concludes by providing a brief comparative assessment (Section 4.5).

4.2 POLAND

Poland's transition to democracy resulted from a·series of negotiations between the incumbent communists and the political opposition (Batt 1991, pp. 31-3). The Magdalenka Agreement of early April 1989, which concluded these negotiations, gave the country a new set of political institutions and called for gradual democratization. The partially free elections in June 1989 resulted in a sweeping electoral victory for the opposition camp. After some manoeuvring, Tadeusz Mazowiecki became Prime Minister and in September 1989 the first non-communist government was formed.

Economic and political conditions at the end of 1989

From the point of view of PEPR, economic and political conditions at the end of 1989 were extremely favourable to the initiation of reforms. A deep economic crisis, a new government with a strong popular mandate and a powerful and coherent change team combined to create a textbook recipe for launching reforms. In this situation the formal constraints on executive authority stemming from the negotiated transition did not really restrict economic reform. As Johnson and Kowalska (1994, p. 198) put it, 'the political conditions for designing a radical programme of reform could not have been more favorable.'

Reform pressure, 1989-90
At the end of 1989, the reform pressure was high. Poland's economic situation was marked by a combination of a partially reformed, yet disintegrating, communist economy and severe macroeconomic imbalances (Kondratowicz and Okolski 1993; Myant 1993, pp. 59-81). In the second half of the 1980s, the communist leadership had launched a series of half-hearted structural reforms to address serious economic problems and a fragile political situation. Patterned on Hungarian lines, these measures had strengthened enterprise autonomy and enacted complementary institutional reforms, including the introduction of a two-tier banking system and some changes in taxation. Compared to Hungary, however, reforms had been more cautious and less consistent. Moreover, the stronger position of Polish workers and the higher degree of political mobilization of Polish society contributed to a far-reaching disintegration of the economy and a macroeconomic softening. When the first non-communist government took over in late 1989, Poland was at the brink of hyperinflation. In this context, proposals for drastic fiscal measures were virtually uncontested.

Popular support, 1989-90
Partly due to the dire economic situation, the Mazowiecki government could build on strong popular support. Contrary to expectations, Solidarność had won, by wide margins, almost all competitive seats in the partially free elections to the Sejm and Senate in June 1989. Surveys taken in late 1989 also showed rather broad support both for Prime Minister Mazowiecki and for radical economic reforms (Batt 1991, pp. 84-5). The latter were widely perceived as the country's last chance after a decade of unsuccessful tinkering with gradual reforms. According to one poll in November 1989, 90.3 per cent

of those who had an opinion about the Balcerowicz Programme expressed support, while only 3.1 per cent of all respondents opposed it (Przeworski 1996, p. 523). The net percentage difference between the proportion of respondents who expected the economy to improve and those who expected it to deteriorate rose from –18 in March 1989 to about +50 at the end of the year (Przeworski 1993, p. 158).

Executive authority, 1989-90

On paper, the executive authority of the Mazowiecki government suffered from the compromises made at the Round Table Talks. The Magdalenka Agreement contained a number of guarantees for the incumbent communists. General Jaruzelski was designated to remain President. While the elections to the newly created Senate were completely free, 65 per cent of the seats of the Sejm were reserved for the communist party and its allies. As a result, the democratically elected deputies did not enjoy a majority in the first and more powerful chamber of parliament but depended on the support of incumbent deputies. In order to please the Soviet Union, the Mazowiecki cabinet also included a number of communist ministers. Mazowiecki and his team thus had to co-operate with a communist president, a parliament still dominated by the forces of the old regime and a number of communist ministers. Initially, however, these constraints on executive authority remained weak and were outweighed by a favourable constellation of actors. Solidarność's unexpected triumph at the polls in June threw the communists into disarray. Preoccupied with defining their future role and cautious not to engage in unpopular attacks against the government, they behaved rather passively. At the same time, the government could rely on the support of the two major independent social organizations, the Catholic Church and the re-legalized Solidarność trade union movement, both of which were highly respected at that time.

Position of reformers, 1989-90

Within the Mazowiecki government, economic reformers enjoyed a rather strong position (Balcerowicz 1994a, pp. 169-72; Blejer and Coricelli 1995, pp. 35, 56-7). The acute crisis, combined with the apparent failure of the previous, more gradual reforms, put economic reform at the top of the agenda and underscored the need for quick and radical action. From a political point of view, the commitment to radical economic reform marked a clear break with the past and promised to fill a policy vacuum. This was tempting for a government that had been catapulted unexpectedly into office, had no ready-made programme at hand and found itself politically constrained by compromises with the forces of the old regime (Myant 1993, p. 85; Juchler 1994, p. 201; Sachs 1993, pp. 42-3). Leszek Balcerowicz, who became Finance Minister in September 1989, was assigned overall responsibility for the economy and vested with extraordinary powers. Apart from assuming responsibilities as Deputy Prime Minister and Chair of the Economic Committee of the Cabinet (Council of Ministers), he also received full rein to staff the key economic positions within the government. Balcerowicz seized this opportunity and installed a determined change team of like-minded economists, most of whom had worked together on economic reforms since the late 1970s. In addition, Balcerowicz's position was strengthened by endorsements from Western economists as well as his favourable standing with international creditors and the Washington twins.

The launching of the Balcerowicz Programme

The Mazowiecki government took advantage of the prevailing economic and political conditions.[1] The Balcerowicz Programme, presented to the public in October 1989, called for far-reaching reforms. Although parts of the programme were controversial, Balcerowicz encountered no serious opposition while pushing them through (Johnson and Kowalska 1994, pp. 197-8; Stone 2002, p. 93). Within the government, he enjoyed almost complete free rein.[2] Outside the government, neither the Sejm nor the Solidarność dared to challenge the reforms. The Balcerowicz Programme, as well as earlier preparatory measures in late 1989 and the 1990 budget, sailed through the Sejm. In order to accelerate the programme's passage, the Sejm and the Senate set up a special commission to handle the legislative work. Presented to Parliament on 17 December 1989, the Balcerowicz Programme and a variety of legal amendments passed both chambers of parliament in late December. In January 1990, the Sejm also vested the government with extraordinary budgetary powers to be exercised if the economic assumptions underlying the budget proved incorrect.

The Balcerowicz Programme combined tough up-front stabilization and liberalization with a comprehensive programme of institutional reform. In January 1990, the bulk of the remaining price controls and restrictions on private economic activity were abolished. Foreign trade was liberalized, current account convertibility introduced and the exchange rate unified and devalued. This far-reaching economic liberalization was accompanied by wage restraint and a tight fiscal and monetary policy. In addition, the Balcerowicz Programme envisaged comprehensive institutional reforms and initial steps toward privatization. The programme found the approval of the IMF and served as the basis for a stand-by agreement signed in February 1990 (Bjork 1995; Gomułka 1995).

The Balcerowicz Programme and fiscal reform

Fiscal reform comprised a prominent component of both the agenda of the Mazowiecki government and the Balcerowicz Programme. As a matter of fact, the fiscal deficit was the first target of reform mentioned in Mazowiecki's inaugural speech. The new government moved swiftly to regain control over the budget. The first steps to reduce the increasing fiscal deficit were taken already in late 1989. By a combination of cuts in subsidies, the suspension of investment projects and tougher deadlines for tax payments, the government succeeded in narrowing the 1989 budgetary gap by 2 to 3 per cent of GDP (Wellisz et al. 1993, pp. 29-30).

The Balcerowicz Programme and the 1990 budget called for a further fiscal correction of about 7 per cent of GDP, thereby achieving an almost balanced budget in 1990. Fiscal adjustment was to be achieved by a combination of expenditure cuts and revenue increases (Gomułka 1990, pp. 133-6; Wellisz et al. 1993, p. 30; de Crombrugghe and Lipton 1994, pp. 114-15). On the expenditure side, further cuts in subsidies, partly offset by increased allowances for social outlays, were to result in net savings worth about 3 per cent of GDP. On the revenue side, the Balcerowicz Programme foresaw a revenue increase amounting to 4 per cent of GDP, to be largely accomplished by the elimination of tax exemptions and by further improvements in tax collection.

Concerning expenditures, the Balcerowicz Programme combined general expenditure restraint with deep cuts in subsidies and investments. Social policy reform played a subordinate role. While the 1990 budget contained increases in social spending, the programme itself was virtually silent on social policy reform (Przeworski 1993, p. 142). As a matter of fact, social policy legislation was drafted separately under the guidance of Minister of Labour Jacek Kuroń. Aimed at cushioning the population from social hardships, it contained extremely generous provisions.

On the tax side, the Balcerowicz Programme combined stopgap measures with the announcement of medium-term structural reforms. Reforms could build on the measures introduced under the old regime. As in Hungary, the economic reforms of the late 1980s had included changes in the tax system (Bolkowiak 1993, pp. 7-8). The single most important move had been the reform of profit taxation. The introduction of a uniform corporate income tax with a flat 40 per cent rate in January 1989 had not only reduced the nominal tax burden levied on enterprises; together with amendments to the taxation of incomes derived from private entrepreneurial activities, it also had ended the differentiated treatment of the public and the private sector. In the state-owned sector, the reform of profit taxation had gone hand in hand with a relaxation of wage increase taxation and the introduction of a new asset tax, the *dywidenda*. In addition, the number of turnover tax rates had been reduced.

The short-term tax measures implemented at the beginning of 1990 aimed at closing the budget gap and eliminating some of the more extreme distortions built into the old tax system (Bolkowiak 1993, pp. 14-16). Moreover, tax policy was deployed to support wage restraint and to impose financial discipline on state-owned enterprises. Measures included some reductions in the taxation of personal incomes and a cut in profit tax allowances. The *dywidenda* and the *popiwek*, a tax on wage increases introduced in 1982, were tightened. In order to make tax collection more effective and to reduce collection lags, the dates of tax payment were moved up. In January 1990, the government also decided to increase employers' social security contributions. As part of the medium-term institutional reforms, the Balcerowicz Programme pledged the introduction of VAT and a Western-style personal income tax in early 1991.

4.3   CZECHOSLOVAKIA

In Czechoslovakia the economic and political conditions at the outset of the transformation were less favourable to the initiation of large-scale reform than in Poland: The short-term reform pressure was weaker; the authorization of reformers and reforms took some time, and the federal set-up of Czechoslovakia complicated the formulation of reforms. While these factors did not prevent the launching of radical reforms, they delayed their start.

Economic and political conditions at the outset of the transformation

Czechoslovakia was the penultimate Central East European country to renounce communism. In contrast to Hungary and Poland, the transition to democracy was not negotiated, but took the form of a 'capitulation' (Stark and Bruszt 1998, pp. 17-20). Following demonstrations and strikes in November 1989, the old regime simply collapsed and a 'Government of National Understanding,' dominated by non-communist ministers, was formed (Batt 1991, pp. 38-42). The founding elections in June 1990 brought a sweeping victory for the democratic camp. From a comparative perspective, economic and political conditions at the outset of the transformation were characterized by limited reform pressure, strong popular support for reform, substantial constraints on executive authority and the gradual emergence of a strong change team.

Reform pressure, 1989-90

At the end of 1989, the Czechoslovak economy was a more or less unreconstructed centrally-planned economy that suffered from relatively weak macroeconomic imbalances (Myant 1989, 1993, pp. 155-87; OECD 1991a, pp. 9-15; World Bank 1991). On the one hand, classical central planning with comprehensive price controls and entrepreneurial dinosaurs prevailed, the private sector was virtually non-existent and the economy strongly depended on CMEA trade. On the other hand, the macroeconomic situation at the beginning of the transformation was relatively favourable. Open and hidden inflation were low (Drábek et al. 1994), as were domestic and external debts. The lack of structural reforms and the advantageous macroeconomic situation were two sides of the same coin. Both reflected the 'course of intransigent resistance to reform' (Batt 1991, p. 16) that had characterized the country's economic policy after the repression of the Prague spring. Traumatized by the experience of 1968, the new leadership feared that economic reforms might spin out of control economically as well as politically. The Husak government thus not only refrained from tinkering with economic reform but also pursued a conservative macroeconomic policy.

Popular support, 1989-90

The 'Government of National Understanding' was able to count on broad popular support. The suppression of the Prague spring and the repressive nature of the Husak regime had made the Czechoslovak communist regime less popular than the Hungarian. Czechoslovakia's inter-war history as one of the world's leading industrial countries served as a yardstick to devalue the communist interlude and provided a sense of direction for the future. The widespread feeling that Czechoslovakia was lagging behind Hungary and Poland, the pioneers of economic reform under communism, increased the readiness to support radical leaps. However, pro-reform sentiments were stronger in the Czech Republic than in Slovakia. In the latter, the communist years were seen in a much more favourable light because they represented a period of industrialization and the achievement of economic parity with the originally much richer Czech part of the country. Moreover, the economic structure created by communist industrialization raised concerns that the transition to the market would become more costly than in the Czech Republic.

The 'Government of National Understanding' initially suffered from issues of legitimation since it had not been voted into office or confirmed by elections. But the founding elections in June 1990, with an extremely high voter turnout of almost 96 per cent, brought a sweeping victory for the democratic forces and granted the government a clear mandate for change (Gabal (ed.) 1996). In the Czech Republic, the Civic Forum received over 50 per cent of all votes and won about two thirds of the Czech seats in the two chambers of the Federal Assembly. In Slovakia, Public Against Violence, Civic Forum's sister organization, scored less successfully at the ballot box, yet still emerged as by far the strongest party. Contemporary surveys revealed broad support for market-oriented reform combined with a clear awareness of the associated transitory costs and even some dissatisfaction with the slow start of reforms (Juchler 1994, p. 396; Večerník 1996, pp. 218, 222).

Executive authority, 1989-90
In formal terms, the political position of the 'Government of National Understanding' was weak. Initially, it consisted of a very heterogeneous group of people and had no clear parliamentary base. This only partly changed after the 1990 elections (Stark and Bruszt 1998, pp. 179-83). While the coalition of Civic Forum, Public Against Violence and the Slovak Christian Democratic Movement that was formed after the elections commanded a clear majority of votes and seats, the government continued to suffer from internal heterogeneity. Civic Forum and Public Against Violence were broad-based movement parties with assertive and individualistic deputies, so that party discipline inside and outside parliament was rather weak. Even more important were constraints inherent in the country's federal system with its peculiar 'semi-tricameral' (Batt 1991, p. 98) Federal Assembly. Based on the amended 1968 constitution, this system gave Slovaks strong veto powers. Legislative changes required majorities in the House of People, the lower chamber with proportional representation from the Czech and Slovak Republics, as well as in both sections of the House of Nations, the second chamber composed of two equally strong republican sections. A three-fifths quorum was necessary not only for constitutional amendments, but also for several other issues, including the budget, taxation and the Civil Code. This unique federal structure implied that merely one fifth of the deputies in the House of Nations could effectively block the passage of an important part of legislation (Batt 1991, p. 97-8; Elster 1995, p. 111). Given the Czech-Slovak tensions that were visible from the beginning of the transformation, this system of checks and balances furnished reform opponents with veto points and increased the need for consensus.

Position of reformers, 1989-90
The federal institutional framework in place until the dissolution of Czechoslovakia also infringed on the position of reformers within government, both by restricting the control capable of being exercised from the centre and by creating complex co-ordination requirements. The federal minister of finance was obligated to respect the partial autonomy of the republics, to co-operate with his republican colleagues in the 'Financial

Council' and to shepherd legislation through a highly fragmented parliament. In addition, the government did not crown any economic czar at the beginning of the transformation. Instead, responsibilities were divided between Václav Klaus, the Finance Minister, and Valtr Komárek, the Deputy Prime Minister with overall authority for formulating economic reform. Unlike Balcerowicz in Poland, Klaus was not bestowed with exclusive authority for policy-formulation and policy-making at the outset of the transformation, but gradually emerged as the architect of Czech (oslovak) economic reform (Myant 2003, pp. 16-24).

The absence of an economic super-minister reflected both the more comfortable economic situation in early 1990, which made emergency measures unnecessary, and the initial split within the government on the strategy of economic reform. In the first months of 1990, two camps struggled for hegemony, one led by Klaus, the other by Komárek. As in most other transformation countries, this controversy was framed essentially in terms of shock therapy versus gradualism, even if both camps were keen to dissociate themselves from the more negative connotations of each of the two labels.

In the course of 1990, Klaus and his group managed to consolidate their position. When Komárek left the government in April 1990, the battle over the strategy of economic reform was by and large decided. Despite the gradualist leanings of most of the Civic Forum's leadership, including President Havel, Klaus gradually emerged as the uncontested architect of economic reform. For one thing, Klaus could rely on a coherent change team. Consisting of several economists who had attended Klaus' famous economic seminar in the 1980s and shared a similar outlook, the group soon controlled key economic positions within the three governments. Moreover, Klaus proved to be a skillful and charismatic political leader (Saxonberg 1999). This became visible as early as October 1990 when he beat Martin Palouš, Havel's candidate, in an election for the chair of the Civic Forum. When the Civic Forum split in early 1991, the vast majority of its members rallied around Klaus. Unlike Balcerowicz in Poland, Klaus could rely on a strong political constituency.

The way to the launching of reforms

The overall economic and political situation after the demise of communism was not very conducive to a rapid initiation of reforms: Unlike Poland, Czechoslovakia did not find itself in an acute economic crisis that would have underlined the urgency of reforms; although popular support for reforms was strong, the government enjoyed only a 'revolutionary' mandate until the 1990 elections; executive authority was heavily constrained by Czechoslovakia's unique federal system and Czech-Slovak quarrels over the shape of the federation; finally, reformers were initially in a relatively weak position within government.

Given these conditions, it is not surprising that economic reform was delayed and took off only after the government had been confirmed at the ballot box, Klaus and his team had consolidated their position within government and an understanding on the future shape of the Federation had been achieved.[3] Before the founding elections in June 1990, only a few interim measures were adopted. These measures included the abolition of the old planning apparatus, the liberalization of market entry, the introduction of a two-tier banking system and a devaluation of the Czechoslovak currency. A majority within the 'Government of National Understanding' hesitated to launch major reforms without prior confirmation by the voters and rejected calls for an acceleration of reforms.

Reforms gained momentum after the elections. Following vague earlier announcements, the government submitted a comprehensive reform programme to parliament in July 1990. Approved by the Federal Assembly in mid-September after intense discussions, the 'Scenario for Economic Reform' became the main script for Czechoslovak economic transformation (Martin 1990; Myant 1993, pp. 174-83; 2003, pp. 18-21; Havel et al. 1998, pp. 248-9). A broad outline rather than a precise programme, the 'Scenario' comprised seven main sections which dealt with macroeconomic stabilization, privatization, price liberalization, convertibility, agriculture, social policy and structural policy.

The passage of the 'Scenario' indicated the consolidation of Klaus's position as well as the persisting limits to his power. The document bore the signature of Klaus and his group yet also contained elements of compromise. In line with Klaus's convictions, the 'Scenario' assigned top priority to macroeconomic stabilization and envisaged a comprehensive price liberalization along with the introduction of internal convertibility. The other sections were less clear-cut. The section on privatization confined itself to emphasizing the need for property reform and listing a variety of different strategies. Although it mentioned the distribution of shares 'below costs,' it did not contain a commitment to a particular privatization strategy, let alone a detailed plan for what later became Czechoslovakia's famous programme of voucher privatization. The sections of the 'Scenario' on agriculture, social policy and structural policy, although vague, were full of calls for smoothing transition costs through state interventions which ran counter to Klaus's beliefs. The limits of Klaus's control over the agenda also became clear in the 'Scenario for Social Reform,' a programme prepared by a group around Petr Miller, the determined Minister of Labour and Social Affairs, and passed parallel to the 'Scenario for Economic Reform' (Orenstein 1996, pp. 16-17).

The implementation of the reforms proposed in the 'Scenario for Economic Reform' was complicated by Czech-Slovak tensions. Present since the 'velvet revolution,' these pressures were aggravated by the results of the 1990 elections which underlined differences between the two republics. The Slovaks' more sceptical stance toward radical economic reform and the disputes over the separation of powers among the Republics and the Federation meant that Czech-Slovak conflicts also bore strong implications for economic reform (Batt 1991, pp. 99-102). To avoid the perception of economic reform as something 'Czech-made' being 'imposed' upon Slovakia, Czech and Slovak politicians first had to achieve a consensus about the federal modus vivendi. Complicated negotiations over an amendment of the 1968 constitution lasted from August to December (Obrman and Pehe 1990). It took the so-called Competence Law to pave the way for the eventual start of economic reform. Approved by the Federal Assembly on 12 December 1990, it provisionally assigned responsibilities to the Federation and the two republics until the passage of a new constitution. While the new law extended the power of the republics and replaced federal transfers with 'own' shares in taxes, it left the responsibility for key issues of economic reform with the Federation.

The enactment of a comprehensive stabilization and reform programme on the basis of the 'Scenario' eventually came in January 1991 (Aghevli et al. 1992; OECD 1991a; Myant 1993, pp. 187-205). This programme was patterned on the Polish 1990 programme. Backed by a stand-by agreement with the IMF and a social accord with the trade unions, it included a comprehensive liberalization of prices and foreign trade, the introduction of internal convertibility, a strong up-front devaluation, the imposition of a temporary import surcharge and tight income, fiscal and monetary policies. In addition, the programme initiated the privatization of state assets. After passing laws on small-scale privatization and restitution, the government laid the legal foundations of large-scale privatization, including the voucher programme, in February 1991.

The fiscal side of economic reform

Fiscal probity played a prominent role in Czechoslovak economic reform right from the beginning. It reflected Klaus's emphasis on macroeconomic stability and fit well into Czechoslovak traditions of fiscal conservatism.[4] The new government's commitment to fiscal discipline, which went far beyond IMF recommendations, became visible as early as March 1990 when the government amended the 1990 budget that it had inherited from the old regime. While Klaus was forced to grant some concessions, he managed to push through expenditure cuts that helped to turn the originally projected small deficit into a surplus (Martin 1991, pp. 12-13; Myant 1993, pp. 172-3; Štěpánek et al. 1995, pp. 14-15). The May 1990 reform programme and the 'Scenario' codified this policy of fiscal restraint and called for fiscal surpluses. In line with these programmatic statements, the 1991 budget, which the Federal Assembly unanimously approved in December 1990 after the passage of the Competence Law, projected a small surplus along with substantial reductions in fiscal intermediation (Martin 1991).

As for tax reform, Czechoslovak reformers opted for a two-stage approach that combined interim measures with the introduction of a completely new Western-style tax system as of 1 January 1993 (Heady and Smith 1995; Heady et al. 1994; Lichnowská et al. 1994; Zamrazilova 1994). The measures mentioned in the 'Scenario' differed in levels of specificity. With regard to the new medium-term tax system, the programme listed a set of taxes and of legislative acts to be adopted but was rather brief on the design of the new taxes and the legislative schedule. Curiously, the overall schedule also went beyond the term of the new parliament. The peculiar strategy of tax reform was motivated largely by pragmatic concerns. Reformers felt that the complex legislative and administrative requirements might not be fulfilled earlier. In addition, the phased introduction of the new tax system gave the government a higher degree of flexibility in the early stage of the transformation, making it easier to weather the transformation crisis and to subordinate tax reform to macroeconomic policy.

At the outset of the transformation, Czechoslovakia had an unreconstructed communist tax system. In contrast to Hungary and Poland, a differentiated turnover tax system with 1506 separate rates, including 428 negative ones, was still in effect. The government had not made any moves toward parametric, uniform profit taxation, let alone the wholesale adoption of a Western-style tax system as Hungary had done. Against this background, initial reforms focused on those taxes that had been particularly 'contaminated' by communism, that is, on profit and turnover taxes. The first interim measures were adopted already in December 1989 when the new government started to reduce and unify profit taxation. In 1990, the government virtually eliminated the arbitrary levies on profits that branch ministries had hitherto imposed as part of the discretionary cross-subsidization of enterprises. Profit tax rates, which originally ranged from 75 to 85 per cent, were standardized and reduced to 65 per cent for non-financial enterprises and 55 per cent for banks. In July 1990, the abolition of negative turnover tax rates on foodstuffs, equivalent to eliminating subsidies, brought the repeal of about two thirds of all negative rates. The resulting jump in food prices was compensated by the introduction of a universal lump-sum transfer payment. Unsuccessfully opposed by Klaus, this compensation made the whole operation revenue-neutral (Myant 1993, p. 174).

Further tax reforms were implemented as part of the 1991 reform programme. The remaining negative turnover tax rates were eliminated and the number of positive ones reduced to four levels, initially set at 0, 12, 22 and 32 per cent, plus some higher rates on a number of typical excise items. The basic corporate income tax was reduced to 55 per cent. In order to support the nascent private sector, private enterprises were given a reduced rate of 20 per cent on the first 200 000 CZK of profits. Finally, the old wage tax was complemented by a special personal income tax on non-wage incomes.

On the expenditure side, initial measures concentrated on cuts in subsidies (van der Willigen 1994, p. 177). The first subsidies to go were enterprise subsidies that previously had been left to the discretion of branch ministries and had been financed from discretionary levies on profits. Along with some cuts in defence and security spending, the elimination of this arbitrary cross-subsidization accounted for the roughly 10 per cent decline in the expenditure-to-GDP ratio in 1990. Expenditure reform gained momentum with the phasing out of most food subsidies in July 1990. The 1991 budget envisaged a further decrease in the expenditure-to-GDP ratio by 12 per cent (Aghevli et al. 1992, p. 11; OECD 1991a, pp. 70-71). Given the 5 per cent decline in GDP originally projected, real spending was budgeted to shrink even more. The bulk of this adjustment was to fall on subsidies whose share of the GDP was set to drop by 9 per cent. The least severe cuts in real spending were imposed on social expenditures.

4.4   HUNGARY

In Hungary the initial reforms after the fall of communism were less radical than in Czechoslovakia and Poland. Differences in starting conditions are part of the explanation. In Hungary the far-reaching economic reforms that had been adopted before 1989 reduced the need for reforms. Hungary not only found itself in a relatively comfortable short-term macroeconomic situation, but unlike Czechoslovakia and Poland, it also already had a Western-style tax system. However, these differences in the reform agenda are not the whole story. Compared to Czechoslovakia and Poland, Hungarian policy-makers also faced stronger political constraints, which complicated the initiation of reform.

Economic and political conditions in 1990

Like in Poland, Hungary's transition to democracy resulted from negotiations between the incumbent communists and the political opposition (Batt 1991, pp. 34-8; Stark and Bruszt 1998, pp. 15-48). Following the Round Table Talks from June to September 1989, free parliamentary elections were held in late March and early April 1990. These elections made the conservative Hungarian Democratic Forum (MDF) the strongest party and brought a centre-right coalition led by Prime Minister József Antall to power. Owing to the comprehensive pre-1990 reforms, the new government found itself in a seemingly favourable economic situation. Compared to the Mazowiecki government in Poland and the 'Government of National Understanding' in Czechoslovakia, the Antall government was in a much stronger constitutional position, commanded a more homogeneous parliamentary majority but enjoyed a weaker mandate for change. Within government, reformers were in a relatively weak position.

Reform pressure, 1990
In mid-1990, the Hungarian economy was characterized by the combination of a partially reformed communist economic system and minor macroeconomic imbalances (Berend 1990; Boote and Somogyi 1991). The pre-1990 economic reforms had made the country the – sometimes acclaimed, sometimes condemned – epitome of reform communism within the Soviet bloc, so that reforms did not need to start from scratch. The sectoral structure and the price system were less distorted, the prevailing shortages smaller and the private sector and the share of foreign trade with OECD countries larger than in most other transition countries. With the bulk of prices already liberalized, the government did not have to fear the negative economic, social and political effects of a comprehensive price decontrol. Moreover, Hungary had already started to rebuild her economic institutions along Western lines. The radicalization of economic reforms in the course of the 1980s had brought far-reaching institutional reforms, including the introduction of a competition law (1984), a bankruptcy law (1986), a two-tier banking system (1987), a corporate law (1988) and a Western-style tax system (1988/89). Thus, an important part of the legal infrastructure of a market economy was already in place at the end of 1989. As a consequence, Hungary was widely perceived as enjoying a head start and as being destined to become the success story among the transition countries.

The macroeconomic situation in mid-1990 was somewhat less comfortable but still much better than in Poland. When the Antall government came to power, Hungary's external position was fragile. Due to the overshooting of current account and fiscal deficits, as well as to some uncertainties over the country's foreign debt strategy after the elections, capital inflows and foreign exchange reserves dropped in the first months of 1990. With some mid-year fiscal adjustment on the basis of a stand-by agreement with the IMF, and with a little help from World Bank and European Union, however, the new government managed to avert the spectre of a currency crisis and to restore confidence in the country's creditworthiness. Both the current account and the fiscal balance improved in the second half of 1990.

Popular support, 1990

As in Czechoslovakia and Poland, Hungary's founding elections documented a clear rejection of the old regime (Tóka (ed.) 1995). In spite of the communists' record of economic and political reform, the opposition forces triumphed and the Hungarian Socialist Party (MSZP), the successor of the old communist party, attracted only a tiny 10 per cent of votes. However, popular support for the new government and for economic reforms was weaker and more fragile than in the neighbouring countries. One piece of evidence is the low voter turnout, which did not exceed 63 per cent in the first and was a mere 46 per cent in the second round of the elections, thus being significantly lower than in the founding elections in Poland and Czechoslovakia. Moreover, almost all comparative surveys document a relatively modest reform enthusiasm. So does the fact that the MDF was elected on the basis of a gradualist platform that promised 'calm strength' and a painless transformation.

The relatively weak reform mandate highlights the ambiguous effects of Hungary's pre-1990 reforms. While these reforms arguably made for favourable economic starting conditions, they came with substantial political costs (Marer 1999, p. 162). The many reforms and the even more frequent reform announcements ever since 1968 nurtured reform fatigue and scepticism. The country's head start and the apparently favourable economic situation made reforms appear less urgent. Finally, the relatively high levels of consumption in the past increased the sensitivity to the 'costs of reform.' Hungary's 'goulash-communism' was much more prone to ex post glorification than other brands of communism. For all these reasons, popular support for radical economic reform was weaker in Hungary than in other transition countries.

Executive authority, 1990

From a comparative perspective, the Antall government enjoyed a rather strong executive authority. Unlike in Czechoslovakia and Poland, the contours of the new political system were almost settled when the Antall government came to power. The new institutional framework, as it emerged from the Round Table Talks and the constitutional deal between the two biggest parliamentary factions, the MDF and the liberal Alliance of Free Democrats (SZDSZ), at the end of April, put a premium on a strong executive authority (Elster et al. 1998, pp. 95-8, 122-4; Bartlett 1997, pp. 141-63; Stark and Bruszt 1998, pp. 170-71). By providing for a 4 per cent threshold and by combining proportional representation and majority voting, Hungary's peculiar electoral system worked against fragmentation of the parliament and the party system. Further, the unicameral parliamentary system with a weak president left the Constitutional Court as the main institutional veto player. Finally, the requirement of a German-style constructive vote of no-confidence, complemented by the prime minister's right to select the members of cabinet, strengthened the position of government against parliament and the standing of the prime minister within cabinet.

Executive authority was further enhanced by the combination of a weak system of interest associations with a rather cohesive party system. In 1990, trade unions were in a shape worse than in the other Central East European countries. Fragmented and consumed with fighting each other, they were weaker than their Czechoslovak and Polish counterparts which both benefited from their involvement in the extrication from communism. This weakness of interest associations coincided with an early differentiation of the party system. Unlike in Czechoslovakia and Poland, the Hungarian anticommunist opposition had already split into separate parties before the founding elections. The main contenders in the 1990 elections were not a more or less reformed communist party and a heterogeneous anticommunist umbrella party, but the conservative MDF and the liberal SZDSZ. As a consequence, the first democratic government was internally more cohesive than in other countries. Although made up of three parties, the government was clearly dominated by the MDF which, thanks to Hungary's peculiar electoral law, accounted for 43 per cent of all seats. With a comfortable majority of seats within parliament, a dominating party and coalition partners with relatively compatible political orientations, the Antall government thus had a rather strong parliamentary basis.

Position of reformers, 1990
The transition to democracy strengthened the position of the Ministry of Finance within government (Bartlett 1997, p. 195). The elimination of the National Planning Office and the diminution of the branch ministries concentrated budgetary authority in the Ministry of Finance. However, the latter's position suffered from the extremely decentralized structure of the public sector. One consequence of the pre-1990 economic reforms was the proliferation of extra-budgetary funds and so-called central budgetary units vested with a high degree of fiscal autonomy. The far-reaching spending, cash management and even borrowing powers of the funds made a large part of overall fiscal activities intransparent even for the Ministry of Finance, thereby complicating debt management and the preparation and execution of the budget.

More importantly, competencies for economic reform were fragmented and that no coherent and uncontested change team existed. Suffering from internal divisions over the course of economic reform and a lack of economic expertise, the MDF had no designated 'economic czar' (Batt 1991, p. 90; Csaba 1992, pp. 952-3; Greskovits 2001, pp. 119-23). The Antall government's first finance minister, Ferenc Rabár, a relatively obscure academic, lacked determination and did not bring a team of committed collaborators with him. Nor was he bestowed with special competencies to oversee reforms by Prime Minister Antall.

From the founding elections to the Kupa Programme

The economic and political conditions in mid-1990 were not very favourable to the launching of reform. Neither an escalating open crisis nor the fear of falling behind underscored the case for reform. The government enjoyed a strong constitutional position and a relatively homogeneous parliamentary majority but only a relatively weak popular mandate. Finally, there was no determined change team ready and able to promote reforms. As a result, the economic policy of the new government suffered from drift (Batt 1991, pp. 88-92; Csaba 1992; Lengyel 1991, pp. 50-54). The new government was quick to distance itself from some of the more populist demands from within the centre-right coalition but failed to commit itself to a clear course. This was partly due to inexperience and the controversies within government over the direction of reforms. Yet what set Hungary apart from other countries was not simply the pluralism of views. Similar debates on the virtues of gradualism and big bang took place in all transition countries. More importantly, the seemingly comfortable economic situation, the open disinterest of the Prime Minister in economic issues and the lack of a determined change team within government were inimical to settling these debates.

The long-awaited 'Economic Programme for National Renewal,' eventually presented in September 1990, was rather vague. Moreover, it fell victim to the taxi driver strike that shattered the country in October 1990. Provoked by the government's plan to cut fuel subsidies, this strike and the public resonance it found once more highlighted the gulf between the government and the population and indicated the fragile mandate the government could count on. Forced into negotiations and concessions, the government reacted by retreating from earlier announcements. A new programme presented in November contained only a third of all subsidy cuts envisaged in the September draft and postponed all social security reforms (Szamuely and Csaba 1998, p. 199).

Reforms gained momentum in December 1990 when Prime Minister Antall, in a move to counter irritations over the bad start of the government, made Mihályi Kupa, a well-respected technocrat and one of the fathers of the 1988/89 tax reform, Minister of Finance (Greskovits 2001, pp. 123-5). Unlike Rabár, Kupa was bestowed with broader competencies and put in charge of overseeing economic policy. Initially backed by the Prime Minister, Kupa drew up a new medium-term reform programme. This so-called Kupa Programme was presented to the public in February 1991. Although still vague, it went beyond earlier proclamations in that it comprised a rough legislative time-table and a detailed medium-term macroeconomic projection. The Kupa Programme also served as the basis for a three-year agreement with the IMF which replaced the 1990 stand-by agreement concluded under the outgoing Németh government.

Fiscal reform in 1990

Given Hungary's particular economic situation, the initial agenda of fiscal reform differed from those in Czechoslovakia and Poland. The need for a tough fiscal adjustment was weaker since the short-term macroeconomic situation was more comfortable and the inflationary effects to be expected from the liberalization of prices were much more limited. Unlike Czechoslovakia and Poland, Hungary also had a tax system roughly in line with Western standards. These peculiarities notwithstanding, most economists agreed upon the need for a continuation of fiscal reform. With off-budget activities abounding, fiscal institutions were fragmented and intransparent. Government spending and the public debt reached high levels, and the tax system was a 'troubled brew of the paternalistic redistribution of a socialist economy, the fiscal impotence of a destitute Third World country, and the refined progressive tax system of a Scandinavian welfare state' (Kornai 1990, pp. 116-17). The high burden of foreign debt and the anticipated fiscal pressures during the transformational recession further strengthened the case for fiscal reform. Hence, almost all early 'blueprints' for Hungarian economic reform, including the well-known programmes by the Blue Ribbon Commission, the Bridge Group or Kornai (1990), converged in emphasizing the importance of fiscal reform (Csaba 1992, p. 952).

However, fiscal reform progressed slowly under the Antall government. The first measures aimed at securing the fulfilment of the 1990 budget target. This was accomplished by a combination of increased excises, higher dividend payments by state-owned enterprises and some reductions in subsidies and enterprise tax reliefs. At the end of the year, fiscal performance was even better than projected in the original budget. Instead of the budgeted general government surplus of 0.5 per cent of GDP, a surplus of 0.9 per cent was achieved, largely due to stronger than expected revenues (NBH 1990, pp. 26-32; OECD 1991b, pp. 41-3).

The 1991 budget, the first one prepared by the Antall government, brought some organizational changes. A number of former off-budget items were consolidated with the central government budget. Given the positive 1990 fiscal outcome and in line with the government's cautious overall approach, the 1991 budget set rather modest targets and implied some fiscal softening by projecting a small deficit for 1991 (Okolicsanyi 1991; OECD 1991b, pp. 43-4). On the expenditure side, the budget called for minor cuts in real expenditures, largely falling on subsidies; on the tax side, the number of personal income tax brackets to be applied in 1991 were increased and the bottom rate reduced to 12 per cent. For revenue concerns, brackets were not adjusted to inflation, thus increasing effective taxation. These amendments were accompanied by minor changes in the corporate income tax, including the elimination of some tax reliefs and the imposition of a temporary surcharge on the profit tax rate. As the budget's targets were built upon rather optimistic assumptions, the budget was widely regarded as not credible. Kupa himself, who became Finance Minister in the midst of the budget debate, criticized the government's draft for being 'not very good' (cited in Okolicsanyi 1991, p. 18). The Kupa Programme was rather brief on fiscal reform. It projected small fiscal deficits from 1991 to 1993, followed by an almost balanced budget in 1994. The expenditure-to-GDP ratio was to fall by 6 percentage points until 1994, almost exclusively through cuts in subsidies.

4.5   CONCLUSION

This chapter has dealt with the initiation of post-communist fiscal reform in Czechoslovakia, Hungary and Poland. The analysis suggests that differences in political constraints and in the political feasibility of reforms played an important role in shaping reform trajectories. The economic and political conditions in Czechoslovakia and Poland after the demise of communism were politically more conducive to launching radical reforms than the conditions in Hungary. From a comparative perspective, Czechoslovak and Polish reformers benefited from the combination of a more 'critical' economic situation, a broader mandate and a stronger position within government. In both countries the old regime was more strongly discredited, the case for a radical break with the past more deeply felt and the readiness to support drastic reforms more widespread than in Hungary. In Poland the macroeconomic crisis underscored the case for reform; in Czechoslovakia the fear of falling behind the other, seemingly more advanced transition countries fulfilled a similar function. These conditions rendered the initiation of bold economic reforms politically feasible. Conversely, the seemingly more favourable economic situation and the less enthusiastic popular support for reforms in Hungary led the government to shy away from the radical measures supported by many economists.

Variations in the intensity of reform pressure, the strength of mandates and the position of reformers also account for many of the differences between Poland and Czechoslovakia and help explain why reforms began more quickly in Poland than in Czechoslovakia. Given the acute macroeconomic crisis, reforms were perceived to be more urgent in Poland than in Czechoslovakia. The Mazowiecki government enjoyed a stronger mandate, since it was elected into office and did not have to wait for an ex post legitimization at the polls. Polish reformers initially were in a stronger position within government than their Czechoslovak colleagues. Unlike Balcerowicz, Klaus was not vested with extraordinary competencies from the outset of the transformation, but gradually emerged as the uncontested architect of Czechoslovak economic and fiscal reform.

The analysis also indicates that national differences in executive authority did not play a major role in shaping the initiation of fiscal reform. In Poland and Czechoslovakia the internal heterogeneity of the new governments did not prevent the adoption of reforms. The broad political bases on which the Polish and the Czechoslovak government relied even favoured the launching of reforms by boosting the governments' legitimacy. Other constraints on executive authority also did not impede the passage of radical reforms. In Poland the concessions made to the communists did not pose major obstacles in the short-term. Given Solidarność's triumphant victory at the polls and the dire economic situation, President Jaruzelski, the communist cabinet members and the incumbent majority in the Sejm behaved rather passively and did not dare to challenge the Mazowiecki government. In Czechoslovakia the debates over the future of the federation delayed the start of reforms. Yet the federal institutional framework, with its intricate checks and balances, did not become a major hindrance to reform. Ironically the Hungarian government, the one with the strongest constitutional position and the most ideologically coherent parliamentary majority, proceeded the most slowly.

NOTES

1. There is a vast literature on the formulation, design and effects of the Balcerowicz Programme. My personal selection includes Balcerowicz 1994a, pp. 159-64; Johnson and Kowalska 1994; Lipton and Sachs 1990; Myant 1993, pp. 81-126; Przeworski 1993; Sachs 1993; Wellisz et al. 1993.

2. In this respect, it was symptomatic that the Balcerowicz Programme was presented to the public before the cabinet formally approved it.
3. For the initiation of economic reform in Czechoslovakia, see Batt 1991, pp. 95-102; Dyba and Svejnar 1994, pp. 98-9; Juchler 1994, pp. 326-34; Myant 1993, pp. 168-86; Svejnar 1993, pp. 26-9.
4. These often-mentioned traditions (and the government's attempt to evoke them) found expression in the portrait of A. Rasin, the first Czechoslovak Finance Minister and architect of the successful orthodox stabilization in the early 1920s, that Klaus hung above his desk (Večerník 1996, p. 239, n. 2).

5.   Staying the course I: fiscal reform during the post-communist fiscal crisis

5.1   INTRODUCTION

After the start of the reforms, economic and political conditions changed. Czechoslovakia, Hungary and Poland all experienced a severe drop in GDP. As the countries entered the 'valley of tears,' discontent with reforms grew and popular support became tenuous. At the same time the initial improvement in the fiscal stance soon gave way to substantial fiscal tensions (Campbell 1992; Kornai 1992a; Mizsei and Rostowski 1994; Dąbrowski 1997). The emerging post-communist fiscal crisis was caused by contradictory developments on the revenue and the expenditure side of the budget. On the one hand, the drop in output and employment and the shift to a new tax system resulted in a decline in revenues; on the other, the increase in unemployment and the social hardships associated with the transformational recession led to higher social spending.

The governments in the three countries under analysis reacted differently to these economic and political challenges. The continuation of fiscal reform proceeded smoothly in Czechoslovakia, where the government responded quickly and managed to contain the size of deficits. In Poland tax and expenditure reform slowed after the start of reforms. However the different governments that were in power between 1991 and 1993 succeeded in pushing through substantial short-term austerity measures. Although these measures were not sufficient to prevent the emergence of huge budget deficits in 1991 and 1992, they helped overcome the fiscal crisis. Hungary's conservative government continued to move cautiously. It delayed unpopular tax and expenditure reforms, tolerated the overshooting of the 1991 and 1992 budget deficits and confined itself to the adoption of relatively modest corrective measures. As a result, Hungary's fiscal problems prevailed until 1995/96 when the newly elected centre-left government eventually tackled the issue.

This chapter analyses the continuation of fiscal reform in Czechoslovakia, Hungary and Poland during the post-communist fiscal crisis. As with the previous chapter, it focuses on the role of political constraints and examines how changes and differences in reform pressure, popular support, executive authority and the position of reformers have shaped differences in the continuation of reform over time and between countries. The structure of the chapter is also similar to Chapter 4, with a section on Poland (5.2) followed by sections on Czechoslovakia (5.3) and Hungary (5.4) and a concluding comparative assessment (5.5).

5.2   POLAND

Of the three countries compared, the deterioration of the fiscal stance was the most dramatic in Poland. Moreover, as the front runner of economic transformation, Poland was the first country to experience the post-communist fiscal crisis and could not learn from the experience of other countries.

Economic and political conditions, 1990-93

After the implementation of the Balcerowicz Programme had started, economic and political conditions in Poland dramatically changed. In 1990 the Polish economy entered a severe recession. When the 'social costs' of transformation began to materialize, popular support for reform dwindled. At the same time, political and institutional liabilities associated with Poland's negotiated transition to democracy surfaced. From 1990 to 1993 Poland was governed by a series of short-lived minority governments with fragile parliamentary bases.

Reform pressure, 1990-93
The Balcerowicz Programme originally foresaw a small 3.5 per cent dip in GDP in 1990, followed by the resumption of growth as early as 1991. The actual transformation crisis proved to be more severe than generally expected (Table 5.1). The jump in the price level following the liberalization of prices was higher than expected and the subsequent decline in inflation took longer than projected. In 1990 and 1991 GDP fell by almost 12 and 7 per cent, respectively. Original estimates painted an even darker picture. The official unemployment rate jumped to 6 per cent in 1990, doubled in 1991 to 12 per cent, and peaked at 16 per cent in 1993. Real wages plummeted by 25 per cent in 1990 and stagnated from 1991 to 1993.

Like most other transiton countries, Poland witnessed a brief fiscal honeymoon after the reforms began. Despite the large contraction in output, profits and profit tax revenues were considerably higher than anticipated. However, the fiscal situation began to deteriorate as early as 1990 (de Crombrugghe and Lipton 1994, pp. 115-20). The unfolding fiscal pressures were stronger than in Hungary or Czechoslovakia. Owing to the more volatile inflation rate, both the initial increase and the subsequent drop in profit tax revenues were more pronounced than in the two other countries. At the same time, the consequences of two decisions – the indexation of pensions on wages adopted in early 1990 and the indexation of public sector wages agreed on at the Round Table Talks – increased pressures on expenditures (de Crombrugghe 1997).

Table 5.1   *Economic and fiscal conditions in Poland, 1990-93*

	1990	1991	1992	1993
GDP growth (real)	-11.6	-7.0	2.6	3.8
Inflation rate (CPI, annual average)	585.8	70.3	43.0	35.3
Unemployment rate (end-year)	6.3	11.8	13.6	16.4
Current account (% of GDP)	1.0	-2.6	1.1	0.7
General government balance (% of GDP)	3.1	-6.7	-6.7	-3.1
General government expenditure (% of GDP)	39.8	49.0	49.5	50.5

Sources: EBRD, Transition Report, various issues.

Popular support, 1990-93

With the massive and higher-than-expected social costs of transformation, reform fatigue increased (Rose 1999a). The popularity of the Balcerowicz Programme declined rapidly. In the second quarter of 1990, the difference between the percentages of those supporting and those opposing reforms had already decreased by 50 per cent; in the course of 1991, opponents began to outnumber supporters (Przeworski 1993, p. 160, Table 3.4; Johnson and Kowalska 1994, pp. 211-14). The results of the 1990 presidential and the 1991 parliamentary elections further reflected the rising discontent with the state of economic reform. Prime Minister Mazowiecki suffered a humiliating defeat in the presidential elections. In the 1991 elections, the parties that had campaigned against the Balcerowicz Programme scored well, while the Democratic Union (UD) and the Liberal-Democratic Congress (KLD), the standard-bearers of economic reform, received less than a quarter of the vote. A final indicator of the spread of dissatisfaction was the resurgence of strikes and other forms of social unrest. Although Solidarność supported the Balcerowicz Programme, a major wave of strikes began as early as May 1990; protests by farmers intensified in the summer. By all accounts, social unrest was stronger in Poland than in the other transition countries (Ekiert 1998).

Executive authority, 1990-93

The various governments in office between 1990 and 1993 were rather vulnerable to the increasing reform fatigue. Their position suffered from a combination of frequent elections, a fractured parliament, shaky majorities and frequent changes in government. From 1990 to 1993 three national elections were held – presidential elections in November 1990 and parliamentary elections in October 1991 and September 1993. During this period, Poland had a total of five different governments, none of whom commanded a clear majority within the Sejm.

In the course of 1990, relations between the government and the Sejm worsened. The government could no longer count on the Sejm's cooperation. Growing reform fatigue and decay of the anticommunist opposition resulted in a more fragmented and more assertive parliament. The election of President Wałęsa in November 1990 had an ambivalent effect on the government's authority. On the one hand, the new government under Prime Minister Jan Bielecki, which had been formed after Mazowiecki's resignation, could rely on the president's support and benefit from his democratic legitimation. On the other hand, the government's relations with the Sejm suffered from the escalating struggle between Wałęsa and parliament. In 1991, the government thus faced an increasingly hostile and antagonistic Sejm.

The 1991 elections produced an extremely fragmented Sejm (Michta 1997, pp. 78-80). Unrestricted proportional representation resulted in a parliament composed of 29 parties. The strongest party, the liberal UD, controlled a mere 13.5 per cent of the seats. Any majority coalition had to contain at least five parties. This fragmentation led to a sequence of short-lived governments. The first of these, the centre-right Olszewski government, was sworn in after a two-month stalemate at the end of December 1991 but was voted out of office on 5 June 1992 after a fierce confrontation with President Wałęsa over the release of communist secret police files. Following a brief interregnum, a minority government was formed. Headed by Prime Minister Hanna Suchocka and backed by President Wałęsa, it was based on a coalition of not less than seven parties. To the surprise of many observers, this government survived until the end of May 1993 when it narrowly lost a vote of no-confidence.

Position of reformers, 1990-93
While executive authority weakened, the position of reformers within government remained strong. Backed by President Wałęsa, Finance Minister Balcerowicz stayed in office after the resignation of the Mazowiecki government and retained responsibility for economic reform. When Balcerowicz left the government after the 1991 elections, the new Prime Minister Olszewski experienced difficulties in finding a new Finance Minister. In December 1991 Olszewski eventually presented Karol Lutkowski, a relatively unknown adviser to Balcerowicz, as Finance Minister. However, Lutkowski resigned in February, partly due to clashes with Jerzy Eysymontt, the new head of the Central Planning Office. Andrzej Olechowski and Jerzy Osiatyński, Lutkowski's successors, enjoyed the backing of their respective Prime Ministers and could rely on the remnants of the Balcerowicz team inside and outside the government.

The continuation of fiscal reform, 1990-93

From the perspective of PEPR, the economic and political conditions from 1990 to 1993 looked extremely unfavourable for the continuation of fiscal reform. The drop in public support for reforms and the temporary improvement of the fiscal stance right after the start of reforms favoured a relaxation of fiscal policy and a postponement and watering down of unpopular expenditure and revenue reforms. The heavy constraints on executive authority reduced the government's capacity to act. In view of these conditions, Polish reformers were surprisingly successful in continuing reform. Contrary to contemporary fears and to what PEPR would suggest, reforms slowed, but did not go off track.

This surprising outcome can be explained by several different factors. First, escalating fiscal pressures kept fiscal reform on the agenda and underlined the need for further reforms. Second, the IMF exercised a strong 'disciplining' effect (Stone 2002, pp. 98-102; Bjork 1995, pp. 105-12). At that time, the Fund's leverage was high because the Paris Club had made the first tranche of debt reduction conditional on Poland's adherence to an IMF-approved reform programme, so that the price for abandoning reforms was high. Third, some alterations in the composition of the change team notwithstanding, Poland continued to have strong and determined reformers. Fourth, some of the apparent constraints on executive authority turned out to be blessings in disguise and helped reformers to stay the course. This applies to the frequent changes in government as well as to the strong fragmentation of the Sejm. While the changes in government in many respects complicated the continuation of reform, they also allowed politicians to avoid blame for problems which they allegedly inherited from previous governments. Likewise, the strong fragmentation of the Sejm rendered it difficult to forge a pro-reform majority, but also reduced the Sejm's potential to act against the government.

Budgets and deficits, 1990-93
The struggles over the 1991-1993 budgets illustrate these ambiguities. On the one hand, they show how the three elections, the frequent changes in government and the fragile parliamentary majorities complicated the continuation of fiscal reform. On the other hand, the three budgets document that the governments in office between 1990 and September 1993 succeeded in adopting substantial short-term measures and managed to prevent potentially much higher fiscal deficits.

The Balcerowicz Programme originally foresaw a fiscal deficit in the first half of 1990 followed by a balanced budget in the second half of the year. In reality, the budget initially performed much better than expected. During the first six months of 1990, profit tax payments exceeded the budgeted level by about 50 per cent, more than compensating for shortfalls in other revenues (Wellisz et al. 1993, p. 35). The underlying surge in profits stemmed from various sources (Schaffer 1992a): the burst of corrective inflation at the beginning of 1990 depressed real wages and, along with historical cost accounting, caused heavy paper profits by boosting the nominal value of inventories. In addition, the massive up-front złoty devaluation increased the value of the substantial foreign exchange holdings of enterprises and banks.

Given the severity of the economic slump and the large overfulfilment of the programme's criteria that had been agreed upon with the IMF, the higher-than-expected fiscal surpluses invited calls for a relaxation of fiscal policy. The upcoming presidential elections made the government receptive to these economically controversial demands. Despite the opposition of the majority of top economic advisers, macroeconomic policy was eased in mid-1990 (Johnson and Kowalska 1994, pp. 209-10; Wellisz et al. 1993, pp. 49-50). In terms of fiscal policy, this meant tax reductions, additional budgetary support for housing and increased preferential credit for farmers. In September 1990 the original budget was amended. The new budget draft still foresaw a balanced budget but revised revenue estimates and expenditure authorizations upwards.

Although it had almost no effect on output, the mid-1990 policy correction contributed to a renewed increase in inflation. As wages rapidly recovered and the positive effects of inflation on government revenues evaporated in the second half of 1990, profits and profit tax revenues started to decline by late

1990 (Schaffer 1992b). Consequently, the fiscal surplus disappeared faster than expected and overall government revenues eventually fell short of the supplementary budget's optimistic forecast. In order to prevent the state budget from plunging into the red, the government had to exercise its extraordinary budgetary competencies and to impose additional spending cuts.

The passage of the 1991 budget reflected the new political conditions after the presidential elections. In contrast to the previous year, negotiations over the budget became a tense and difficult process. Confronted with a more assertive Sejm, the government was forced into substantial compromises (Myant 1993, p. 104). Approved in February 1991, the budget proposed a small deficit. This deficit rested on extremely optimistic assumptions. Revenue calculations assumed a 5 per cent increase in GDP and the persistence of high enterprise profits.

As a matter of fact, the budget performed more poorly than most sceptics had feared (Bolkowiak 1993, pp. 18-23; OECD 1992, pp. 33-6; Owsiak 1994, pp. 254-60; WERI 1992, pp. 47-57)(Table 5.1). Due to continuing declines in output and profits after the official demise of the CMEA, tax intakes, still highly dependent on enterprise profits, remained far behind expectations. By the end of June, revenues stood at a mere 34 per cent of the level projected for the year; they reached no more than 73 per cent by the end of the year. Profit tax revenues were among the revenues hit most strongly. Amounting to no more than 39 per cent of the budgeted level, they were about 6 per cent of GDP less than expected. This massive revenue shortfall was only partly offset by higher-than-expected revenues from excess wage taxation and import duties. As a result, the deficit soared and Poland slipped into a period of severe fiscal stress. Estimates in late 1991 put the 1992 budget deficit in the absence of corrective measures at about 10 per cent of GDP.

The political context complicated the government's reaction to the worsening fiscal crisis. Because of the changes in government and the fragmentation of the Sejm, all budgets and supplementary budgets that were adopted from 1991 to 1993 experienced a rather rocky passage through the Sejm. By 1991, two supplementary budgets had already been approved that provided for overall reductions in government expenditures of approximately 5 per cent of GDP (Gomułka 1992, p. 368). These savings were achieved largely by further cuts in subsidies and delayed increases in pensions and public sector wages. These cuts were highly controversial within the Sejm (Johnson and Kowalska 1994, pp. 224-5; Myant 1993, p. 105). Those actors against retrenchment argued for the toleration of higher deficits. The Bielecki government had to threaten to resign in order to ensure the passage of the August supplementary budget.

Difficulties in installing a new government also shaped the formulation of fiscal policy in 1992 (OECD 1994, pp. 33-4). The 1992 budget was finally presented to the Sejm in early April and approved in June, ironically just one day after the ousting of the Olszewski government. This delay turned out to be a blessing in disguise because it resulted in the implementation of a tough provisional budget that had been drafted for the first quarter of 1992 by the outgoing government. The Olszewski government used this budget to buy time and to avoid the blame for unpopular measures. The final 1992 budget envisaged a state budget deficit of 5 per cent of GDP. While implying an increase in the deficit, the budget provided for some expenditure cuts and revenue increases. Pressure by the IMF facilitated the forging of a relatively broad coalition in favour of the budget draft (Bjork 1995, pp. 107-10).

Similar to its predecessor, however, the 1992 budget turned out to be overly optimistic (WERI 1993, pp. 83-90). Soon after its adoption, it became clear that the actual deficit was likely to exceed the level set by the budget. The incoming Suchocka government quickly blamed its predecessors and submitted a supplementary budget which enlarged the state budget deficit by about a fourth. The actual deficit turned out to be slightly above the original budget target but below the deficit projected in the November supplementary budget. This partly reflected a margin of safety built into the latter. Moreover, financing problems at the end of 1992 prevented a further increase in the deficit (OECD 1994, pp. 33-4; WERI 1993, p. 84).

Submitted to the Sejm at almost the same time as the 1992 supplementary budget, the 1993 budget aimed at stabilizing the nominal deficit (Gomułka 1994, pp. 59-60; OECD 1994, p. 34). To this end, the budget incorporated revenue increases and expenditure cuts worth about 6 per cent of GDP. On the revenue side, measures included an increase in indirect taxes, the introduction of a temporary 6 per cent import surcharge and a freeze in personal income tax brackets. On the expenditure side, the package envisaged cuts in government spending on goods and services along with a further tightening of pensions and public sector wages. The Suchocka government's fragile parliamentary majority caused the adoption of the budget to become a protracted process (Vinton 1993). Despite a series of defeats in earlier ballots, the budget was eventually approved by a narrow margin in February 1993. Parliamentary approval was secured by Prime Minister Suchocka's threats to resign and President Wałęsa's threats to dissolve the parliament. In the end, the 1993 fiscal outcome was considerably better than expected (WERI 1994, pp. 100-11). The general government deficit shrank from 8 per cent of GDP in 1992 to 4 per cent in 1993. This was due, in part, to the adjustment package adopted. More important, however, were unexpectedly favourable revenue and expenditure trends.

Expenditure reform, 1990-93

The change in political constraints after the launching of the Balcerowicz Programme also affected the field of expenditure reform. The favourable fiscal situation in the first half of 1990 and the fragile parliamentary majorities between 1990 and 1993 led to a delay of reforms. At the same time, the strong fiscal pressures allowed reformers to impose substantial short-term measures.

In 1990 the combination of an initially favourable fiscal situation and a strong decline in employment and wages led the government to shy away from further expenditure reforms. In particular, the government did not tackle the time bombs that were associated with generous provisions concerning either social benefits or the indexation of public sector wages. Except for unemployment benefits, which were tightened in September 1990, social programmes were by and large left unchanged. The 1991 budget refrained from further cuts in overall real spending.

The decision to leave social benefits and wages untouched contributed to a drastic increase of the expenditure-to-GDP ratio (Table 5.1). After decreasing from about 49 per cent in 1989 to about 40 per cent in 1990, the ratio rebounded in 1991 and jumped to 48 per cent in 1992 and 52 per cent in 1993. This increase was driven largely by a 'meteoric rise' (Gomułka 1993, p. 194) in social spending, particularly pensions. Propelled by a combination of rising unemployment and rather generous provisions concerning benefits, the share of social security transfers in GDP jumped from 10.6 per cent in 1990 to 17.3 per cent in 1991 and increased by two more percentage points during the next two years.

Beginning in 1991, the government reacted by resorting to short-term measures. Supplementary budgets provided for across-the-board cuts and temporary freezes in public sector wages and transfer payments. Although these measures brought some savings, they did not prevent the expenditure-to-GDP ratio from rising. Moreover, part of the measures created only short-term relief, since the Constitutional Court later declared them unconstitutional. However, the political situation prevented the passage of more structural expenditure reforms (Schwartz 1994, pp. 9-12; World Bank 1994, pp. 28-9).

The slow progress with pension reform epitomizes the problems with expenditure reform (Götting 1998, pp. 164-6). Between 1990 and 1993, little progress was made in either reforming the inherited communist social policy regime or streamlining the generous provisions hastily introduced at the outset of the transformation. Facing a vocal 'grey lobby' capable of mobilizing the Sejm, governments were in a predicament, especially because they lacked a clear reform concept. The first serious reform measures were adopted in late 1991 when the government suspended the indexation of pensions for the rest of the year and eventually succeeded in shepherding a pension law through the Sejm. However, the Constitutional Court overturned both provisions in 1992. In a vote which led to the resignation of Finance Minister Olechowski, the government failed to muster the two-thirds majority in the Sejm needed to override the Court. The Court's decisions further weakened the reformers' position by limiting their room to manoeuvre. While the Suchocka government managed to push through a reduction in the replacement ratio and to avert the reintroduction of the branch privileges that had been adopted by the Sejm in early 1993, it was forced to shelve more extensive reforms.

Tax reform, 1990-93
On the revenue side, the initial fiscal honeymoon and the political volatility after the start of reforms resulted in substantial delays in tax reform. While a Western-style tax system was successfully introduced before the 1993 elections, reforms took much longer than originally expected. These delays aggravated Poland's fiscal problems (de Crombrugghe 1994, pp. 69-70; Dąbrowski 1992, pp. 307-8; Johnson and Kowalska 1994, pp. 222-3). Until the enactment of VAT in 1993, the Polish tax system was rather narrowly based and highly depended on the taxation of enterprise profits. In 1990 the share of profit taxes in total revenues stood at about a third, up from a fourth a year ago. This dependence on enterprise profits made the Polish budget extremely vulnerable to a decline in profits, such as the one that began in the second half of 1990. Following the inflation-induced surge in 1990, the share of profit tax revenues in GDP fell by almost 8 percentage points in 1991 and continued to decline in 1992 and 1993. Partly due to slow progress with tax reform, this shrinking of profit tax revenues was compensated only gradually by increases in other taxes. In effect, the Polish revenue-to-GDP ratio fell in 1991 and recovered only modestly in 1992.

The Balcerowicz Programme had foreseen a combination of stopgap measures with a fundamental medium-term overhaul of the tax system. Deadlines were rather ambitious, with the introduction of VAT and personal income tax scheduled for January 1991. Preparations began quickly since the new laws could build on communist plans from the late 1980s. Already in 1990 the government submitted draft laws for a personal income tax and a VAT to the Sejm. However, tax reform soon became a protracted process and the original deadlines were missed by a wide margin.

In 1990 the favourable fiscal situation nourished overly optimistic expectations and made tax reform appear less urgent. Instead of concentrating on personal income tax and VAT, debates began to focus on minor and more ideological issues such as tax preferences for the private sector or the *popiwek* (Bolkowiak 1993, p. 18). As the fiscal crisis unfolded, the prevailing political conditions hindered the acceleration of tax reform, even though observers became increasingly aware of the need for it. None of the submitted draft laws was adopted on schedule. While the law on personal income tax finally passed the Sejm before the 1991 elections and went into effect in January 1992, the reform of indirect taxation suffered severely from the political turbulence of 1992/93. The Olszewski and the Suchocka government were forced to postpone the imposition of higher turnover and sales taxes and the introduction of VAT several times (Slay 1992, p. 53). VAT was eventually introduced in July 1993, two and a half years behind the schedule in the Balcerowicz Programme and more than one year behind the Olszewski government's original schedule. The fragile parliamentary majorities not only delayed the enactment of tax reform, but also made it difficult for reformers to prevent the adoption of various tax exemptions. For instance, defections within the governing coalition forced the Suchocka government to accept preferential VAT rates for coal, electricity and other forms of energy.

5.3   CZECHOSLOVAKIA

In Czechoslovakia fiscal reform progressed more smoothly than in Poland. The government managed to keep deficits under control and to continue the comprehensive tax and expenditure reforms initiated in 1990 without major delays and concessions.

Economic and political conditions, 1991-92

The economic and political conditions that prevailed in Czechoslovakia during the post-communist fiscal crisis were in many respects similar to those in Poland. Like its neighbour, the continuation of reform was complicated by the initial fiscal honeymoon, spreading reform fatigue and substantial constraints on executive authority. Compared to Poland, however, Czechoslovak reformers faced weaker fiscal tensions and were able to maintain a higher degree of popular support for reforms.

Reform pressure, 1991-92
In Czechoslovakia the 1991 budget had assumed a 5 per cent decline in GDP. Instead, GDP fell by more than 10 per cent in 1991 and continued to decline in 1992 (Myant 2003, Chapter 3). Due to the combination of wage restraint and higher-than-expected inflation, real wages fell by about a quarter in 1991. While Czechoslovakia did not escape a transformational recession, it enjoyed a relatively advantageous economic situation (Table 5.2). Compared to other transition countries, it excelled especially in two areas: inflation and

unemployment. With regard to inflation, Czechoslovakia represented an almost 'textbook case' (Bruno 1993, p. 219) of stabilization. The stronger-than-expected increase in prices in the wake of the liberalization of prices and the strong devaluation in January 1991 was arrested swiftly and did not lead to persistent inflation. As early as 1992, inflation had decreased to about 13 per cent. At the same time, recorded unemployment remained at a rather low level. Contrary to initial fears, Czechoslovak unemployment never reached the 8 to 12 per cent assumed in the 1992 budget, but instead peaked at 6.6 per cent in the fourth quarter of 1991. In the Czech Republic, unemployment was even lower.[1]

Table 5.2   *Economic and fiscal conditions in the Czech Republic, 1990-92**

	1990	1991	1992
GDP growth (real)	-1.2	-11.5	-3.3
Inflation rate (CPI, annual average)	10.8	56.5	11.1
Unemployment rate (end-year)	0.8	4.1	2.6
Current account (% of GDP)	-2.8	1.2	-0.1
General government balance (% of GDP)	-0.2	-1.9	-3.1
General government expenditure (% of GDP)	61.5	57.1	55.2

Notes: * Figures for 1990 refer to former Czechoslovakia.

Sources: EBRD, Transition Report, various issues.

As in Poland, in Czechoslovakia the start of reforms went hand in hand with a temporary fiscal honeymoon, albeit on a smaller scale. Given the weaker burst of inflation, the jump in profits and the concomitant rise in profit tax revenues were less pronounced than in Poland (IMF 1995, p. 119, Table A2). Due to an increase in prices in early 1991 that went substantially beyond expectations, the fiscal stance in the first half of 1991 was much better than anticipated in the 1991 budget.

With the initial fiscal honeymoon fading during the course of 1991, a period of fiscal stress set in. Similar to other transformation countries, Czechoslovakia began to face strong strains on both the revenue and the expenditure side of the budget. However, these pressures were somewhat weaker than in Poland as the the less volatile inflation rate made the fiscal swings after the start of reforms less pronounced, the lower unemployment helped stabilized revenues and expenditures, and the absence of generous

Polish-style indexation rules reduced the pressure on the expenditure side of the budget.

Popular support, 1991-92

Partly due to low unemployment, popular support for the continuation of economic reform remained relatively high, particularly in the Czech Republic. Several indicators show that support dropped after the start of reforms yet began to rise as early as the end of 1991 (Juchler 1994, pp. 389-400, 409-22; Večerník 1996, p. 218-22). The results of the 1992 parliamentary elections underlined the relative lack of reform fatigue. In contrast to Poland, pro-reform parties were not voted out of office, but scored well, at least in the Czech part of the country. Having garnered about a third of all votes, the party associated with economic reform, Václav Klaus's Civic Democratic Party (ODS), became by far the strongest party in the Czech Republic.

The low unemployment in the Czech Republic was only one reason for the strong showing of the ODS. Other quickly palpable economic successes such as the taming of inflation or the early recovery of wages worked in the same direction. Owing to the voucher privatization and egalitarian social policies, the Czech transformation was perceived as relatively 'fair' and egalitarian.[2] In addition, Klaus's determination, decisiveness and economic expertise played a role in the ODS's success. Many voters felt that such characteristics made Klaus the ideal person to handle the economic transformation and articulate Czech interests vis-à-vis the Slovaks (Orenstein 1998; Saxonberg 1999).

Executive authority, 1991-92

While the federal government thus enjoyed strong popular support, especially in the Czech Republic, it remained weak on other counts (Elster et al. 1998, pp. 125-6). Following the split of the Civic Forum in early 1991, the federal government encompassed five parties with quite different programmes. Moreover, the short term of the first parliament, which was scheduled to end as early as mid-1992, raised concerns about 'the ability of those in office today to commit to tough policies' (Begg 1991, p. 249). Precisely for this reason, Klaus and others originally had argued for a longer parliamentary term. A further constraint on executive authority stemmed from the fact that the failure to adopt a new constitution left the old federal institutional framework intact. As a result, Czechoslovakia's political system continued to contain an enormous potential for deadlock, and this at a time when negotiations over the future of the Federation had begun.

Position of reformers, 1991-92

As opposed to the government's overall authority, the position of reformers within government strengthened after the start of reforms. While Klaus was the only representative of the ODS in the cabinet and remained surrounded by social-liberals until the end of the 1990-92 term, the apparent success and relative acceptance of reforms strengthened his control over economic reform. His personal popularity and his political clout as leader of the ODS further consolidated his position. Widely regarded and praised as the 'father' of reforms, Klaus was able to capitalize on the smooth Czechoslovak transformation. His ODS soon emerged as the strongest Czech party by far, leading in the polls and being the only non-communist party with a strong grassroots organisation (Kroupa and Kostelecky 1996).

The continuation of fiscal reform in 1991 and 1992

At first sight, the economic and political conditions after the start of reforms were not conducive to their continuation. Given the heavy constraints on executive authority, concerns over the government's capacity to sustain reforms loomed large (Begg 1991, p. 249; OECD 1991a, p. 37). The short term of the first parliament nurtured doubts about the government's commitment to reform. Even more widespread were fears that escalating Czech-Slovak tensions might produce disintegration and/or deadlock and thus derail economic reform.

Despite relatively weak executive authority and the hesitant start of reforms, however, Czechoslovakia was the transition country in which the continuation of reform during the transformational recession went most smoothly (Bönker 1995, pp. 195-203, Elster et al. 1998, Chapter 5). A strong change team and a set of economically successful and politically popular policies were responsible for the success (Holmes 1995, 1996, p. 61-8; Orenstein 1998). Positive reform outcomes helped to strengthen the position of reformers who in turn continued reforms, renewing the self-reinforcing cycle. This benevolent circle enabled the government to proceed with economic reform in 1991 and 1992 and facilitated the maintenance of a tight macroeconomic policy and the continuation of structural reforms.

The set of policies that contributed to the initial successes of Czechoslovak economic reform and relatively weak reform fatigue comprised elements as diverse as a restrictive macroeconomic policy, wage restraint, an undervalued currency, voucher privatization, an active labour market policy and egalitarian social policies (Orenstein 1994; Raiser 1994; Kosta 1997). This combination of measures resulted not from any grand design masterminded by Klaus and his team but rather from improvization and compromise. In fact, some of the policies that contributed to the relative popularity of

Czechoslovak economic reform, especially labour market and social policies, were drafted by the social-democratic and social-liberal social policy reformers within government and were originally more or less imposed on Klaus (Orenstein 1996, pp. 17-18, 1998). Yet Klaus managed to receive credit for the results. Thanks to their strong position, reformers were able to continue the tight fiscal policy and consolidate tax and expenditure reforms.

Budgets and deficits, 1991-92
The Czechoslovak government managed to contain deficits during the transformational recession. While the fiscal stance deteriorated from 1990 to 1992, deficits remained smaller than in most other transition countries. This relatively favourable fiscal performance partly stemmed from factors exogenous to fiscal reform, such as the low unemployment. However, it also reflected the implementation of tough discretionary measures and the smooth continuation of the reforms launched in 1990.

Despite the Polish precedent, the initial fiscal honeymoon hit the Czechoslovak government by surprise. In June, projections by the federal ministry of finance showed an unexpected surplus of 5 to 6 per cent of GDP for 1991. The government reacted to the combination of a higher-than-projected fiscal surplus and a worse-than-feared drop in GDP with an expansionary package worth about 47 bn CZK, equivalent to more than 10 per cent of the expenditures originally budgeted (Aghevli et al. 1992, p. 11; OECD 1991a, pp. 36-7, 68-9; Kupka et al. 1993, pp. 51-2). On the expenditure side, the government enacted additional spending on health, education and infrastructure as well as increases in public sector salaries. On the revenue side, turnover tax rates were reduced. The nominal surplus target was maintained.

Also, as in Poland, the fiscal relaxation turned out to be premature. The initial period of fiscal overperformance did not last long. Partly due to dwindling revenues, partly due to a spending spree at the end of the year, the fiscal balance deteriorated in the second half of 1991 and plunged into the red in November. The government missed its original fiscal target: instead of an 8 bn CZK surplus, the budget posted a deficit of 10 bn CZK. At the end of the year, the general government deficit stood at 2.1 per cent of GDP.

The government quickly learned its lesson. Lengthy negotiations over the distribution of revenues among the Federal and the Republican budgets notwithstanding, Klaus managed to push through a tough 1992 budget (Svitek 1992a). Based on the assumption of a further 5 to 10 per cent decline in GDP, the state budget was to be balanced. In order to reach this ambitious target, real spending was set to decline by another 7 per cent. The adoption of the budget was combined with the institutionalization of strict expenditure controls (Kočárník 1992, pp. 9, 22-3; Caiden 1993, pp. 69-70). In order to prevent an expenditure overrun like the one that had occurred at the end of 1991, quarterly expenditure ceilings were imposed on spending ministries.

The tough budget notwithstanding, Czechoslovakia ran into fiscal problems in 1992. Revenues, most notably turnover tax revenues, remained behind expectations. The government responded by capping spending. At mid-year, expenditure cuts worth about 4 per cent of total spending were adopted in order to contain the deficit. Adjustment was strongest in the Czech Republic and at the federal level. The new Slovak government that assumed office after the 1992 elections, however, largely refrained from cuts and accommodated the underperformance of revenues by incurring a higher deficit.

Expenditure reform, 1991-92

Czechoslovakia was one of the few transition countries that did not experience an increase of the expenditure-to-GDP ratio in the course of the transformational recession (Table 5.2). As opposed to Hungary and Poland, the shares of social security transfers and government consumption in GDP rose only modestly, so that the drastic decline in subsidies translated into a falling overall expenditure ratio. The underlying expenditure restraint was made possible by the government's strong reform mandate and the reformers' uncontested position. Moreover, the absence of Polish-style indexation rules increased the room for manoeuvring.

The decline in the expenditure-to-GDP ratio was achieved by a combination of cuts in subsidies and the freezing of other expenditures. The government managed to limit the growth in public sector wages and pensions. In the case of pensions, the government continued its practice of discretionary adjustments in order to retain an important lever for expenditure control. In addition to this spending restraint, the government streamlined some expenditure programmes. It restricted eligibility for the general income transfer to the economically inactive, which had been introduced in spending programmes in mid 1990. Moreover, the government amended its earlier legislation on unemployment benefits by reducing the replacement ratio, introducing a ceiling on maximum benefits and tightening eligibility.

Tax reform, 1991-92

The continuation of tax reform also went rather smoothly. The government succeeded in implementing a number of revenue-enhancing measures in the short-term and introduced a completely new, Western-style tax system. In 1992 the government adopted a number of short-term tax measures in order to contain the deficit (Štěpánek et al. 1995, p. 17). These measures included an import tax for enterprises that did not pay turnover tax, higher minimum social insurance contributions for private entrepreneurs and increased income tax rates for working pensioners and high-income earners.

The overhaul of the overall tax system posed more difficulties. The original 1990 plans had not specified a detailed schedule for the adoption of the new tax system to be implemented in 1993. While legislative work started early, the passage of the new laws was complicated by ongoing controversies over the future shape of the Federation (Svitek 1992b). Since major legislation fell within the federal domain,[3] tax reform soon became part of Czech-Slovak bargaining. Within the Federal Assembly, curious proposals such as a regionally differentiated VAT were debated. However, reformers managed to push through their measures. Two situational factors proved to be instrumental: First, the weak revenue performance in 1992 highlighted the need for reforms. Second, the upcoming parliamentary elections in 1992 imposed a deadline, since a delay in passing reforms would have prevented the establishment of a new tax system by January 1993. Although the results seemed uncertain for a long time, parliament met the deadline, passing the final piece of legislation, the Income Tax Law, just before the end of the term.

The new legislation envisioned a tax system similar to those of most EU countries (Lichnowská et al. 1994, pp. 134-8; Zamrazilova 1994; John 1998, pp. 26-38). Turnover taxation was to be replaced with specific excises as well as a VAT with a standard rate of 23 per cent and a preferential rate of 5 per cent on foodstuffs and services. A flat 45 per cent tax on corporate income and a uniform personal income tax were introduced. All personal incomes derived from wages and self-employment were taxed on a progressive scale (with marginal rates ranging from 15 to 47 per cent). Interest and dividends as well as capital gains were subjected to flat-rate withholding taxes. The old payroll tax was replaced with individualized social security contributions based on wages and incomes of the self-employed. Furthermore, new taxes on gifts, inheritance and motor vehicles were introduced and the import surcharge imposed in January 1991 was eliminated.

When the Czech and Slovak governments decided to dissolve Czechoslovakia, reformers faced the additional challenge of transforming the new federal tax system into two independent, national ones. The Czech Republic adopted the federal legislation almost unchanged.[4] The transition to a national tax system was facilitated by the fact that tax administration traditionally had rested with the republics. The crowded agenda led some actors to plead for phasing in the new taxes and delaying the introduction of VAT. In the end, however, the government stuck to the original schedule. When the Czech Republic became independent in January 1993, a new tax system was in place. Despite the later start, the first round of post-communist tax reform was thus completed earlier than in Poland.

5.4   HUNGARY

Compared to Czechoslovakia and Poland, the continuation of fiscal reform in Hungary was more protracted. The policy drift that had already characterized the first stage of fiscal reform continued after the onset of the post-communist fiscal crisis. Due to the postponement of reform under the conservative government, fiscal problems were overcome only in 1995/96.

Economic and political conditions, 1991-94

In Hungary, the economic and political conditions during the post-communist fiscal crisis were not very conducive to the passage of reforms. Similar to the situation at the outset of the transformation, a combination of limited reform pressure, low popular support and weak reformers favoured policy drift. In addition, executive authority substantially weakened between 1990 and 1994.

Reform pressure, 1991-94
The 1991 budget and the Kupa Programme had foreseen a decline in real GDP by about 4 per cent in 1991, to be followed by a return to growth in 1992. As in other transition countries, however, the drop in output turned out to be steeper and the transformational recession more protracted than originally thought (Table 5.3). Concomitant with the economic slump, recorded unemployment jumped from 2 per cent in 1990 to 12 per cent in 1992. Inflation fell to about 20 per cent in 1992, but did not recede further. Real wages did not drop as drastically as in Poland and Czechoslovakia after the launching of reforms but continued to decline until 1993.

As in other transition countries, the transformational recession was accompanied by massive fiscal strain. Compared to Poland, however, tensions were less dramatic. Owing to the gradual liberalization of prices, profit tax revenues were less volatile than in most other transition countries. Moreover, an increase in savings eased the financing of the deficit and limited the resulting inflationary pressures.

The high deficits were one of the major reasons why Hungary was one of the first post-communist countries to run into massive external imbalances (Cottarelli 1998, pp. 3-6; Dethier and Orlowski 1998). In the second half of 1992, the current account plunged into red. Driven by an overvalued exchange rate and the combination of a surge in domestic absorption with a weak supply response, current account deficits reached an alarmingly high 10 per cent of GDP in 1993 and 1994. Part of these external imbalances were caused by Hungary's high fiscal deficits. Along with rising wages and the drop in savings, deficits contributed to the increase in domestic demand.

More importantly, the huge borrowing requirements supported the appreciation of the real exchange rate by increasing external government borrowing and by inducing those enterprises that were crowded-out on domestic markets to borrow abroad.

Due to the particular nature of Hungary's macroeconomic problems, the need for fiscal reform was felt much less than it was in Poland and other transition countries. For non-economists, the risks associated with Hungary's external economic imbalances were difficult to identify. Moreover, compared to inflation, the nexus between the fiscal stance and the current account was much more abstract and remained more controversial.

Table 5.3   *Economic and fiscal conditions in Hungary, 1990-96*

	1990	1991	1992	1993	1994	1995	1996
GDP growth (real)	-3.5	-11.9	-3.1	-0.6	2.9	1.5	1.3
Inflation rate (CPI, annual average)	28.9	35.0	23.0	22.5	18.8	28.2	23.6
Unemployment rate (end-year)	1.9	7.5	12.3	12.1	10.4	10.4	10.5
Current account (% of GDP)	0.4	0.8	0.9	-9.0	-9.4	-5.6	-3.7
General government balance (% of GDP)	0.4	-3.7	-7.6	-8.9	-8.6	-6.2	-3.1
General government expenditure (% of GDP)	53.5	52.1	53.7	54.6	52.1	48.7	47.5

Sources: EBRD, Transition Report, various issues.

Popular support, 1991-94

In the Hungarian case, the new government's standing in the polls had already suffered a heavy blow before the unfolding of the transformational recession. The bad start for the new government resulted in what Iván Szelényi dubbed a 'world record loss of popularity' (cf. Batt 1991, p. 91). Confidence in, and support for, the government dwindled drastically in the second half of 1990 and lingered at a rather low level until the end of the term (Kurtán 1994, pp. 121-2). The local elections in September 1990 and all five by-elections during the term went badly for the government (Szarvas 1995, p. 134). So did the 1994 parliamentary elections, in which the governing coalition suffered a smashing defeat. The decline in popular support for the conservative government partly reflected the unexpected economic and social hardships after the start of the transformation. It was further aggravated by the government's indecision and its inclination towards ideological posturing.

Executive authority, 1991-94

As has been shown, Hungary started the transformation with a relatively high degree of executive authority. While the institutional framework, with its premium on 'governability,' remained intact, executive authority weakened in the early 1990s (Haggard et al. 2001, pp. 90-91). For starters, the governing coalition proved to be rather fragile. In the course of the first term, its majority of seats in parliament dropped from 60 to 51 per cent (Kurtán 1994, pp. 122-4). When the Smallholders' Party (FKGP), one of the MDF's coalition partners, broke apart in February 1992, one faction left government. The other partner, the Christian Democrats (KDNP), also became more assertive. The MDF itself suffered from massive internal rifts and experienced a net loss of 7.5 per cent of its MPs between 1990 and 1994 (Szarvas 1995, p. 130, Table 5). Struggles within the MDF peaked in the second half of 1992 when a leader of the party's conservative wing, the writer István Csurka, openly challenged Antall's leadership. These struggles were only partly settled by bullying Csurka out of the party in early 1993. In addition to the governing coalition's fragility, Antall's agony and the upcoming 1994 elections constrained executive authority. Although terminally ill, Antall refrained from handing over office, but stayed on until the very end in December 1993. His temporary physical incapacity and the struggles for authority among his would-be successors infringed upon the government's strategic capacity. With the term progressing, the 1994 elections cast their shadow and put a further premium on the 'putting off' of unpopular reforms.

Position of reformers, 1991-94

The strengthening of reformers that had accompanied Kupa's nomination in late 1990 turned out to be temporary (Csaba 1995, pp. 223-4; Greskovits 2001, pp. 125-8). As early as 1991 Kupa fell into disgrace with Antall and lost prime ministerial support. Antall, an instinctive centralizer, perceived his determined Finance Minister as a potential rival and sought to counter the lingering talk of a 'two-headed government.' Moreover, Kupa fell victim to political balancing. Concerned with holding the fragile governing coalition together, Antall avoided making too strong a commitment to Kupa whose strong resistance to property restitution and whose good standing with the liberal opposition made him an anathema to the right wing within the coalition. Without Antall's backing, however, Kupa became increasingly isolated and lost influence within the cabinet. As early as 1991 the ministry of finance was overturned in key decisions on privatization. At the end of the year, Antall convened a working group in charge of drafting an alternative economic platform. In February 1993 Kupa fell victim to a cabinet reshuffle and was replaced with Iván Szabó, an MDF politician with ambitions to succeed Antall (Greskovits 2001, 128-30).

At the same time, the decentralized structure of the public sector continued to complicate the making of fiscal policy. While the Act on Public Finances, which had been adopted after much haggling in May 1992, reduced the number of extrabudgetary funds, the surviving funds continued to have far-reaching spending, cash management and even borrowing powers (Lutz and Krueger 1995, p. 40). The gradual separation of the social security funds from the budget, which had begun in 1989, even aggravated the problems because the 1991 legislation bestowed the new funds with far-reaching, internationally unprecedented authorities (Götting 1998, pp. 159-60; Pataki 1993; OECD 1995, pp. 33-6, 1997, pp. 41-2). Funds were allowed to run their own apparatus for collecting social security contributions, to independently administer their budgets, to borrow independently from the state budget and even to submit their budgets directly to parliament. This gave the funds a strong voice in the process and severely limited the Finance Minister's control over an important chunk of the budget.

The policy drift under the conservative government

The economic and political conditions that prevailed in Hungary before the 1994 elections were unfavourable to the continuation of fiscal reform. Gradual deterioration of the fiscal stance, relatively easy financing of budget deficits and weak inflationary pressures let fiscal adjustment appear less urgent, reduced readiness to support restraint and favoured the postponement and watering down of reforms. The fact that reformers were isolated within government and could not count on prime ministerial support also hindered efforts at reform. The reaction to the fiscal crisis and the continuation of fiscal reform were complicated further by rifts within the governing coalition, Prime Minister Antall's illness and the upcoming 1994 elections. These factors explain why the conservative government moved slowly.

Budgets and deficits, 1991-94
The conservative government's vacillation resulted in a failure to contain deficits. In 1991 and 1992, the government tolerated the overrun of deficit targets and the build-up of huge deficits (Table 5.2). When the fiscal situation further deteriorated in 1993/94, it confined itself to the adoption of half-hearted measures that were not sufficient to bring down deficits.

The deterioration of the fiscal stance began in 1991. As many critics had foretold, the 1991 budget proved to be unattainable. Partly due to the higher-than-expected decline in GDP, revenues fell short of projected levels. Profit and indirect taxes were especially affected by the economic downturn. While expenditures were below target as well, the underperformance of revenues was not matched by reductions on the expenditure side of the budget (NBH 1991, pp. 43-8). Attributing the deterioration of the fiscal stance to exogenous and transitory factors, the government largely accommodated the growing deficit. By delaying some unpopular energy price rises and by granting higher-than-planned compensation payments, it even aggravated the fiscal problems. As a consequence, the general government fiscal stance deteriorated by 4 percentage points in 1991. The resulting violation of deficit targets was tolerated by the IMF, which waived the application of the fiscal performance criteria underlying the 1991 agreement.

The government reacted slowly to the emerging fiscal tensions. While the 1992 budget posted a 50 per cent reduction of the budget deficit, the projected fiscal adjustment did not rest on expenditure and revenue measures, but was to result from an improving economic situation. The underlying macroeconomic assumptions were politically motivated were widely held to be dubious (Csaba 1992, pp. 956-7). As a matter of fact, projections soon turned out to be far off the mark. As in 1991, revenues fell short of expectations. The general effects of the economic slump were aggravated by the unforeseen consequences of the 1991 accounting, bankruptcy and banking legislation (NBH 1992, pp. 47-8; OECD 1993, pp. 36-7; Okolicsanyi 1992, p. 54): The surge in bankruptcy filings triggered by the new bankruptcy law heavily reduced tax intakes since firms engaged in bankruptcy proceedings were not obliged to pay taxes. The Banking Act of December 1991 substantially squeezed profits and profit tax payments by requiring strict provisioning. The higher than expected provisions set aside by the banks, along with substantial rebates of excess taxes paid in 1991, resulted in a drop in net tax revenue from the financial sector in 1992 equivalent to 2 per cent of GDP. Due to the resulting weak revenue performance, the state budget had already surpassed the level targeted for 1992 by the end of May. At the end of the year, the general government deficit stood at close to 7 per cent of GDP, up by 4 percentage points compared to 1991.

As in 1991, the government did not react to the overshooting deficit, even though the IMF was increasingly concerned with deficits and eventually froze the disbursement of stand-by facilities. During the first half of 1992, the government resisted growing calls for corrective measures. When it eventually drew up a supplementary budget, the government largely confined itself to ratifying the higher deficit and did not undertake any serious attempt at counteracting the continuing revenue decline. The supplementary budget explicitly ruled out tax increases, and the expenditure cuts adopted in the second half of 1992 were tiny and insufficient to prevent expenditures from growing well beyond expectations. Unlike in the previous year, revenue shortfalls went hand in hand with expenditure overruns, with the latter accounting for more than a third of the deficit increase.

The government's inaction had different sources. In mid-1992, the government was already preoccupied with the preparation of the 1993 budget. In addition, the case for fiscal adjustment was controversial. Given the decline in inflation from a peak of 40 per cent in June 1991 to around 20 per cent in July 1992, a current account surplus and a declining net foreign debt, calls for a fiscal boost had grown louder (OECD 1995, pp. 1-2). At the same time, the government's political capacity was fragile. It was precisely in the second half of 1992 that the internal rifts within the government reached their peak. Absorbed with maintaining control and with securing its position, the government ducked away from controversial measures. The conflicts within the governing coalition also infringed upon the position of Finance Minister Kupa. Cautious to hold the coalition and his own party together, Prime Minister Antall was keen to distance himself from Kupa, a key target of the populist wing within government.

Kupa's weak position became increasingly visible in the second half of 1992 when he failed to push through a fiscal adjustment package that he had prepared for 1993 (Csaba 1995, p. 225; Haggard et al. 2001, pp. 91-2). His proposal, which combined tax increases and expenditure cuts, provoked strong resistance both inside and outside the government. Internally split, anxious not to antagonize voters and confronted with some signs of incipient social unrest, the government decided to enter in negotiations over the reform package with the trade unions, so as to gain additional legitimisation. Not surprisingly in view of the government's lack of determination, however, negotiations at the Interest Reconciliation Council led to a watering down of Kupa's original plans (Greskovits 1998, Chapter 9; Pataki 1993). The social contract that the government and the unions eventually agreed upon and signed at the end of November 1992 brought no net relief for the budget.

The 1993 budget projected a slight reduction in the deficit (OECD 1995, pp. 36-8). As early as in the second quarter, however, it became evident that revenue shortfalls and expenditure overruns would render the original deficit target unattainable. This time, the government responded more quickly than in 1992. In May, Iván Szabó, the new Finance Minister, submitted a supplementary budget which was eventually adopted in July (Okolicsanyi 1993). While this supplementary budget increased the deficit target by about 10 per cent, it also contained a number of revenue and expenditure measures, including an increase in VAT and unemployment contributions as well as cuts in pharmaceutical subsidies and overall spending. Many elements of the supplementary budget had already been part of the original Kupa package. Together with the measures already included in the original 1993 budget, the value of the 1993 supplementary budget was estimated at about 4 per cent of GDP on a full-year basis. Most of the adjustment was to be accomplished on the revenue side of the budget. At the end of the day, the actual 1993 deficit came in between the original and the corrected 1993 target.

The 1994 budget had already been submitted to parliament before the passage of the 1993 supplementary budget. The government hoped that the 1993 supplementary budget and the 1994 budget might together serve as the basis for a politically welcome agreement with the IMF. In order to please the IMF, the 1994 budget projected a small decline in the overall deficit. For the first time, adjustment was to fall proportionally on expenditures and revenues. Although Hungary's commitment to reform was highly controversial within the IMF, the Hungarian government eventually succeeded in forging a new agreement. However, this agreement proved to be rather short-lived. In the run-up to the 1994 elections, the Hungarian government failed to implement important parts of the announced measures and the resulting violation of the fiscal targets soon led the IMF to suspend the agreement.

Expenditure reform, 1991-94
On the expenditure side, the conservative government's postponement of fiscal reform resulted in a failure to bring down expenditures. While the government succeeded in reducing government spending in real terms, the decline was not sufficient to ward off an increase in the expenditure-to-GDP ratio. Moreover, medium-term expenditure reforms slowed.

Antall's 1990 state of the nation address and the Kupa Programme called for a reduction of the expenditure ratio by about 6 per cent of GDP, largely to be realized by cuts in subsidies. As a matter of fact, budgetary subsidies were gradually brought down from 12 per cent in 1989 to 5.5 per cent in 1993, eventually reaching a level similar to Western countries (Gyulavári and Neményi 1996, pp. II/48-50; Schaffer 1995). Except for public transportation, the government eliminated almost all consumer price subsidies. Subsidies to enterprises and housing subsidies were substantially reduced. Part of these cuts, however, were compensated by an increase in tax arrears and the costly bank recapitalization schemes in 1992 and 1993, which manifested themselves not in budgeted subsidies, but in revenue losses and increasing interest payments respectively.

With regard to other types of spending, the conservative government acted more cautiously. Government consumption initially fell, but increased from 1991 to 1994. Given the high unemployment, the government refrained from reducing Hungary's relatively high level of public employment (Gyulavári and Neményi 1996, pp. II/50). The 1992 Civil Service Act, intended to restore a strong bureaucracy, further curtailed the room for manoeuvre and increased the costs of lay-offs. As a consequence, the decline in public sector employment remained far behind the general drop in employment. Moreover, the grip on public sector wages and government spending on goods and services was softened in 1992. As a pre-election give-away the government even conceded a substantial pay rise in 1994 which amounted to an ex ante increase in real wages by 6 per cent (OECD 1995, p. 38).[5]

In addition to interest payments, the single most important factor contributing to Hungary's resilient level of expenditures was the high share of social security benefits in GDP. Already high at the outset of the transformation, this share further grew in the early years of the transformation and stabilized at a rather high level. The deficit of the social security funds rose in 1993 and amounted to 1 per cent in 1993 and 1994.

The conservative government reacted reluctantly to these expenditure pressures and the well-known deficiencies of the country's 'generous' social security system (Bartlett 1997, pp. 200-202; Gedeon 1995; Götting 1998; World Bank 1995, pp. 25-56; Marer 1999, pp. 171-5). Although the need for reforms was widely acknowledged and reform proposals had abounded since 1989, the government largely refrained from unpopular reforms. Even the deterioration of the fiscal situation did not suffice to trigger more than timid reform attempts.

In the case of pensions, the biggest chunk of social spending, some savings were achieved by only partly adjusting pensions to inflation. However, reformers failed to launch the comprehensive structural reforms promised in 1991. More importantly, from a short-term perspective, was that the government also refrained from tackling the widespread misuse of disability pensions and from raising the retirement age. The delayed increase in retirement age nicely illustrates the government's dilatory approach to pension reform (Götting 1998, p. 161). Under communism, retirement age was rather low. Women could retire at 55, men at 60. Not surprisingly, these provisions became the target of the IMF and the Ministry of Finance soon after the start of the transformation. Following the presentation of its White Paper in October 1991, the government proposed an increase in retirement age. However, this proposal was watered down at the Interest Reconciliation Council. The law that was passed in 1992 envisaged a gradual increase in the retirement age to be phased in, beginning in January 1994. In a first step, the age of retirement for women was to be brought in line with the age for men until the year 2003. In the end, the conservative government even retreated from this schedule. With the approaching elections in mind, the enactment of the law was postponed for another year in December 1993.

A similar dithering on expenditure reform can be observed in other fields of social policy. As for health care, the conservative government failed to address the overcapacity of hospital beds and to increase co-payments for medicine and medical treatment; as for education, it several times postponed the introduction of tuition in education. The low levels of reforms regarding sick pay and family benefits also epitomize the Antall government's irresolution.

At the outset of the transformation, provisions on state-paid sick pay in Hungary were extremely generous by international standards. The replacement ratio amounted to 85 per cent of the gross wage. Benefits were available for a maximum period of one year, with only the first three days covered by the employer. This construction invited abuse. On the one hand, the high replacement ratio made sick pay highly attractive in financial terms. On the other, the 3 days-clause reduced incentives for employers to control and to contain abuses. Against this background, it is not surprising that Hungary reported one of the highest numbers of paid sick days in Europe in the early 1990s and that payments accounted for a relatively high 1 per cent of GDP. In spite of early calls by the ministry of finance and international organizations, however, the conservative government addressed the problem but reluctantly. In January 1992, the number of days of sick leave to be paid by the employer was increased from three to ten. The replacement rate remained unchanged until 1993, when it was gradually reduced to 75 per cent. More far-reaching reforms were contemplated, but eventually rejected (OECD 1995, p. 52).

Family benefits, including an allowance for families with children, a number of maternity benefits and payments for child care for young children, are another case in point. Accounting for about 4 per cent of GDP, they reached a rather high level in the early 1990s. High expenditures stemmed from a combination of generous benefit levels, long eligibility periods and universal coverage. It was especially this lack of 'targeting' which drew heavy criticism and which made family benefits an often named candidate for expenditure cuts. Notwithstanding all reform proposals, however, the conservative government stuck to universalism and refrained from all attempts at streamlining entitlements, be it through means-testing or through taxing benefits. Instead, the measures adopted until the 1994 elections boiled down to an erosion of real benefits through delayed and partial inflation adjustment (Götting 1998, pp. 226-7; Sipos and Tóth 1998, pp. 303-4).

Tax reform, 1991-94

On the revenue side, the policy drift typical of the conservative government manifested itself in the slow pace of tax reform. The postponement of major tax reforms not only stifled growth and employment but, by inducing tax avoidance and tax evasion, it also directly contributed to the poor showing of revenues and aggravated Hungary's fiscal problems (World Bank 1995, pp. 15-24; Semjén 1995; Hétenyi 1994, pp. 198-200).

Part of Hungary's pre-1989 economic reforms had been the overhaul of the fiscal system (Felkai 1996; Gergely 1988; Koltay 1993; Newbery 1991; Varga 1989; John 1998, pp. 36-9). In autumn 1987, the National Assembly passed a comprehensive tax reform which envisaged the introduction of a Western-style tax system. In January 1988, the old turnover tax system was replaced by a VAT with three rates (0, 15, 25 per cent), complemented by a number of excises. Simultaneously, a uniform personal income tax was adopted, which combined the progressive taxation of wage incomes with a linear withholding tax of 20 per cent on interest and dividend incomes. In 1989, various profit taxes were substituted by a parametric corporate income tax at a uniform rate of 50 per cent. Along with taxes, social security contributions were overhauled. Employers' contributions were raised twice and employees' formerly progressive contributions replaced by flat ones.

Although patterned upon Western tax systems, Hungary's new tax system still bore the imprints of communism. In particular, it suffered from a high degree of non-neutrality stemming from numerous preferences. As for VAT, products covering about 40 per cent of total household consumption expenditure, mostly consumer staples, were zero-rated. The bulk of other expenditures were subject to the rather high 25 per cent rate and only a few items fell in the intermediate category of 15 per cent. The same held true for personal income tax and social security contributions. Almost all cash and in-kind transfer incomes provided by the government, employer-paid fringe benefits, as well as incomes from agricultural activities and 'intellectual activity,' were exempt from taxation, so that personal income tax and employees' social security contributions were in fact levied on a mere 40 per cent of total household incomes in 1989. The corporate income tax likewise suffered from a plethora of tax reliefs, targeted toward specific sectors and activities and reducing the effective unification of tax rates. At the same time, restrictive provisions on depreciation, provisioning and loss carry-over made effective tax rates on profits rather high (Andersson 1991).

As has been shown in Section 4.4, the initial tax reform moves by the Antall government were modest. Tax reform gained momentum after the arrival of Kupa. Income tax policy changed course. For 1992, the number of tax brackets was reduced again, the top marginal tax rate was cut to 40 per cent and an adjustment of brackets was undertaken. As new accounting law was introduced, corporate income taxation was also restructured. The law on the new Company Tax, which was to replace the old corporate income tax, brought the rules for depreciation, provisioning and loss carry-overs closer to Western standards. At the same time, a further tightening of tax reliefs took place, partly offset by the introduction of new preferences. Notwithstanding these changes, the amount of profit tax reliefs rose from 26 per cent of all collected profit tax revenues in 1991 to 36 per cent in 1993 (Semjén 1995, p. 27).

The unpopular broadening of the bases of personal income tax and VAT progressed more slowly. It took the fiscal pressures and the overshooting deficits in 1991 and 1992 to induce the government to initiate reforms. A substantial broadening of the personal income tax base was adopted only in late 1992. Starting in 1993, about one third of estimated fringe benefits were made taxable. At the same time, preferences for income from 'intellectual activity' and agricultural production were curtailed. VAT reform also had a rocky passage. Original plans by the Ministry of Finance proposed a system with a 10 and a 20 per cent rate which would have brought Hungary's value-added tax closer to EU patterns. Owing to resistance from within the government, however, this plan was shelved. Kupa's subsequent proposal, part of the reform package that he suggested in autumn 1992, envisaged a replacement of the 0 and 15 per cent rates with a new bottom rate of 8 per cent. This proposal fell victim to the compromise reached with the unions in November 1992 (Greskovits 1998, Chapter 9; Pataki 1993). Following negotiations with the trade unions, the new bottom rate was set at 6 instead of 8 per cent. Moreover, only part of Kupa's reclassification plans survived. In particular, the abolition of VAT tax exemptions for pharmaceuticals, household energy and housing construction and refurbishing were postponed. At the end, however, the new provisions proved to be short-lived. Given the fiscal problems in 1993, the 1993 supplementary budget raised the lower VAT rate from 6 to 10 per cent and subjected household energy to the 10 per cent rate.

In the run-up to the parliamentary elections in May 1994, the government partly rescinded earlier reforms. Departing from the policy pursued in the previous years, the number of personal income tax brackets was re-increased from four to six. In an attempt to raise wages and pensions, the government made employees' social security contributions tax deductible, thus re-narrowing the personal income tax base. Finally, the government switched to a more redistributive course. By raising tax brackets selectively and by increasing the top personal income tax rate, it increased the tax burden falling on higher income strata.

The move to reform after the 1994 elections

Hungary's fiscal problems were eventually tackled in March 1995 when the new government adopted the famous Bokros Package. The initiation of reform took some time. During the first months of the new government, the policy drift that had characterized the first legislative term continued (Barany 1995).

Economic and political conditions, 1994-95

The parliamentary elections in May 1994 radically changed the political scene (Elster et al. 1998, pp. 123-4; Arato 1994). The hitherto governing coalition suffered a heavy blow. The MDF was decimated and retained but a tiny 10 per cent of seats. In contrast, the post-communist MSZP more than tripled its share of votes from 10 per cent in 1990 to about 33 per cent and, with a little help from Hungarian electoral law, captured 54 per cent of seats. Notwithstanding its absolute majority in parliament, the MSZP leadership opted for an oversized coalition with the second-strongest party in parliament, the liberal Alliance of Free Democrats (SZDSZ), partly in order to counter concerns over a 'return of communists,' partly in order to contain the influence of the MSZP's traditionalist wing. The new government was led by Gyula Horn, the chairman of the MSZP.

The strong parliamentary majority provided for a high degree of *executive authority*. Until early 1995, however, other conditions were less favourable to the launching of reforms. For starters, despite the overwhelming victory at the polls, *popular support* for reforms was limited. The MSZP had not campaigned on a platform of austerity, but had won the elections as a staunch defender of living standards and a guarantee against radical change (Kornai 1996, p. 143; Stark and Bruszt 1998, pp. 171-2). It had also restricted its room for manoeuvre by a strong commitment to a social pact with the unions.

A second obstacle to the launching of reforms was the apparent improvement in the economic situation and the resulting weakening of *reform pressure*. In 1994, GDP and investment picked up more strongly than expected and inflation and unemployment remained behind expectations. This 'light at the end of the tunnel' raised some doubts about the need for drastic measures and nourished the futile hope that the country could escape from retrenchment by eventually growing out of its problems.

Finally, the *position of reformers* within government suffered from a number of constraints (Lengyel 1995, pp. 35-41; Szilagyi 1995, p. 62; Greskovits 2001, pp. 130-32). László Békesi, the new Finance Minister, the leading exponent of the MSZP's liberal wing, was vested with strong formal powers and enjoyed the support of the SZDSZ. At the same time, however, Békesi was only half-heartedly backed by Prime Minister Horn, who perceived the Finance Minister to be a countervailing power, if not a rival. Keen to demonstrate his authority and sensitive to all attempts at confining his constitutional position, Horn only reluctantly supported Békesi in his struggle for reform. Given the pivotal role of the Hungarian Prime Minister within the cabinet, this lack of support strongly infringed upon Békesi's position. The conflicts between Horn and Békesi culminated in the resignation of the Finance Minister in January 1995.

Economic and political conditions changed in early 1995. Developments in both spheres combined to increase the pressure for reform and to pave the way for the installation of a new change team. Békesi's resignation followed on top of two other resignations. In December 1994, the new government had eventually succeeded in bullying Péter Ákos Bod, the conservative central bank governor, out of office. In January 1995, Ferenc Bartha, the Privatization Commissioner, had resigned in the wake of Horn's resistance to the privatization of HungarHotels. This series of resignations, the resulting vacancies in key economic positions and the meagre record of the new government raised strong doubts about the government's reform commitment and its strategic capacity. These concerns mushroomed as the economic situation deteriorated. In February, disappointing economic figures for 1994 were released and the 1995 fiscal and current account deficits were well ahead of projections. Against the backdrop of the Mexican currency crisis of December 1994, investors became increasingly nervous and the incipient crisis of confidence threatened to translate into a full-blown currency crisis (Kornai 1997, pp. 181-91; Lengyel 1995, pp. 42-6; Cook and Orenstein 1999, pp. 91-3; Haggard et al. 2001, p. 98). Prime Minister Horn reacted to the growing reform pressure by putting two well-known liberal economists in charge of running economic policy. György Surányi, President of the National Bank of Hungary in 1990/91, became the new central bank governor; Lajos Bokros, at that time chairman of the Budapest Bank, was appointed Minister of Finance. Bokros was vested with extraordinary powers and received full rein to prepare a reform programme (Kornai 1996, p. 145; Haggard et al. 2001, pp. 97-9).

The way to the Bokros Package
The changing economic and political conditions strongly shaped economic policy-making. In the first months into the new government, the relatively weak reform pressure and the conflicts between Horn and Békesi worked against the initiation of reforms. Contrary to expectations, the presentation of a medium-term economic programme took until January 1995, more than half a year after the elections. Neither the announced social pact nor the intended agreement with the IMF materialized. Privatization came almost to a halt (Csillag 1995). As for fiscal reform, both the 1994 supplementary budget and the original 1995 budget remained behind expectations and did not suffice to overcome Hungary's fiscal problems.

At the time the new government came to power it was evident that the 1994 budget could not be attained. Mid-year estimates put the 1994 deficit at about a fifth above the targeted level and the increasing financing problems raised further concerns. Against this background, the long-awaited supplementary budget adopted in October 1994 was rather modest. Providing for revenue and expenditure measures worth about 1.3 per cent of GDP on a full year basis, it did not go beyond keeping the budget within the original target. Spending cuts were much lower than originally announced and agreed upon in the coalition programme. As with the previous governments' budgets, the bulk of adjustment fell on the revenue side. Békesi failed to push through more far-reaching measures in cabinet, including increases in VAT and a smaller retroactive adjustment of pensions.

The 1995 budget, adopted in December 1994, was more ambitious (OECD 1995, pp. 39-41). As for consolidated general government, it envisaged a reduction in the overall deficit by 2 percentage points and a decline in the primary deficit by about 4 percentage points. Adjustment was to be achieved by a combination of increased privatization revenues and cuts in real non-interest spending. Privatization revenues were budgeted to increase by almost 2 per cent of GDP; non-interest spending was targeted to decline by 6 per cent in real terms. The brunt of adjustment was to be borne by public sector wages. On the revenue side, increases in indirect taxation and the conversion of personal income tax deductions into tax credits aimed at stabilizing revenues.

The snag with the 1995 budget was its strong reliance on privatization revenues (OECD 1995, pp. 39-41). Cuts in non-interest spending, estimated at about 2 per cent of GDP, only sufficed to balance the surging interest payments, thus making the decline of the overall deficit contingent upon the achievement of rather ambitious privatization goals. This vulnerability of the deficit target was aggravated by the fact that privatization revenues were projected to materialize only towards the end of 1995. This timing raised severe financing and credibility problems. Observers had to trust in the government's privatization policy and a high deficit had to be 'tolerated' and financed up until privatization revenues would come in. It was for these problems that the 1995 budget was deemed unsustainable by critics and that within the ministry of finance the preparation of a supplementary budget started almost immediately after the passage of the budget.

Fiscal reform gained new momentum after the resignation of Békesi. On March 12 ('black sunday' in Hungarian parlance), Lajos Bokros, the new finance minister, announced a drastic adjustment programme at an extraordinary cabinet meeting. The 'Bokros Package' combined an up-front devaluation of the forint by 9 per cent, coupled with the imposition of an import surcharge and the move to a pre-announced crawling peg, with some fiscal adjustment, wage restraint and the call for an acceleration of privatization (OECD 1995, pp. 41-3; World Bank 1995, pp. 11-12). Part of the fiscal adjustment was to be achieved by a mix of revenue increases adding up to 2.2 per cent of GDP and expenditure cuts worth 0.8 per cent of GDP. The principal fiscal measures comprised the already mentioned introduction of an import surcharge, increases in excises, a broadening of social security contributions, cuts in personnel spending, cost savings in the health system, the introduction of tuition in education and reductions in sick pay, family and child allowances. In addition, the government imposed a freeze on nominal spending which, given the expected surge in inflation in the wake of the devaluation, implied a substantial decline in real expenditures and real public sector wages. By exercising its ownership rights in state-owned enterprises and by moral suasion, the government sought to extend wage restraint to the enterprise sector.

Both in substance and, even more, in style, the Bokros Package marked a clear departure from the economic policy that had been pursued in Hungary since 1990, if not since 1956. The adoption of the programme was favoured by the strong executive position of the Hungarian prime minister, who backed Bokros and Surányi and allowed them to draw up their programme outside of cabinet. Neither the government's parliamentary factions, the Ministry of Welfare nor the socialist trade unions were informed about the programme in advance, let alone incorporated into its preparation (Kornai 1996, p. 145; Haggard et al. 2001, pp. 97-9).

The Bokros Package was highly unpopular. The announced cuts in social spending led to the first mass protests and demonstrations in Hungary since the 1990 taxi driver strike. One public opinion poll found that two thirds of Hungarians were 'outraged' at the reform package (cited in Cook and Orenstein 1999, p. 95). Popular support for the MSZP declined from 33 per cent in 1994 to less than 20 per cent in early 1996 (Szilagyi 1996, p. 43). Despite these protests and the resignation of a number of socialist ministers, the government essentially held the line. Backed by Prime Minister Horn and benefiting from the strong parliamentary position of the government, reformers were able to implement the bulk of the announced measures. After minor modifications, only a handful of socialist deputies dared to vote against the government, so that the two major legal acts had a safe passage through parliament. However, part of the legislation fell victim to a couple of rulings by the Hungarian Constitutional Court between May and October 1995 (Sajó 1996; Dethier and Shapiro 1998).

While the court decisions forced the government to withdraw expenditure cuts estimated at 0.5 per cent of GDP, they did not derail reforms. The government defied all sceptics and succeeded in enforcing the tough freeze of nominal budgetary allocations. Due to this inflation-induced erosion of real spending, the expenditure-to-GDP ratio declined drastically after the launching of reforms. This decline translated into a substantial improvement in the fiscal stance. In 1995, the general government primary balance improved by almost 3 per cent and the overall fiscal balance by 1.2 per cent of GDP.

The adoption of the Bokros Package resulted in an 'adjustment without recession' (Kornai 1997). Despite the fiscal tightening, GDP recovered quickly and fell only in the second and third quarters in 1995. The current account deficit shrank from 9.7 per cent in 1994 to 5.7 per cent in 1995 and 3.8 per cent in 1996. These favourable economic developments coincided with a substantial drop in real wages. In contrast, unemployment remained more or less constant.

The combination of quickly receding fiscal and current account deficits on the one hand and plummeting living standards on the other complicated the consolidation of reform, especially the adoption of the announced pension and health care reforms. The quick improvement of the macroeconomic situation, along with the approaching parliamentary elections in 1998, favoured a slowing of reforms and contributed to the postponement of health care reform and a relaxation of the fiscal stance in 1997 and 1998 (Orosz et al. 1998; OECD 1999, pp. 48-53). The controversies over the continuation of reforms led to the eventual resignation of Finance Minister Bokros in February 1996.

Despite the slowing of reforms, the Horn government succeeded in locking-in fiscal adjustment and in replacing and complementing the short-term measures that had borne the brunt of adjustment in 1995 with more lasting changes (Ruggiero 1998, pp. 37-40). Reforms adopted included substantial cuts in public personnel, the overhaul of family and child allowances (Sipos and Tóth 1998, pp. 304-13) and a comprehensive pension reform (Müller 1999, Chapter 4). As for tax reform, measures were less consistent and suffered from frequent changes (Ruggiero 1998, pp. 40-42). Yet the government managed to dismantle the import surcharge introduced in 1995 and to reduce the high social security contribution rates from 60.8 per cent in 1994 to 55 per cent in 1997.

The far-reaching consolidation of fiscal reform was favoured by a high degree of executive authority. The government's strong parliamentary majority and the strong position of Horn within cabinet made it relatively easy to overcome resistance inside and outside of government. In addition, the insistence of the IMF on fiscal restraint played some part. Despite the favourable reform outcomes in 1995, the IMF did not endorse an agreement with the Hungarian government until March 1996. As the government was keen on getting IMF approval, the IMF's reluctance, partly caused by the bad experience with the 1993 agreement with the conservative government, strengthened the position of reformers within government.

5.5   CONCLUSION

Like my earlier analysis of the initiation of reform, a comparative reading of the second stage of post-communist fiscal reform underscores the role of political constraints in shaping national trajectories. Due to differing economic and political conditions, the capacity to react to the unfolding fiscal tensions and to continue reforms differed among the sample countries. These capacities were highest in Czechoslovakia where the combination of a powerful change team and a greater overall popularity of transformation allowed the government to push through reforms despite heavy constraints on executive authority. The economic and political conditions in Poland were less favourable to a consolidation of reform. Popular support for fiscal reform was substantially weaker than in Czechoslovakia. At the same time executive authority was heavily constrained by fragile parliamentary majorities. These obstacles notwithstanding, the coincidence of strong reform pressures and powerful change teams allowed the adoption of substantial reform measures. Conditions were the least favourable in Hungary, which suffered from a combination of relatively weak fiscal pressures and weak reformers. Gradual deterioration of the fiscal stance, relatively easy financing of budget deficits and weak inflationary pressures let fiscal adjustment appear less urgent, reduced readiness to support restraint and favoured the postponement and watering down of reforms. The fact that reformers were isolated within government and could not count on prime ministerial support also hindered efforts at reform. The reaction to the fiscal crisis and the continuation of fiscal reform were complicated further by rifts within the governing coalition, Prime Minister Antall's illness and the upcoming 1994 elections. As a result, it took until March 1995 for Hungary's fiscal problems to be eventually addressed.

NOTES

1. Much has been written about the reasons for the initially low unemployment in the Czech Republic (Ham et al. 1998; Raiser 1994). Among the factors is certainly the 'luck factor' (Drábek 1995, p. 244) associated with foreign tourists' attraction to Prague and the long border with Bavaria. The country's macroeconomic and political stability comprises another reason. Also widely acknowledged as contributing factors are an efficient labour market policy and the 'two cushions' (Klaus) associated with an undervalued currency and wage restraint. Observers continue to disagree about the extent to which the low Czech unemployment reflected delayed restructuring and continued hoarding of labour.
2. For the impact of voucher privatization on the support for reforms, see Earle et al. 1997.
3. The 1990 Competence Law assigned the legislation on personal and corporate income taxes, VAT and excises to the Federation. In contrast, responsibility for property, road, inheritance and environmental taxes rested with the republics.
4. In the Slovak Republic, the standard VAT rate was increased from 23 to 25 per cent.

5. The 1993 peak in government spending on goods and services is due to a special purchase of Russian military equipment worth about 2 per cent of GDP. This one-off transaction was part of an intergovernmental agreement with Russia on the cancellation of outstanding debt obligations incurred by the former Soviet Union.

6. Staying the course II: fiscal reform from the end of the post-communist fiscal crisis to EU accession

6.1 INTRODUCTION

After the end of the transformational recession and the associated post-communist fiscal crisis, the economic context and the agenda of fiscal reform once more changed. The heroic challenges during early transformation gave way to more mundane problems. Short-term fiscal pressures have receded, and tax and expenditure reforms have no longer been pre-occupied with laying the foundations of a market system, but have been about streamlining an already existing system.

Since the overcoming of the fiscal crisis, the reform trajectories of the Czech Republic, Hungary and Poland have converged. The Czech Republic's reputation as a pace-setter in fiscal reform suffered a heavy blow from the 1997 currency crisis and the subsequent deterioration of the fiscal stance (Bönker 2006b). Today, all three countries under analysis are among the new EU members with the biggest fiscal problems. Compared to the Baltics and Slovenia, they are characterized by relatively huge fiscal deficits and rather high levels of spending and taxes (Bönker 2003b; Dyson 2006). While they have succeeded in becoming EU members, they are unlikely to enter the Euro-zone before the end of the decade if current membership criteria, including the magic 3 per cent deficit threshold, are kept.

This chapter continues the comparative analysis of fiscal reform in Hungary, Poland and the Czech Republic by examining the developments since the end of the post-communist fiscal crisis. It seeks to account for the striking convergence between the three countries and to learn about the role of political constraints during the most recent stage of post-communist fiscal reform. Section 6.2 looks at the continuation of fiscal reform in Poland after the 1993 elections. Section 6.3 covers fiscal reform in Hungary since the 1998 elections. Section 6.4 examines how the Czech Republic has turned from pace-setter to laggard. Section 6.5 draws some comparative conclusions.

6.2 POLAND

Poland was the first post-communist country to overcome the transformational recession. With the return to growth, the strong short-term fiscal pressures characteristic of the early 1990s receded. Notwithstanding the improved fiscal stance, however, fiscal reform has progressed relatively slowly. This applies both to the centre-left and the centre-right governments that were in office from 1993 to 2005 (for an overview of the political development in Poland during this period, see Table 6.1).

Fiscal reform under the first SLD/PSL government, 1993-97

The parliamentary elections in September 1993 resulted in a spectacular change in government and catapulted the post-communist Democratic Left Alliance (SLD) and the Polish Peasant Party (PSL) into office. The 'return of the communists' raised some concerns about a turnaround in economic policy. However, dire scenarios of a derailing transition and spiralling inflation did not materialize (Blazyca and Rapacki 1996; Kołodko and Nuti 1997). The new government managed to keep fiscal deficits low, to gradually reduce inflation and to limit the external economic imbalances. Moreover, it adopted a number of structural reforms, most notably the much-acclaimed 1997 pension reform, one of the first systemic pension reforms in the region. Upon closer inspection, however, the reform record of the first SLD/PSL government looks less impressive. Given the high rates of economic growth in the mid-1990s, the fiscal targets of the SLD/PSL government appear very modest. Tax and expenditure reforms suffered from delays and a lack of ambition and progressed rather slowly.

Economic and political conditions, 1993-97
The economic and political situation between 1993 and 1997 was inimical to an acceleration of fiscal reform. Soon after the change in government, reform pressure receded. Popular support for reforms continued to be limited, and while the 1993 elections ended a period of short-lived minority governments and highly fragmented parliaments, a number of constraints on executive authority existed. Finally, reformers were not uncontested within government.

Table 6.1   The political scene in Poland, 1993-2005

Parliaments	Parties in government	Prime ministers	Finance ministers
9/1993-9/1997	SLD, PSL	Waldemar Pawlak (PSL) *9/1993-3/1995*	Marek Borowski *10/1993-2/1994*
		Józef Oleksy (SLD) *3/1995-2/1996*	Grzegorz Kołodko *3/1994-2/1997*
		Włodzimierz Cimoszewicz (SLD) *2/1996-9/1997*	Marek Belka *2/1997-9/1997*
9/1997-9/2001	AWS, UW	Jerzy Buzek (AWS) *9/1997-6/2000*	Leszek Balcerowicz *9/1997-6/2000*
	AWS (minority government)	Jerzy Buzek (AWS) *6/2000-9/2001*	Jarosław Bauc *6/2000-9/2001*
9/2001-9/2005	SLD, UP, PSL	Leszek Miller *9/2001-3/2004*	Marek Belka *9/2001-7/2002*
			Grzegorz Kołodko *7/2002-7/2003*
			Andrzej Raczko *7/2003-3/2004*
		Marek Belka *3/2004-9/2005*	Mirosław Gronicki *3/2004-9/2005*

Sources: Zubek 2006; press releases.

When the new government came to office, the *pressure to reform* was relatively high. Estimates at that time emphasized the need for substantial corrective measures if the fiscal deficit was to be kept at a level of 4 per cent of GDP. The pressure to contain the deficit was increased by Poland's negotiations with the IMF. Since Poland's 1991 agreement with the Paris Club had made the second tranche of debt relief conditional on adherence to an IMF-supported reform programme, controversies with the IMF over the size of the deficit threatened to put a substantial reduction of Poland's foreign debt in 1994 at risk.

In 1994/95, the reform pressure substantially weakened (Table 6.2). The acceleration of economic growth that set in in 1994 allowed Poland to grow out of its fiscal problems, as the combination of strong economic growth and a new tax system with relatively high rates pushed up government revenues. The economic recovery was accompanied by a gradual decline in inflation and unemployment. The current account showed a surplus in 1994 and 1995 and plunged into the red only in 1996.

Table 6.2   Economic and fiscal conditions in Poland, 1993-97

	1993	1994	1995	1996	1997
GDP growth (real)	3.8	5.2	7.0	6.1	6.9
Inflation rate (CPI, annual average)	35.3	32.2	27.8	19.9	14.9
Unemployment rate (end-year)	16.4	16.0	14.9	13.2	8.6
Current account (% of GDP)	-0.7	0.7	4.5	-1.0	-3.2
General government balance (% of GDP)	-2.4	-2.2	-3.1	-3.3	-3.1
General government expenditure (% of GDP)	49.9	50.5	49.2	49.3	48.0

Sources: EBRD, Transition Report, various issues.

This limited reform pressure coincided with weak *popular support* for a continuation of fiscal reform. Given the social hardships during the early 1990s and the recovering economy, the readiness for further belt-tightening among the population was limited. Since both the SLD and the PSL had campaigned on a platform of higher social spending, the results of the 1993 elections were widely perceived as a manifestation of reform fatigue.

The 1993 elections eliminated a number of constraints on *executive authority* that had complicated fiscal reform during the post-communist fiscal crisis. Unlike previous elections, the 1993 parliamentary elections gave rise to a 'fairly unproblematic parliamentary majority' (Stone 2002, p. 110). With almost two thirds of the seats in the Sejm, the governing coalition dominated the parliament. Despite clear parliamentary majorities, however, executive authority suffered from a number of important constraints. First, the fact that presidential elections took place in November 1995, half-way into the term, favoured electioneering and made it more difficult to adopt unpopular measures during the first part of the parliamentary term. Second, until the 1995 presidential elections the SLD/PSL government had to deal with a president from a different political camp. Keen to exploit rivalries within the governing coalition and to obstruct government initiatives, President Wałęsa tested the limits of presidential power. The period of 'divided government' came to an end in November 1995 when Aleksander Kwaśniewski, a leading SLD politician, succeeded Wałęsa as president. Finally, the government's capacity to act suffered from strong internal rifts. For one thing, the SLD consisted of different factions. For another, the relationship between SLD and PSL was strained. The struggles between SLD and PSL were particularly intense between October 1993 and March 1995, when the government was led by Waldemar Pawlak the chairman of the PSL.

Like executive authority, the *position of reformers* within the government changed over time. Marek Borowski, the first finance minister of the SLD/PSL government, was widely recognized as a leading spokesman of the reformist wing of the SLD and enjoyed a strong standing in the SLD. However, his position in the government suffered from conflicts with Prime Minister Pawlak, which led to Borowski's resignation in February 1994. Grzegorz Kołodko, a well-known economist who succeeded Borowski, tried to strengthen his position within government by formally committing the government to this 'Strategy for Poland'. Until the end of 1995, however, his position in the cabinet was weakened by conflicts with President Wałęsa and Prime Ministers Pawlak and Oleksy. In contrast, Prime Minister Cimoszewicz and President Kwaśniewski tended to back Kołodko. In February 1997, Kołodko resigned for personal reasons. Marek Belka, his successor, another professor of economics, was also supported strongly by Cimoszewicz and Kwaśniewski.

Fiscal reform, 1993-97
The economic and political conditions that prevailed between 1993 and 1997 made it relatively easy to contain fiscal deficits, but were less favourable to the passage of unpopular tax and expenditure reforms and a more radical fiscal tightening.

When the new government came to office, short-term fiscal pressures were still substantial. The new government thus struggled hard to reconcile its promises of higher spending with its commitment to macroeconomic stability and disinflation. Submitted to parliament in December 1993, the 1994 budget draft posted a substantial increase in spending, most notably social spending. However, Finance Minister Borowski succeeded in limiting the planned deficit to 4.2 per cent of GDP, i.e. only slightly higher than planned by the outgoing Suchocka government. The additional spending was financed by higher taxes. The measures adopted included a broadening of the VAT base, an introduction of a presumptive income tax for hard-to-tax sectors and a temporary increase in personal income tax rates from 20, 30 and 40 per cent to 21, 33 and 45 per cent, respectively. Part of these measures had already been prepared by the outgoing Suchocka government.

In his struggle to limit the budget deficit, Borowski benefited greatly from the IMF's insistence on fiscal restraint (Bjork 1995, pp. 115-17; Stone 2002, pp. 110, 114). At that time, the position of the IMF was rather strong. The new government was keen to defy critics and to demonstrate its respectability by not falling from grace with the IMF. Moreover, conflicts with the IMF threatened to put a substantial reduction of Poland's foreign debt in 1994 at risk since Poland's 1991 agreement with the Paris Club had made the second tranche of debt relief conditional on the adherence to an IMF-supported reform programme. This nexus strengthened Borowski's position in the negotiations on the 1994 budget and helped him to ward off demands for further increases in spending. The government's desire not to risk IMF support also became visible after the resignation of Borowski in February 1994 (Vinton 1994, pp. 5-7). Owing to struggles between Prime Minister Pawlak, President Wałęsa and the SLD, the position of the Minister of Finance remained vacant for almost three months. Yet the government managed to hold the line and to prevent a renegotiation of the budget during the interregnum.

Fiscal reform gained momentum when Grzegorz Kołodko became Finance Minister. Kołodko brought with him a medium-term reform programme. Approved by the government and the Sejm in June 1994, the 'Strategy for Poland' projected a gradual decline in deficits and a medium-term decline in the share of government spending in GDP (Stone 2002, p. 112; Kołodko and Nuti 1997). The programme called for a change in the indexation of pensions and the move to a multi-pillar pension system. Tax reform featured less prominently on Kołodko's original agenda, yet became an important part of 'Package 2000', an update of the 'Strategy for Poland' adopted in March 1996. The new programme called for the gradual phasing-in of substantial cuts in corporate and personal income taxes. The corporate income tax rate was scheduled to fall from 40 per cent in 1996 to 32 per cent in 2000. Personal income tax rates were set to be reduced to their 1993 levels in 1997, followed by further cuts in subsequent years. Part of these cuts were to be financed by a broadening of tax bases through changes in depreciation rules, tax deductions and tax exemptions.

Kołodko's fiscal targets helped to dispel concerns about the economic policy of the SLD/PSL government. Taking into account the tigerish growth of the Polish economy in the mid-1990s, however, they were not very ambitious. The original targets for the deficit-to-GDP ratio left scope for a substantial increase in real spending and were only modestly updated when the economic recovery proved to be stronger than expected. Despite the strong GDP growth, the 1996 and 1997 budgets left the deficit almost unchanged (OECD 1998, pp. 36-45). In the end, the fiscal stance even slightly worsened in 1996 and 1997. The lack of fiscal tightening represented a major reason for the slow disinflation and the increase in the current account deficit.

Kołodko's cautious stance was partly motivated by the fear that lower deficits might infringe on economic growth. However, it also reflected the limited pressure to reform, weak popular support for more radical reforms and some constraints on executive authority. With the fiscal deficit and inflation under control and current account deficits still relatively low, short-term economic problems were limited. At the same time, the readiness of the population to tolerate further hardships was limited. Moreover, expenditure reforms threatened to hit core constituencies of the governing coalition among farmers, industrial workers, public employees and pensioners. Finally, executive authority suffered from the prospect of the upcoming 1997 elections and from some conflicts within the governing coalition.

The obstacles to fiscal reform are visible in the fields of expenditure and tax reform. Regarding expenditure reform, Kołodko had focused on pensions, which accounted for about a third of all government spending in the mid-1990s. However, pension reform had a long gestation (Götting 1998, pp. 165-6; Müller 1999, pp. 108-11; Orenstein 2000, pp. 46-59; Hausner 2001). Until early 1996, Kołodko failed to commit the government to his reform plans. Facing strong resistance by the SLD's traditionalist wing, he lacked prime ministerial support. Pension reform did not gain momentum until February 1996 when Prime Minister Cimoszewicz became prime minister and replaced Labour Minister Leszek Miller, the leading spokesman of the SLD's traditionalist wing, with Andrzej Bączkowski, an independent with a *Solidarność* background. Backed by Cimoszewicz and President Kwaśniewski, Bączkowski submitted plans for a systemic pension reform along the lines suggested by Kołodko. When Bączkowski died unexpectedly in November, Jerzy Hausner, a former adviser to Kołodko, was put in charge of finalizing pension reform. In 1997, a number of laws laid the foundations of a multi-pillar pension system. With a view to the upcoming elections, however, the government postponed most of the controversial reforms of the first pillar and did not touch the retirement age, the mininum pension, the indexation of pensions and the traditional privileges for particular occupations.

In other fields, expenditure reform also progressed slowly. In the case of health care, the passage of reform took until February 1997. Moreover, the bill approved by the Sejm established only the broad outlines of a new national health-insurance system, but did not go into details (Nelson 2001, pp. 255-6). The government also shied away from restructuring the coal, steel and railway sectors, which were strongholds of the unions. In the run-up to the 1997 elections, it granted substantial increases in public sector wages and other give-aways.

Tax reform also turned out to be a protracted process. The prolongation of the higher income tax rates introduced in 1994 provoked fierce struggles between the government and President Wałęsa, who tried to capitalize on the government's violation of earlier promises. With an eye to the upcoming presidential elections, Wałęsa vetoed the bill and appealed to the Constitutional Court twice. In March 1995, the Constitutional Court declared the maintenance of the higher rates unconstitutional because of procedural failures. In the end, the governing coalition managed to override the Court.

However, the taxation of personal income remained plagued with uncertainties. In October 1995, the parliamentary factions of the SLD and the PSL passed a reform of personal income tax which ran against the will of the government. The adopted measures sought to make the personal income tax more differentiated and more redistributive and would have resulted in unplanned revenue losses. For that reason the measures were strongly opposed by Kołodko. However, the Finance Minister failed to bring the coalition in line. Eventually, the enactment of the new provisions could nevertheless be avoided. In one of his last moves, President Wałęsa vetoed the bill, and the resulting delay allowed Kołodko to maintain the old rate structure by decree.

While the reform of corporate income taxation was uncontroversial and passed parliament without complications, Kołodko's plans for the personal income tax stirred severe conflicts within the governing coalition. In late 1996, when Kołodko eventually had succeeded in committing the government to the cuts, the PSL defected in the Sejm in late 1996. In a desperate attempt to demonstrate its independence from the SLD and to strengthen its profile in the run-up to the 1997 elections, the PSL managed to forge a majority with the opposition and to pass a four-tier tax system with rates of 17, 20, 33 and 45 per cent. Like in the previous year, Kołodko strongly opposed the vote. This time, President Kwaśniewski and Prime Minister Cimoszewicz joined his side. Kwaśniewski threatened to veto the Sejm's decision; Cimoszewicz threatened to resign. At the end, the SLD and the liberal Freedom Union (UW) teamed up in the Senate and hammered out a different scheme (20, 32 and 44 per cent), which was then accepted by the Sejm.

Marek Belka, Kołodko's successor, stayed in office only from February to October 1997, thus having little time to shape fiscal policy. Despite the approaching elections, however, he succeeded in limiting the adverse budgetary impact of the summer floods of 1997 on the budget. The success of his attempts to tighten the fiscal stance was favoured by the further deterioration of the current account and the Czech currency crisis in May 1997, which increased the reform pressure (Belka 1997).

The return of Balcerowicz: fiscal reform under the AWS/UW government, 1997-2001

The 1997 elections brought a further change in government. The SLD/PSL government was replaced by a centre-right government consisting of the conservative Electoral Action Solidarity (AWS) and the liberal Freedom Union (UW). The new government committed itself to an ambitious reform programme that called for a tightening of the fiscal stance and an acceleration of tax and expenditure reform. This programme was strongly shaped by the UW, the smaller coalition partner. Leszek Balcerowicz, its chairman, became Finance Minister for a second time. Due to unfavourable economic and political conditions, however, only part of the envisioned reforms could be implemented.

Economic and political conditions, 1997-2001
The economic and political conditions that prevailed from 1997 to 2001 were characterized by the combination of an increased reform pressure, weak popular support for reforms, limited executive authority and relatively strong reformers.

The increasing *reform pressure* largely stemmed from the deteriorating external balance (Table 6.3). The current account deficit grew from 1.0 per cent in 1996 and 3.2 per cent in 1997 to 8.1 per cent in 1999. At the same time, the currency crises in Asia and Russia increased the nervousness of investors. As many observers saw Poland at the brink of a currency crisis, calls for fiscal adjustment grew louder.

While the pressure to reform increased, *popular support* for reforms remained relatively weak. Due to the relatively strong showing of the liberal UW, the new government enjoyed some kind of mandate for reform. However, most of its voters questioned the need for radical reforms. The initial mandate quickly eroded due to the increasing unemployment, the perceived incompetence of the new government and severe problems with implementing the adopted reforms.

Executive authority also suffered from a number of constraints (Zubek 2001, pp. 914-25). For starters, the government was weakened by the fact that Marian Krzaklewski, the leader of the AWS, preferred to stay outside the cabinet with a view to increasing his chances of becoming president. Second, the government had to cooperate with President Kwaśniewski, whose authority had been curbed by the new 1997 constitution, but who was still able to veto part of the legislation. Third and most importantly, the governing coalition showed strong internal rifts. Not only did the liberal UW and the conservative AWS disagree on many issues, but the AWS itself was a conglomerate of heterogeneous centre-right forces with little cohesion and discipline. These rifts, which culminated in the disintegration of the governing coalition and the AWS in 2001, manifested itself in a fragile parliamentary majority.

Table 6.3   *Economic and fiscal conditions in Poland, 1997-2001*

	1997	1998	1999	2000	2001
GDP growth (real)	6.9	4.8	4.1	4.0	1.0
Inflation rate (CPI, annual average)	14.9	11.8	7.3	10.1	5.5
Unemployment rate (end-year)	8.6	10.2	13.4	16.4	18.5
Current account (% of GDP)	-3.2	-4.4	-8.1	-6.1	-2.9
General government balance (% of GDP)	-3.1	-2.3	-1.5	-1.8	-3.5
General government expenditure (% of GDP)	48.0	42.7	42.8	41.7	43.6

Sources: EBRD, Transition Report, various issues.

Compared to the position of government, the *position of reformers* within cabinet was relative strong. Finance Minister Balcerowicz could rely on a well-rehearsed team of experts. Moreover, his international reputation and his double role as Finance Minister and party leader strengthened his position within cabinet. By and large, he was also backed by Prime Minister Jerzy Buzek.

Fiscal reform, 1997-2001
At the outset of the term, the conditions were relatively favourable to the launching of reforms. The government enjoyed some kind of mandate and benefited from the sense of crisis created by the deteriorating external balance and the currency crises in other countries. Moreover, Balcerowicz and his team had a clear reform agenda and could draw on elaborate reform concepts. In the end, however, the government only partly succeeded in pushing through its ambitious reform programme. The implementation of pension, health care and education reforms suffered from administrative difficulties, and the existing constraints on executive authority led to some backtracking.

The incoming government was quick to emphasize its commitment to fiscal tightening. One of its first moves was to make the 1998 budget more restrictive. In 1999, the new government also adopted a medium-term fiscal framework that went beyond the plans of the SLD/PSL-government and envisaged a balanced budget as early as in 2003. However, the government's fragile parliamentary majority complicated reform. A number of MPs from the AWS consistently opposed Balcerowicz's plans and several times threatened to defect. This lack of support forced Balcerowicz to compromise on part of the originally planned cuts in the deficit. The government's fragile position was indicated by the dubious way the 1999 deficit overrun was financed (IMF 2000, p. 14): instead of financing the higher-than-expected deficit of the social insurance fund through transfers from the central government's budget, the government resorted to off-budget funds. This decision was largely motivated by the wish to circumvent the Sejm since the government feared that parliament would use the approval of a higher central government deficit to vote for extra spending.

The new government had also promised to speed up expenditure reform. In 1997/98, it completed the pension and health care reforms initiated by the SLD/PSL government, so that reforms could take effect in 1999. Moreover, the government launched ambitious restructuring programmes for the coal and steel sector (IMF 2000, pp. 58-9). Supported by the EU, these programmes aimed at closing inefficient production sites and at reducing overstaffing. While implying additional government spending for severance packages in the short-run, these programmes were to reduce medium-term fiscal pressures by reducing the need for subsidies.

The passage of these reforms was complicated by rifts within the governing coalition. Supported by the parliamentary opposition and the trade unions, the labour wing of the AWS opposed part of the more unpopular measures. As for pension reform, the government had to withdraw from its plans to equalize the retirement age for men and women until the year 2035, to restrict pensioners' rights to go on working and to abolish part of the privileges of certain occupations, most notably the 'uniformed services' (Müller 1999, p. 113). As for the restructuring of the coal and steel sector, opposition from within the governing coalition forced the government to delay the restructuring and to grant higher severance payments. These concessions contributed to a watering down of reforms and reduced the envisaged positive fiscal effects.

The political constraints on fiscal reform can also be seen in the field of tax reform (OECD 2000a, pp. 140-47; Zubek 2001, pp. 925-7). When coming to office, the new AWS/UW-government pledged vigorous tax reforms. In 1998, the Ministry of Finance published a White Book with proposals for a comprehensive tax reform to be implemented in the second part of the term.

However, both the rifts within the governing coalition and the opposition of President Kwaśniewski made the passage of reforms a rocky process. At a first stage, opposition from within the governing coalition, in particular the AWS, forced Balcerowicz into concessions. As early as 1998, he had to drop his original plan to introduce a flat-rate income tax. Owing to controversies within the government, it took until June 1999 before the government officially committed itself to a reform package. This package foresaw a gradual cut in corporate income tax rates from 34 per cent in 1999 to 22 per cent in 2004, while personal income tax rates were scheduled to come down in stages from 19, 30 and 40 per cent in 1999 to 18 and 28 per cent in 2001. At the same time, the reform included the wiping out of most income deductions and tax credits within the framework of the personal income tax, the elimination of most tax incentives and loopholes within the framework of the corporate income tax and the imposition of the standard VAT rate on a number of products and services.

However, the endorsement of reform by the government and by the leaders of the coalition was not sufficient to ensure parliamentary approval. In a number of late night meetings in the run-up to the parliamentary vote, the government made additional concessions to the AWS dissenters. The eventually submitted draft laws stretched the cuts in personal income tax rates over time and kept various popular tax exemptions. Even after these concessions, however, it remained unclear until the very end whether the government's plan eventually would find a majority. In the end, Balcerowicz had to threaten his resignation and the end of the AWS/UW coalition in order to forge a majority for the government's tax reform.

After the parliamentary approval, tax reform faced a further obstacle. In late November 1999, President Kwaśniewski vetoed the enactment of the law on personal income tax. According to Kwaśniewski, the new provisions were biased towards the rich. Kwaśniewski's veto not only delayed the much needed further reform of the personal income tax. As the new provisions on corporate income tax and VAT were enacted in schedule, the veto also led to severe inconsistencies between the (reformed) corporate income tax and the (unreformed) personal income tax.

The controversies over tax reform contributed to the eventual split of the governing coalition and the resignation of Balcerowicz in June 2000. After the break, fiscal reform slowed (Zubek 2006). With the UW out of government and the AWS disintegrating, the government lacked a clear majority; Jarosław Bauc, the new Finance Minister, had much less clout than his predecessor; finally, the parliamentary elections scheduled for September 2001 reduced the readiness to adopt unpopular measures.

The break-down of the coalition came at a time when the Polish economy started to slow (Table 6.3). The stuttering growth increased the pressure on the budget and led to a strong increase in the fiscal deficit in 2001. When Finance Minister Bauc proposed spending cuts worth 1 per cent of GDP in May 2001, the cabinet rejected his proposal. Later on, some reforms were announced. However, proclamations remained lofty.

The failure of fiscal reform under the second SLD/PSl government, 2001-2005

The postponement of fiscal reform did not help the AWS to prevent an electoral disaster. In the 2001 elections, the UW and the remainder of the AWS did not get enough votes to enter parliament. Contrary to expectations, however, the post-communist SLD and its social-democratic ally, the Labour Union (UP), also failed to muster a majority, so that they were forced to forge a coalition with the agrarian PSL. From 2001 to 2005, Poland was thus governed by a 'red-green' coalition for the second time. The new government took over in a situation of escalating fiscal pressures. However, a number of attempts at fiscal reform failed (for the following, see Zubek 2006).

Economic and political conditions, 2001-2005

After the 2001 elections, the pressure to reform remained relatively high. At the same, however, limited popular support for reforms, an eroding executive authority and a weak position of reformers complicated the initiation of reform.

With the current account under control, the main *pressure to reform* stemmed from the strong fiscal tensions (Table 6.4). The huge budget deficits that re-emerged in 2001 severely undermined the credibility of Poland's commitment to a quick Euro-zone entry. Moreover, the Polish central bank used the deficits as justification for sticking to its tight monetary policy. Finally, the deficits raised fears that Poland might violate the restrictions on the size of the public debt enshrined in the 1997 constitution.

Despite these economic and political problems, *popular support* for reforms remained relatively weak. Large parts of the population were still fed up with the ambitious reform projects of the early Buzek government. As in 1993, the SLD had campaigned as an defender of social entitlements. Not only the population, but also the majority of the business community did not regard the postponement of Euro-zone entry as a major problem.

Executive authority was limited by the strong rifts within the SLD. They stemmed from conflicts between the regional party bosses and the supporters of President Kwaśniewski in the party and were aggravated by a string of major corruption scandals that involved senior SLD politicians, including Prime Minister Leszek Miller. The scandals contributed to the bad showing of the SLD in the 2002 local elections and the elections to the European

Parliament in 2004 and eventually led to the disintegration of the SLD. Starting in March 2004, a number of prominent politicians defected from the SLD and set up competing parties. The rifts within the SLD substantially reduced the authority of Prime Minister Miller and his successor Marek Belka.

Table 6.4   Economic and fiscal conditions in Poland, 2001-2005

	2001	*2002*	*2003*	*2004*	*2005*
GDP growth (real)	1.0	1.4	3.8	5.4	3.5
Inflation rate (CPI, annual average)	5.5	1.7	0.7	3.5	2.2
Unemployment rate (end-year)	18.5	19.8	19.2	19.0	na
Current account (% of GDP)	-2.9	-2.6	-2.2	-1.5	-1.3
General government balance (% of GDP)	-3.7	-3.3	-4.8	-3.9	-3.7
General government expenditure (% of GDP)	43.0	43.4	44.2	44.6	na

Sources: EBRD, Transition Report, various issues.

The limited capacity of the government also infringed upon the *position of reformers*. The latter were only half-heartedly backed by Prime Minister Miller and the rest of the cabinet. The lack of support is evidenced by a string of resignations by frustrated reformers. Marek Belka, the first Finance Minister of the Miller government, resigned in July 2002; Grzegorz Kołodko, his successor, stayed for less than a year; Jerzy Hausner, the Economics and Labour Minister who drew up the most recent plan for fiscal reform, left the government in March 2005.

Fiscal reform, 2001-2005
The strong rifts within the governing coalition complicated the adoption of fiscal reform. From 2001 to 2005, three major reform initiatives were undertaken. All eventually failed, as they were only half-heartedly backed by the Prime Minister or faced strong opposition in the Sejm.

The first attempt at fiscal reform was initiated by Finance Minister Belka. Benefiting from the strong sense of crisis in late 2001, he managed to gain support for a bundle of short- and medium-term measures. By combining a freeze on public sector wages and other cuts in spending with moderate income tax increases and the introduction of a capital gains tax, Belka succeeded in tightening the 2002 budget. More importantly, he committed the cabinet to limiting spending growth in the years from 2002 to 2006 to 1 per cent above inflation. However, Belka's 'fiscal contract' did not hold for long. As early as mid 2002, the cabinet agreed upon higher spending targets. The failure of the contract was largely motivated by the weak approval ratings of the SLD in the run-up to the 2002 local elections.

Kolodko, Belka's successor, was the second Finance Minister to initiate fiscal reform. Compared to Belka, his strategy was slightly different. For one thing, Kolodko aggressively 'sold' fiscal reform in order to achieve fast Euro-zone entry. For another, he put less emphasis on the expenditure side and assigned a greater role to tax increases and the mobilization of extraordinary revenues. Notwithstanding earlier promises, however, Prime Minister Miller and the cabinet eventually rejected the comprehensive reform programme presented by Kolodko in March 2003. Again, the shying away from reform was primarily driven by fears that a fiscal tightening would further reduce the popular support for the government.

The third and final attempt at fiscal reform was launched by Jerzy Hausner, the Economics and Labour Minister, who was put in charge of coordinating economic policy in May 2003. His so-called 'Hausner Plan,' which included a reduction in overall social spending by about 4 per cent of GDP between 2004 and 2007, was adopted by the cabinet in January 2004. The adoption of the Hausner plan was favoured by EU pressure, which forced the Polish government to submit a credible medium-term fiscal strategy. Moreover, in late 2003 a number of analyses suggested that Poland was at risk of exceeding the constitutional limit on public debt as early as 2005. At the end, however, the Hausner plan was only partly implemented. For one thing, the better-than-expected performance of revenues in 2004 and 2005 reduced the short-term reform pressure. For another, the upcoming parliamentary elections in September 2005 and the increasingly fragile parliamentary majority led the government to back away from part of the most unpopular measures.

6.3   HUNGARY

Like Poland, Hungary has seen a relatively cautious continuation of fiscal reform since the end of the post-communist fiscal crisis. Both the 1998-2002 centre-right government and its centre-left successor have shied away from unpopular expenditure and tax reforms and strong cuts in the deficit. Unlike in Poland, the main cause of the low level of fiscal reform has been a high degree of political polarization and party competition rather than the fragmentation of the governing coalition (for the political developments between 1998 and 2002, see Table 6.5).

Table 6.5   *The political scene in Hungary, 1998-2005*

Parliaments	Parties in government	Prime ministers	Finance ministers
5/1998-5/2002	Fidesz-MPP, FKGP, MDF	Viktor Orbán (Fidesz-MPP)	Zsigmond Járai *7/1998-12/2000*
			Mihály Varga *1/2001-5/2002*
5/2002-	MSZP, SZDSZ	Péter Medgyessy (MSZP) *5/2002-9/2004*	Csaba László *6/2002-2/2004*
			Tibor Draskovics *3/2004-4/2005*
		Ferenc Gyurcsány (MSZP) *9/2004-*	
			János Veres *5/2005-*

Sources: Greskovits 2006; press releases.

Fiscal reform under the Orbán government, 1998-2002

The 1998 parliamentary elections brought a change in government. The centre-left government was replaced by a centre-right government led by Viktor Orbán, the leader of the Alliance of Young Democrats/ Hungarian Civic Party (Fidesz-MPP).

Economic and political conditions, 1998-2002
As for the continuation of fiscal reform, the economic and political conditions between 1998 and 2002 were ambivalent. On the one hand, Prime Minister Orbán enjoyed a rather strong position in the cabinet. On the other, the pressure to reform, the popular support for reforms and the position of reformers within government was weak. Moreover, electoral pressures were strong, as the approval ratings of the two main political camps were rather close.

Between 1998 and 2002, the *pressure to reform* was relatively low. After the 1995/96 adjustment, the Hungarian economy showed a strong performance (Table 6.6). Despite the turbulent international economic environment, Hungary recorded high rates of economic growth, which reduced the short-term pressure on the budget. The reappearance of high current account deficits raised some concerns about the sustainability of the external stance and led to calls for fiscal adjustment. However, strong FDI inflows eased the financing of the current account deficit and reduced the danger of a currency crisis.

Table 6.6   *Economic and fiscal conditions in Hungary, 1998-2002*

	1998	1999	2000	2001	2002
GDP growth (real)	4.9	4.2	5.2	3.8	3.5
Inflation rate (CPI, annual average)	14.3	10.0	9.8	9.2	4.8
Unemployment rate (end-year)	7.8	7.0	6.4	5.7	5.8
Current account (% of GDP)	-7.2	-7.9	-8.7	-6.2	-7.2
General government balance (% of GDP)	-8.0	-5.6	-3.0	-4.4	-9.3
General government expenditure (% of GDP)	50.4	47.4	47.0	51.8	50.7

Sources: EBRD, Transition Report, various issues.

Popular support for reforms was also weak. Fidesz-MPP had heavily criticized the Bokros Package as unjust and unnecessary and had campaigned on a populist platform. The booming economy reduced the readiness to support restraint and favoured calls for compensating the social hardships associated with earlier reforms.

As for *executive authority*, the picture was mixed. On the one hand, the government had a clear parliamentary majority and an extremely strong and dominating Prime Minister. Orbán was the uncontested leader of the government and made heavy use of the strong constitutional position of his office. The centralization of authority in the cabinet went so far that the prime minister was granted the right to impose spending caps on the budgets of the ministers (Brusis and Dimitrov 2001, p. 900). On the other hand, the authority of the government was limited by strong electoral pressures. Opinions polls showed a neck-and-neck race between the two main political camps during most of the term. The parliamentary elections in 2002 thus created strong incentives to cater to voters and to shy away from unpopular measures.

The strong position of Prime Minister Orbán also infringed upon the *position of reformers* within government. Orbán's dominance meant that the two Finance Ministers of the centre-right government played only a limited role as independent agenda-setters. Both Zsigmond Járai and, even more so, Mihály Varga, who succeeded Jarai after the latter had become governor of the National Bank of Hungary in January 2001, refrained from coming up with their own ambitious reform plans and largely confined themselves to accommodating the wishes of Prime Minister Orbán.

Fiscal reform, 1998-2002

Owing to its clear parliamentary majority and the strong position of the Prime Minister, the centre-right government in principle was in a favourable position to engage in fiscal reform. In fact, however, the government took a modest approach. Despite steady admonitions by many economists and the international financial organizations, it set itself only very modest fiscal targets and shied away from unpopular tax and expenditure reforms.

The low level of fiscal reform can partly be explained by the weak reform pressure and the low popular support for reforms. In addition, the lack of a strong independent Finance Minister pushing for reform played a role. The single most important factor, however, was the strong party competition and the atmosphere of permanent electioneering. It severely reduced the capacity of reformers to adopt unpopular measures and favoured the postponement of fiscal reform.

With a view to the election-induced fiscal expansion in 1998 and the deteriorating current account, the incoming government initially undertook some fiscal tightening. The 1998 deficit was slightly reduced, and the 1999 budget provided for another small decline in the deficit (OECD 1999, pp. 48, 55). In order to be on the safe side, the government made part of the spending contingent on the macroeconomic development.

The government's initial attempts at fiscal tightening coincided with the enactment of new entitlements and substantial tax cuts. The 1999 budget reintroduced universal child benefits, reduced income taxes and lowered social security contributions (Kiss and Szápary 2000, p. 253). A substantial part of these reforms with their permanent effects was financed by short-term measures such as a delay in investment projects and wage restraint (OECD 2000b, p. 62). Moreover, the government reneged on the 1996/97 pension reform and refrained from increasing the share of individual social security contributions going to private pension funds from 6 to 7 per cent (Müller 2003, p. 79). This freeze improved the short-term fiscal situation of the public pension scheme, but increased medium- and long-term fiscal risks because of unchanged state guarantees for the returns of private pensions.

The Orbán government's reluctance to engage in structural expenditure reform was also evidenced by its medium-term fiscal programme (World Bank 1999, pp. 39-42). Adopted in July 1999, it envisioned a decline in the fiscal deficit by about 1.5 percentage points from 1999 to 2002. However, this decrease was to be achieved almost exclusively by the projected drop in inflation and the resulting decline in nominal interest payments. Moreover, the programme provided for a slight reduction in the primary surplus in 2001 and 2002.

The government's joint budget for 2001 and 2002, which was brought in in September 2000, was highly shaped by the upcoming elections (OECD 2000b, pp. 71-5, 2004, p. 47). It provided for a number of popular tax cuts and spending inceases. The adopted measures included a quadrupling of the personal income tax credit for families with three or more children, reductions in employers' social security contributions, the introduction of generous housing subsidies, strong increases in public sector wages and higher spending on infrastructure, most notably motorways. The government's infrastructure initiatives were summarized in the Széchenyi Plan, a medium-term national development plan, which called for additional infrastructure spending of about 0.5 per cent of GDP. These tax and expenditure measures were difficult to reconcile with the official 2002 deficit target of 4.9 per cent and contributed strongly to the spectacular soaring of the Hungarian fiscal deficit in 2002.

Fiscal reform under the second MSZP/SDSZ government, 2002-2005

The shying away from fiscal reform continued after the 2002 elections, which brought the Hungarian Socialist Party (MSZP) and the centre-left Alliance of Free Democrats (SDSZ) back into office. As during the previous term, electoral pressures complicated the adoption of reforms (Greskovits 2006).

Economic and political conditions, 2002-2005
After the 2002 election, economic and political conditions partly changed. While the popular support for reforms and the position of reformers within government remained weak and electoral pressures continued to loom large, the reform pressure substantially increased. At the same time, executive authority further suffered from the weakening position of Péter Medgyessy, the first Prime Minister of the new government, within the MSZP and the government.

The *pressure to reform* largely stemmed from rising fiscal and current account deficits (Table 6.7). The erratic policy of the Hungarian National Bank and a number of speculative attacks on the Hungarian forint further nurtured fears of a currency crisis. Morever, the huge fiscal deficits raised concerns about Hungary's Euro-zone entry and provoked conflicts with the European Commission, which launched the excessive deficit procedure against Hungary upon accession. Finally, the case for fiscal reform was strengthened by the fact that the Hungarian National Bank took them as a justification for continuing its tight economic policy.

Table 6.7   *Economic and fiscal conditions in Hungary, 2002-2005*

	2002	*2003*	*2004*	*2005*
GDP growth (real)	3.5	2.9	4.2	3.5
Inflation rate (CPI, annual average)	4.8	4.9	6.8	3.8
Unemployment rate (% of labour force, end-year)	5.8	5.9	6.3	na
Current account (% of GDP)	-7.2	-8.9	-8.9	-8.0
General government balance (% of GDP)	-8.5	-6.5	-5.4	-6.0
General government expenditure (% of GDP)	52.6	50.2	48.9	na

Sources: EBRD, Transition Report, various issues.

While the reform pressure increased, *popular support* for reform remained limited after the 2002 elections. Both political camps had campaigned on populist platforms and had downplayed the need for adjustment before the elections. Like in Poland, large parts of the business community, the trade unions and even many economists did not view the postponement of Euro-zone entry as a major problem.

Executive authority continued to suffer from the strong electoral pressures associated with the strong party competition in Hungary. In addition, the position of Prime Minister Medgyessy was much less uncontested than that of his predecessor. Medgyessy, who had served as a minister in the past, but had not even been a member of the MSZP before his election, enjoyed a much weaker position in his party. Moreover, his standing suffered from revelations about his cooperation with the Hungarian secret service before 1989. Medgyessy's weak position became evident in September 2004 when he was forced to resign by younger party leaders, who were concerned about the outcome of the 2006 elections. Ferenc Gyurcsány, Medgyessy's successor, was able to capitalize on his own popularity. He was widely seen as the only socialist capable of boosting the electoral prospects of the governing coalition.

As in the previous term, the *position of reformers* within government remained weak. The three subsequent Finance Ministers of the centre-left government shied away from propagating more radical reforms and focused on implementing rather than shaping the cabinet's line. This accomodative approach was favoured by the strong political polarization in Hungary. Moreover, because of their professional background and its crucial electoral importance, both Prime Ministers claimed a strong role in drawing up the government's programme of economic reform.

Fiscal reform, 2002-2005
Like its predecessor, the post-2002 centre-left government has shied away from fiscal reform. Despite the rising reform pressure, as well as a number of reform announcements by the government, little progress with reform has been achieved (OECD 2004, pp. 47-57; 2005a, pp. 51-62). Like under the Orbán government, the single most important reason has been the electoral pressures stemming from the high degree of party competition (Greskovits 2006).

These pressures were felt right after the elections. During its first months in office, the new government increased the already high 2002 fiscal deficit by implementing a number of expensive campaign promises including additional money for pensioners, higher child care benefits, a pay-rise for all public employees and tax relief for low-income earners. The unusal honoring of expensive campaign promises at the beginning of the term, which went contrary to all conventional political wisdom, was motivated by the upcoming local elections scheduled for autumn 2002. Confronted with high popular expectations and a strong political mobilization by the opposition, the government did not dare to resort to normal political practice and to retreat from its campaign promises.

Following the spending splurge in 2002, the government committed itself to a gradual reduction in the deficit aimed at putting the fiscal deficits below 3 per cent in 2007 in order to allow for Euro-zone entry in 2008. In September 2003, the government adopted a stabilization programme that called for savings worth 1.5 per cent of GDP in 2003 and 2004. However, fiscal targets were persistently missed, largely due to spending overruns. The impressive decline in the deficit from 2002 to 2004 was achieved primarily by one-off operations and by changes in accounting methods (OECD 2005a, pp. 51-4). The 2004 deficit was one of the highest in the EU, second only to Greece.

Under Prime Minister Gyurcsány, the commitment to fiscal reform has been watered down further. Gyurcsány not only has tinkered with a rhetoric of fiscal expansionism, but he has openly questioned the case for a fast Euro-zone entry and the rationale of the Maastricht criteria. In spite of fierce criticism by the European Commission, the 2005 and 2006 budgets provided for additional spending on infrastructure and substantial tax cuts. These measures were motivated by electoral considerations and aimed at boosting the popularity of the governing coalition.

6.4   CZECH REPUBLIC

The Czech Republic was long regarded as a pace-setter in fiscal reform. Up to the mid-1990s, low official fiscal deficits and a smooth passage of tax and expenditure reforms made the country a much envied paragon of 'sound money and finance' in the region. Since then, however, the reputation of the Czech Republic has eroded (Bönker 2006b). In 1997, the Czech Republic was the first Central-East European country to experience a major currency crisis. Ever since, it has run fiscal deficits above the average of the Central-East European countries. Moreover, the Czech Republic is widely perceived as one of those new member states of the EU that have reached relatively little progress with tax and expenditure reform (for the political developments in the Czech Republic from 1993 to 2005, see Table 6.8).

Fiscal reform from Czech independence to the 1997 currency crisis

In the Czech case, the end of the post-communist fiscal crisis coincided with the dissolution of Czechoslovakia. The era from the heydays of the Czech 'economic miracle' during the first years of independence to the 1997 currency crisis was characterized by a creeping policy drift.

Economic and political conditions, 1993-97
Between 1993 and 1997 the economic and political conditions in the Czech Republic underwent substantial changes (Tables 6.8, 6.9). The year 1996 marks a watershed in both economic and political terms.

From 1993 to 1996, the *pressure to reform* was relatively limited. The Czech economy grew strongly. Other macroeconomic indicators remained favourable, too. The government managed to tame the inflationary effects of the newly introduced VAT and to return to a single-digit inflation rate in 1994. Unemployment stayed low by all standards, making the Czech Republic a 'low unemployment oasis' (Munich and Sorm 1996) in the region

Table 6.8   *The political scene in the Czech Republic, 1993-2005*

Parliaments	Parties in government	Prime ministers	Finance ministers
1/1993-6/1996*	ODS, KDS, KDU-ČSL, ODA	Václav Klaus (ODS)	Ivan Kočárník
7/1996-6/1998	ODS, KDU-ČSL, ODA *7/1996-11/1997*	Václav Klaus (ODS)	Ivan Kočárník *7/1996-5/1997*
			Ivan Pilip *6/1997-11/1997*
	caretaker government *12/1997-7/1998*	Josef Tošovský	Ivan Pilip
7/1998-6/2002	ČSSD (minority government)	Miloš Zeman (ČSSD)	Ivo Svoboda *7/1998-7/1999*
			Pavel Mertlík *7/1999-4/2001*
			Jiří Rusnok *4/2001-6/2002*
7/2002-	ČSSD, KDU-ČSL, US-DEU	Vladimír Špidla (ČSSD) *7/2002-7/2004*	Bohuslav Sobotka *7/2002-present*
		Stanislav Gross (ČSSD) *7/2004-4/2005*	
		Jiří Paroubek (ČSSD) *4/ 2005-*	

Source: Bönker 2006b.

until 1996. With the economy recovering and a new tax system with relatively high tax rates in place, pressure on the budget receded.

The economic situation deteriorated in the mid-1990s. Compared to Poland, the economic recovery was accompanied by stronger external imbalances. From 1994 to 1996, the current account deteriorated by more than 5 per cent of GDP. The growing external imbalances were favoured by the government's decision to keep the nominal exchange rate at its 1991 level and the resulting real appreciation. Moreover, Czech privatization had led to opaque structures of corporate governance that delayed the restructuring of the Czech economy and contributed to a gradual erosion of competitiveness and export performance.

Table 6.9   *Economic and fiscal conditions in the Czech Republic, 1993-97*

	1993	*1994*	*1995*	*1996*	*1997*
GDP growth (real)	0.1	2.2	5.9	4.8	-1.0
Inflation rate (CPI, annual average)	20.8	11.0	9.1	8.8	8.5
Unemployment rate (end-year)	3.5	3.2	2.9	3.5	5.2
Current account (% of GDP)	1.3	-1.9	-2.6	-7.4	-6.1
General government balance (% of GDP)	0.5	-1.1	-1.4	-0.9	-1.7
General government expenditure (% of GDP)	41.2	41.8	41.5	40.6	40.9

Sources: EBRD, Transition Report, various issues.

As for *popular support* for reforms, the situation was ambivalent. Given the favourable situation after 1993, it comes as no surprise that surveys registered an increasing satisfaction with the economic situation as well as stable support for the ODS and the government during the entire 1992-96 term (Olson 1997, pp. 166-7). Comparative analyses consistently suggest that the Czechs were more satisfied with the results of the economic transformation in the mid-1990s than Hungarians or Poles (Večerník 1996, pp. 228-30, 238, 245-6). At the same time, however, some signs of discontent surfaced. From 1993 to 1996, the commitment to 'leftist' values increased. Numerous strikes documented the erosion of the initial consensus. Ironically, these developments were nourished by the government's steady success stories. Given the economic recovery and Prime Minister Klaus's declarations of an 'end of transformation,' many citizens felt that the time for belt-tightening was over and began to articulate hitherto deferred demands. The 1996 parliamentary elections partly documented the changing mood (Pehe 1996; Turnovec 1997). While the incumbent centre-right coalition slightly increased its share of votes, it lost its majority of seats because the Czech Social Democratic Party (ČSSD) overcame the fragmentation of the left and more than quadrupled its votes. This spectacular increase made the ČSSD the main winner of the 1996 elections and weakened the mandate of the 'old' coalition, which hung on as a minority government until the end of 1997.

Executive authority was strong until 1996, but declined afterwards. The new Czech constitution, adopted in December 1992, not only removed all the constraints that had been associated with Czechoslovak federalism, but also encouraged the formation of a strong government. While it provided for a bicameral parliament, the new second chamber, the Senate, enjoyed only limited legislative powers (Olson 1996). Moreover, since the Senate did not constitute itself before the end of 1996, the Czech Republic effectively had a unicameral parliament during its initial years of independence. Several other features of the Czech institutional framework also bolstered executive authority: despite President Havel's attempts to extend his position, the Czech Republic maintained a parliamentary system with a relatively weak president; a 5 per cent threshold limited the fragmenting effects of proportional representation; finally, the constitution strengthened the position of government vis-à-vis parliament and vested the prime minister with a strong position within cabinet.

The actor constellation that prevailed from 1993 to 1996 further strengthened executive authority. Klaus's ODS had garnered 30 per cent of the votes in the 1992 elections, making it by far the strongest party in the governing coalition. Moreover, the opposition was split and the ODS enjoyed a pivotal role because no majority coalition, excluding extremist parties on the right or the left, could be assembled without it. The ODS also controlled a clear majority of portfolios within the cabinet.

The 1996 parliamentary elections substantially weakened executive authority. While the 'old' coalition hung on as a minority government and Klaus remained prime minister, the government now suffered from the lack of a parliamentary majority. Not only did it become dependent on support by deputies from other parties, but the new distribution of seats also changed the balance within the governing coalition. Courted by the Social Democrats, the smaller coalition partners of the ODS, in particular the Christian Democratic KDU-ČSL, became more assertive. The new division of power within the government was reflected by a reallocation of cabinet portfolios. While the ODS's coalition partners had so far commanded but a minority of portfolios, they now got half of all positions.

The *position of reformers* also underwent some change. In the mid-1990s, it was relatively strong. The dissolution of Czechoslovakia left the economic change team intact because most of its members opted for the Czech Republic. The 'velvet divorce' put an end to the need for coordinating economic and fiscal policy between the federation and the two republics and established unified control over the budget. Above all, the apparent economic and political successes of Czech economic reform made it difficult to challenge its architects.

Over time, however, the position of reformers weakened. The spreading cracks in the Czech model and the growing conflicts between the government and the central bank reduced the authority of Prime Minister Klaus and Finance Minister Kočárník. This made it more difficult for them to compensate for the relatively weak legal position of the Czech finance minister, which has suffered from the institutional fragmentation of the public sector and his limited control over the preparation and implementation of the budget (Gleich 2003; Brusis and Dimitrov 2001; Dimitrov 2006).

Fiscal reform, 1993-97
The changing economic and political conditions are reflected in the course of fiscal reform. From 1993 to 1996, the dominating role of Prime Minister Klaus eased the continuation of fiscal reform. The emerging policy drift was caused not so much by fragile parliamentary majorities or by conflicts within the governing coalition, but stemmed from electoral considerations and a certain smugness of Klaus and his team. The situation changed in mid-1996 when the elections deprived the government of its parliamentary majority and weakened the position of Klaus within government.

After independence, the Czech government reconfirmed its commitment to fiscal reform. Fiscal prudence continued to be one of the 'trademarks.' From 1993 to 1996, the government submitted balanced budgets which were approved by the governing coalition's majority in parliament almost without discussion. In 1994, Klaus even toyed with the idea of enshrining a balanced budget rule in the constitution. From 1993 to 1995, the economic growth facilitated the implementation of the budget. Instead of breaking even as projected, the official state budget regularly reported surpluses.

The government also committed itself to comprehensive tax and expenditure reforms. The government's medium-term fiscal programme called for a progressive decline in the expenditure-to-GDP ratio by 3 to 5 percentage points by the end of 2000. In line with this target, the 1994 to 1996 state budgets envisioned declines in fiscal intermediation, to be achieved largely by further cuts in subsidies and across-the-board constraints on spending growth.

Owing to its strong position, the government also was able to substantially change spending programmes. Starting in 1993, it embarked upon a fundamental overhaul of social policy designed to eliminate 'leftist' remnants from both the communist era and the 'social-liberal' period from 1990 to 1992 (Orenstein 1996, pp. 18-19). Most of these measures were unpopular and were opposed by trade unions; some of the reforms were controversial within the governing coalition as well. Despite some compromises, however, Klaus succeeded in implementing a substantial portion of his programme.

Capitalizing on its strong overall position, the Czech government was the first Central East European government to pass a major pension reform (Götting 1998, pp. 168-72; Müller 1999, pp. 136-9). In February 1994, a non-obligatory, state-subsidized private scheme was added to the traditional pay-as-you-go system. One year later, the 1995 Pension Insurance Act eventually abolished branch privileges, adopted a gradual increase in retirement age and substantially altered pension formulas and indexation rules.

Unlike most other governments in the region at that time, the Klaus government also adopted a comprehensive health care reform (Götting 1998, pp. 193-8; OECD 1996, pp. 89-98; Orenstein 1996, p. 18). Driven by the strong doctors' lobby within ODS and supported by the government's laissez-faire ideology, initial reforms brought about a far-reaching liberalization of health care. However, the measures were ill-conceived and resulted in cost increases and expensive bail-outs of shady private health insurance funds. These problems led to a second round of more incremental reforms.

Economic and political conditions also were conducive to a smooth continuation of tax reform. From 1993 to 1996, the government gradually cut tax rates. These cuts comprised part of the government's programme of scaling back the role of the state in the economy and complemented the gradual reduction in government spending. Corporate and personal income tax rates were reduced by 1-3 percentage points every year. From 1993 to 1996, the corporate income tax rate fell from 45 to 39 per cent. During the same period, the top personal income tax rate was cut from 47 per cent to 40 per cent. In 1995, the standard VAT rate was brought down from 23 to 22 per cent. Social security contributions remained high, yet were also reduced.

The smooth passage of reforms in the Czech Republic contrasted favourably with the much more protracted reform process in Hungary and Poland during the mid-1990s. However, these reforms masked a gradual policy drift (Pehe 1997). As is now well-known, the Czech government increasingly failed to address weak corporate governance in voucher-privatized enterprises and widening economic imbalances. In the field of fiscal reform, the policy drift primarily manifested itself in substantial quasi-fiscal activities, the reliance on dubious accounting practices and a lack of fiscal tightening.

The extent of these problems is evidenced by the discrepancies between the 'official' and the 'real' fiscal figures. Starting in 1994, the government departed from previous practice and channelled part of the privatization revenues from the National Property Fund to the state budget. Contrary to conventions and the government's lauded earlier practice, these funds were now budgeted as revenues (rather than as financing). In a similar fashion, the government used the bulk of the accumulated 1993 and 1994 state budget surpluses to finance current expenditures and counted these funds as revenues. Given the non-negligible spending from these two sources, the 1994 and 1995 state budgets thus clearly masked a substantial loosening of fiscal policy.

The deterioration of the fiscal stance was not merely a matter of accounting. Given the booming economy and the widening current account deficit, it clearly marked a step in the wrong direction. While fiscal deficits certainly did not represent the main cause of the external economic imbalances, the failure to tighten fiscal policy aggravated Czech economic problems (Begg 1998, pp. 682-4). A stricter fiscal policy not only would have reduced domestic absorption, but also would have allowed a loosening of monetary policy in order to abate capital inflows.

After the 1996 elections, political constraints on fiscal reform increased (Brusis and Dimitrov 2001, p. 903). While a minor budget adjustment in August 1996 went relatively smoothly, the passage of the 1997 budget was a tenuous process, accompanied by much haggling and repeated threats by all coalition partners to leave the government. Eventually the government managed to shepherd the budget through parliament with the support of two defecting social democrats, which were later expelled from their party. Following past practice, the 1997 budget was a balanced one. However, the budget rested on shaky assumptions and was overtaken by reality almost immediately after its passage. In the first months of 1997, a bigger-than-expected deficit began to accumulate.

The rifts within government and the lack of a parliamentary majority reduced the government's capacity to react to the growing economic and fiscal problems. It was not until April 1997 that the government agreed upon a stabilization programme. This programme included a small fiscal correction, but was insufficient to prevent the outbreak of the Czech currency crisis.

Fiscal reform after the 1997 currency crisis

Since the 1997 currency crisis, Czech fiscal reform has continued to drift. The prevailing economic and political conditions have been inimical to an acceleration of fiscal reform. Governments and reformers have been in a weak position. Moreover, both the pressure to and the popular support for reform have been low.

Economic and political conditions, 1997-2005
After the 1997 currency crisis, both the economic and the political conditions changed dramatically (Table 6.10). From 1997 to 1998, the Czech economy

went through a recession, which was followed by a relatively modest recovery. On the political front, the currency crisis paved the way for a change in government and ended the political dominance of the ODS. Both post-1998 governments have been led by the Social Democrats.

Ever since the late 1990s, Czech fiscal deficits have been among the highest in the new member states and have clearly exceeded the ceilings set by the Maastricht criteria and the Stability and Growth Pact. The high deficits have implied a postponement of Euro-zone entry and have led the European Commission to launch the excessive deficit procedure against the Czech Republic upon accession. Because of stable current account deficits, strong capital inflows and a low inflation rate, however, the overall *pressure to reform* has been relatively weak.

Popular support for reform also has been low. After the social hardships of the recession, there has been little enthusiasm about cuts in spending, especially among the constituency of the ČSSD. Moreover, for a long time the recession and the slow economic recovery weakened the case for fiscal tightening. Finally, the Czech Republic has been characterized by a high level of EU-scepticism on the mass level. This scepticism has extended to the Euro and has reduced the scope for justifying fiscal reform as a precondition for quick Euro-zone entry.

The two post-1998 governments also have suffered from weak *executive authority*. While being the strongest party in parliament, the ČSSD has not commanded a parliamentary majority on its own. From 1998 to 2002, Prime Minister Miloš Zeman led a minority government. Although an agreement with the centre-right ODS, the so-called 'Opposition Agreement', provided for some degree of stability, the government was forced to find outside support for most of its policies (Roberts 2003). After 2002, the ČSSD formed a centre-left coalition with the christian-democratic KDU-ČSL and the liberal US-DEU but enjoyed a mere one-vote majority in parliament. This narrow majority has made the government vulnerable to threats of defection by individual deputies, thus limiting its room to manoeuvre. A second constraint on executive authority has stemmed from the strong rifts within the ČSSD. The existence of strong factions within the party and the limited authority of the party leadership have made it quite difficult for Social Democratic party leaders and prime ministers to bring the party and its parliamentary group 'in line' and to commit them to controversial policies such as fiscal reform. Finally, the position of the Czech Prime Minister has been constrained by the collegial nature of the Czech cabinet and the lack of a strong Prime Minister's office (Goetz and Wollmann 2001, pp. 869-71).

Table 6.10   *Economic and fiscal conditions in the Czech Republic,*
                  1997-2005

	1997	1998	1999	2000	2001	2002	2003	2004	2005
GDP growth (real)	-1.0	-1.0	0.5	3.9	2.6	1.5	3.2	4.4	5.0
Inflation rate (CPI, annual average)	8.5	10.6	2.1	4.0	4.7	1.8	0.2	2.8	2.0
Unemployment rate (end-year)	5.2	6.5	8.7	8.8	8.1	7.3	7.8	8.3	na
Current account (% of GDP)	-6.1	-2.1	-2.5	-4.9	-5.4	-5.6	-6.2	-5.2	-3.5
General government balance (% of GDP)	-1.7	-4.2	-3.4	-4.5	-5.9	-6.8	-11.6	-3.3	-4.5
General government expenditure (% of GDP)	40.9	38.4	39.0	40.4	41.6	43.9	43.7	41.9	na

Sources: EBRD, Transition Report, various issues.

The *position of reformers* within government has been limited by the relatively weak institutional authority of the Finance Minister (Gleich 2003; Dimitrov 2006). While the passage of a new budget framework in 2002 has reduced the fragmentation of the public sector, the position of the Finance Minister vis-à-vis parliament has remained weak. Moreover, given their limited authority, Prime Minister Miloš Zeman and his successors have hesitated to back the Finance Minister too strongly.

Fiscal reform, 1997-2005
The economic and political conditions after the 1997 currency crisis have complicated the continuation of fiscal reform. Both the 1998-2002 social democratic minority government and the post-2002 centre-left government have moved on cautiously.

When the social democrats came to office in 1998, their economic policy platform was vague and ambiguous. Within the party and even at the top of the Ministry of Finance, there were wildly diverging views. Whereas one camp argued for higher public spending and fiscal expansion, others took a more orthodox position. The latter group was led by Pavel Mertlík, who started as Deputy Prime Minister responsible for economic policy and became Finance Minister in July 1999. However, Mertlík was only half-heartedly backed by Prime Minister Zeman and could not prevent a loosening of fiscal policy. In April 2001, the conflicts over fiscal reform eventually led Mertlík to resign.

Under the social democratic minority government, public spending was substantially increased. The government increased capital spending, granted significant increases in public sector wages and launched some controversial recapitalization and subsidization schemes. These spending increases, a substantial part of which took place outside the state budget, contributed to a substantial deterioration of the fiscal stance. Despite the recovering economy, the general government fiscal deficit increased by about 3 per cent of GDP from 1999 to 2002. Fiscal expansion was favoured by the lack of short-term reform pressures. Strong privatization proceeds eased the financing of the deficits, the current account deficit grew slowly, and inflation stayed low. In this situation, the government could easily ignore the admonitions by the IMF, the OECD or the EU.

After the 2002 elections, the newly established centre-left government declared fiscal reform to be one of its key priorities. The eventual commitment to reform was motivated by the high 2002 deficit and dire medium-term scenarios. Moreover, a programme for fiscal reform was a precondition for a credible euro-area accession strategy. In their attempt to commit the government to fiscal reform, Prime Minister Špidla and Finance Minister Sobotka faced strong obstacles, which highlighted the tight constraints on the government's reform capacity. The first obstacle was the strong opposition to fiscal reform from the trade unions and from within the ČSSD. Echoing the concerns about a trade-off between nominal and real convergence, the reform opponents questioned the need for cuts in social spending and public-sector wages and warned against the negative effects of fiscal adjustment on economic growth. The opposition to fiscal reform manifested itself in different forms. The trade unions took to the streets. In the ČSSD, reform opponents threatened to vote for a new party leader. Most importantly, part of the ČSSD parliamentary party threatened to vote against some of the proposed measures. One of them even temporarily defected from the parliamentary group, thus ending the governing coalition's narrow one-vote majority.

A second obstacle to the passage of fiscal reform was the referendum on EU membership in June 2003. Given the strong Euro-scepticism in the Czech Republic, a rejection of EU membership was a real option. Against this background, the government was afraid of alienating voters with unpopular reforms and shied away from unveiling its final plans for fiscal reform before the referendum. The eventual approval of Czech membership in the referendum made it easier to announce unpopular reforms. With 77.3 per cent of the voters in favour of the Czech Republic's EU accession, the referendum signalled a much higher support for the EU than expected (Hanley 2004). By reducing the need to please voters, and by strengthening the authority of Prime Minister Špidla within the ČSSD, the referendum paved the way for the eventual move to fiscal reform. On June 23, 2003, about a week after the referendum and almost a year after the installation of the new government, the government finally adopted a programme for fiscal reform, which provided for a gradual fiscal adjustment and targeted a fiscal deficit of 4 per cent of GDP in 2006. More than two-thirds of the envisaged adjustment was to fall on the expenditure side and was to be achieved by cuts in spending, including public-sector wages and social outlays. The key elements of the programme went through parliament in the second half of 2003 (Ministry of Finance 2003; OECD 2005b, pp. 49-57).

The programme, which opened the way for the formulation of a joint 'Euro-area Accession Strategy' with the Czech National Bank (Czech Government and Czech National Bank 2003), provided for a substantial fiscal adjustment. Given the 2003 estimates, it reduced the fiscal deficit in 2006 by about 4 percentage points. Given the resistance to reforms and the limited reform capacity of the centre-left government, the government was not able to push through more ambitious measures. Moreover, it feared that a stronger fiscal tightening might dampen economic growth.

The acceleration of economic growth in 2004 allowed the government to meet its fiscal targets without fully implementing the 2003 reform programme. This fiscal over-performance, symbolized by the unexpected temporary fulfilment of the Maastricht deficit criterion in 2004, reduced the incentives to continue reforms. Incentives to slow down fiscal reform were strengthened by the political situation. The elections to the European Parliament in June 2004 and the forthcoming parliamentary elections in June 2006 reduced the incentives to tackle controversial issues. Moreover, the political turbulence in 2004/2005 reduced the government's capacity to act. Following the bad showing of the ČSSD in the elections to the European Parliament, Prime Minister Špidla was ousted by his own party. Less than one year later, his successor, Stanislav Gross, after some dithering, fell victim to a financial scandal.

Given these favourable economic and unfavourable political conditions, the government slowed down fiscal reform. Despite the acceleration of economic growth, it confined itself to minor changes in the fiscal targets. Reacting to the initiation of the excessive deficit procedure by the European Commision in May 2004, the government reduced the fiscal target for 2006 by a mere 0.2 percentage points. Instead of seizing the opportunity to tackle the country's medium-term fiscal problems and to speed up fiscal convergence, it postponed part of the originally envisioned reforms, most notably in the fields of pensions and health care.

6.5   CONCLUSION

After the end of the post-communist fiscal crisis, political constraints have continued to shape national reform trajectories. Compared to the previous stages, however, these constraints have become more similar among the three countries under analysis. This helps explain why reform trajectories have converged and why Hungary, Poland and the Czech Republic are now struggling with broadly similar problems.

Fiscal reform in all three countries has been complicated by weakening reform pressure and an eroding popular support for reform. The social hardships during early transformation and the strong economic growth after the transformational recession have reduced the readiness to support further adjustment. The risks associated with high current account deficits have been more controversial and more difficult to see than the costs of high inflation or the need for overhauling the communist fiscal system. Finally, the pressure exerted by the IMF has proved to be stronger than the pressure stemming from the Stability and Growth Pact and the accession countries' obligation to enter the Euro-zone.

In all three countries, fiscal reform after the end of the post-communist fiscal crisis has also suffered from strong constraints on executive authority. The latter have taken different forms, which reflect the particular institutional frameworks and actor constellations in each country. In Poland and the Czech Republic, the capacity to engage in unpopular reforms has been limited primarily by unstable parliamentary majorities. In contrast, the main problem in Hungary has been the electoral pressures associated with strong political polarization and party competition.

7. Conclusion: post-communist fiscal reform and the changing nature of political constraints

7.1 INTRODUCTION

This book has addressed post-communist fiscal reform from a PEPR perspective. The analysis has rested on three closely related assumptions. First, fiscal reform, as a politically difficult and unlikely reform project, comes close to a 'mission impossible.' Second, the successful initiation and continuation of reform thus presuppose supportive economic and political conditions. Finally, differences in the patterns of fiscal reform are therefore likely to reflect differences in these conditions and the resulting constraints on the political feasibility of reforms. Based on this set of assumptions, this book has analysed post-communist fiscal reform in Hungary, Poland and the Czech Republic.

Weaving the various stands together, this concluding chapter elaborates on some of the broader implications of the empirical analysis by examining what that analysis adds to the three bodies of literature discussed in the introduction. Section 8.2 explores the insights into national differences in post-communist fiscal reform that the case studies provide. Section 8.3 relates the findings of this study to the controversies and debates within PEPR. Finally, Section 8.4 draws some general conclusions on the peculiarities of post-communist fiscal reform and the changing nature of political constraints during the transformation.

7.2 POLITICAL CONSTRAINTS AND NATIONAL DIFFERENCES IN POST-COMMUNIST FISCAL REFORM

This book has been motivated partly by the dearth of more systematic research into the factors that determine the political feasibility of post-communist fiscal reform. As Chapter 1 noted, most of the available analyses tend to treat the adoption of reforms as a black box or reduce the process to a problem of 'political will.' In contrast to this common yet unsatisfactory approach, this study has examined in detail how economic and political conditions have shaped the paths of fiscal reform by either enabling or hindering the adoption of politically costly reforms. The analysis suggests that political constraints have changed during the transformation, but have featured prominently at all three stages of fiscal reform.

Regarding the outset of the transformation, this study has emphasized differences in the pressure to reform, popular support for the launching of reforms and the position of reformers within government. As Chapter 4 argued, differences in these factors go a long way in accounting for the different reform patterns and help explain why reforms began more quickly in Czechoslovakia and, even more so, Poland than in Hungary. In contrast, national differences in executive authority played only a subordinate role in shaping the initiation of fiscal reform.

In Poland the combination of a deep economic crisis, a new government with a strong popular mandate and a powerful and coherent change team was highly conducive to a quick initiation of radical reforms. It allowed Leszek Balcerowicz to start the implementation of a comprehensive reform programme less than four months after the installation of the first non-communist government and despite a number of guarantees for the incumbent communists.

In Czechoslovakia the economic and political conditions were less favourable to launching reforms than in Poland. While the fear of falling behind the other, seemingly more advanced transition countries, underscored the case for change, the better short-term economic situation attenuated the pressure to reform. While the 'Government of National Understanding' was able to count on broad popular support, it had not been voted into office or confirmed by elections. Finally, Václav Klaus was not vested with extraordinary competencies from the outset of the transformation, so that the emergence of an uncontested change team took some time. For these reasons, the initiation of post-communist economic reform took longer than in Poland.

In Hungary the situation was the least favourable to the launching of reform. Neither an escalating open crisis nor the fear of falling behind underscored the case for moving quickly; the Antall government enjoyed a strong constitutional position and a relatively homogeneous parliamentary majority but only a relatively weak popular mandate; moreover, there was no determined change team ready and able to promote reforms until Finance Minister Mihályi Kupa took office in December 1990. These conditions contributed to the slow start of post-communist economic reform in Hungary.

Differences in political constraints and in the political feasibility of reforms continued to play an important role in shaping reform trajectories during the post-communist fiscal crisis. As Chapter 5 showed, the capacity to react to the unfolding fiscal tensions and to continue reforms differed between Czechoslovakia, Hungary and Poland. Like during the first stage of fiscal reform, national differences were shaped primarily by differences in reform pressure, popular support for reforms and the position of reformers within government. In contrast, executive authority continued to be of less importance. In Czechoslovakia, the combination of a powerful change team and greater popular support for transformation allowed the government to push through far-reaching reforms despite upcoming elections, a multi-party government and a federal system with many checks and balances. In Poland, fragile parliamentary majorities contributed to some slowing of fiscal reform. Like in Czechoslovakia, however, the coincidence of strong reform pressures and powerful change teams limited the negative fall-out of constrained executive authority and made it possible to implement substantial short-term austerity measures. Compared to Czechoslovakia and Poland, Hungary suffered from a combination of relatively limited fiscal pressures and weak reformers. Gradual deterioration of the fiscal stance, relatively easy financing of budget deficits and weak inflationary pressures let fiscal adjustment appear less urgent and reduced readiness to support restraint. At the same time, reformers were isolated within government and could not count on prime ministerial support. Both factors severely reduced the capacity of the Hungarian government to commit itself to the continuation of reforms.

Since the end of the post-communist fiscal crisis, reform trajectories have converged. As Chapter 6 has shown, all three countries have experienced a slowing of reform during the third stage of reform and are now among the new EU members with the biggest fiscal problems. For one thing, weakening reform pressure and an eroding popular support for reform have closed the 'window of opportunity' that has been open during early transformation. For another, constraints on executive authority have gained importance and have complicated the continuation of reform. These constraints have taken different forms. In the Czech Republic and Poland, unstable parliamentary majorities have limited the capacity to engage in unpopular reforms. In Hungary, the electoral pressures that have been associated with strong political polarization and fierce party competition have infringed upon fiscal reform.

The findings of this study are partly in line with the tiny available body of literature on political determinants of fiscal reform in Eastern Europe. The emphasis on the position of reformers echoes the findings by Holger Gleich (2003), Martin Brusis and Vesselin Dimitrov (Brusis and Dimitrov 2001; Dimitrov 2006), who present strong evidence that post-communist fiscal reform has been favoured by a powerful position of the Finance Minister in the cabinet and vis-à-vis parliament.

Regarding the role of executive authority in post-communist fiscal reform, the picture is less clear. The existing studies on this issue arrive at different conclusions. Two studies basically confirm the conventional wisdom. Hallerberg et al. (2002a, 2002b), in an econometric analysis, find some evidence for a fiscal electoral cycle. In a similar vein, in their analysis of fiscal reform in Hungary between 1990 and 1998, Haggard et al. (2001) argue that the single most important determinant of fiscal reform has been the cohesion of the governing coalition. This view has been challenged by John Campbell (2001), who has pointed to the fact that the strong political fragmentation in Czechoslovakia and Poland did not prevent the adoption of radical fiscal reform. This book has provided further evidence for the limited role of executive authority during the first and second stage of the transformation. At the same time, however, it has shown that executive authority has gained importance since the end of the post-communist fiscal crisis.

7.3   POST-COMMUNIST FISCAL REFORM AND PEPR

The second chapter of this book surveyed key debates within PEPR in order to unearth factors that determine the likelihood of reforms. This prompts the question of to what extent the experience with post-communist fiscal reform in Hungary, Poland and the Czech Republic confirms, qualifies or refutes standard PEPR findings on the conditions for the successful initiation and continuation of reforms. The section below elaborates on these issues by going beyond individual cases and by discussing topics that the case studies treated only in passing.

Crises, mandates and the initiation of reform

A prominent tenet of the PEPR literature has been the 'enabling' role of crises and mandates. Both are widely viewed as almost indispensable preconditions for the successful launching of reforms. Section 2.3 provided ample evidence of how crises can open up windows for reform by discrediting entrenched policies and by inducing the delegation of authority. Mandates similarly can help launch reforms by vesting governments with extra legitimation. The experience with post-communist fiscal reform in Hungary, Poland and the Czech Republic sheds light on these issues.

In line with received wisdom, all successful initiations of reform in this study's sample share some combination of an economic crisis before the start of reforms and a government bestowed with a mandate. In the Polish case the adoption of the Balcerowicz Programme in 1989/90 occurred in the face of a disintegrating economy close to hyperinflation. The overwhelming victory of Solidarność in the partially free 1989 Sejm elections brought a new government into office. In Czechoslovakia in 1990/91 the Calfa government could also command strong popular support, as expressed in the 1990 elections. While no short-term macroeconomic crisis existed, the bankruptcy of the old economic system was uncontested, and the fear of falling behind the seemingly more advanced neighbouring transition countries served as an additional catalyst for change. In accordance with these findings, Hungary, the main case in this study's sample of a 'non-initiation' of reform at the outset of reform, was characterized by the combination of an apparently favourable economic and fiscal situation and a government with a relatively weak mandate.

The critical role of crises and mandates in making reforms possible is also confirmed by the experience with fiscal tightening at later stages of the transformation. In Hungary the Horn government was at the brink of a currency crisis in early 1995 and could still draw on at least some form of mandate from the MSZP's victory at the polls in 1994. In the Czech Republic it took the 1997 currency crisis to induce a tightening of the fiscal stance in the face of ballooning current account deficits. In Poland the initiation of reform by Balcerowicz after 1997 and by Belka in 2001/2002 was clearly favoured by the combination of a spreading sense of crisis and some legitimization through the parliamentary elections in 1997 and 2001.

The case studies can help solve the notorious problems with the 'crisis hypothesis' concerning the definition of a crisis and the identification of thresholds and trigger points (Corrales 1998). A comparison of Hungary and Poland demonstrates well how the reaction to apparently similar fiscal problems depends on the particular shape and dynamics of these problems. Both countries faced massive fiscal shocks and incurred large fiscal deficits during the transformational recession. As this book argued, however, fiscal pressures were perceived differently. The more drastic fiscal swing, the more precarious financing and the stronger inflationary effects made the unfolding fiscal tensions in Poland much more alarming and threatening than those in Hungary.

The case studies also cast some light on the issue of pre-emptive reforms, that is, reforms triggered by anticipated crises. Both the launching of reform in Czechoslovakia in 1990/91 and the move towards reform in Hungary in 1995 were driven by the threat of trouble rather than by a full-blown crisis. The short-term macroeconomic situation was stable in Czechoslovakia. In Hungary a currency crisis may have been developing but did not materialize before the start of reforms (Kornai 1997, pp. 183-93). Both cases illuminate some of the ingredients of such a pre-emptive reform.

In the case of Czechoslovakia the demise of communism opened a certain 'window of opportunity.' Since the end of the old regime placed economic reform on the agenda almost automatically, an acute crisis was unnecessary to demonstrate the old policies' lack of viability and the need for change. Czechoslovakia could have it both ways: it benefited from the advantages of a more stable macroeconomic situation but did not have to bear the 'political costs' that normally accompany economic stability. The situation in Hungary in 1995 was different. Five years into the transformation, the initial 'window of opportunity' was no longer open. Instead, two other factors were critical for starting reforms without an acute crisis. First, a series of triggering events made policy-makers more receptive to calls for reform. In December 1994 the example of the Mexican currency crisis recalled the fickleness of capital inflows and raised the danger of contagion. These fears were aggravated further by concerns over the course of economic reform after the resignation of Finance Minister Békesi in January 1995. A second crucial ingredient for starting reforms was strong executive authority, which enabled the Horn government to push through reforms in the absence of an acute crisis and in the face of controversy over their necessity.

The role of change teams

A second prominent theme within the PEPR literature has been the role of change teams (cf. Section 2.4). According to a popular view, the successful initiation and continuation of reforms presupposes the existence of a group of reformers who are bestowed with broad powers and are held together by shared convictions and a determined leader. Such strong and powerful change teams are needed for seizing the opportunities associated with temporary windows for reform. They are also crucial for ensuring policy coherence and staying on course in the face of resistance to reform from both inside and outside the government.

The case studies provide interesting evidence on these issues. As shown in the case studies, strong change teams played a decisive role in both initiating and continuing reforms during and after the fiscal crisis. The pivotal role of change teams in the launching of reforms finds expression in the fact that all episodes of a successful initiation of reforms covered in this study are closely associated with the names of particular Finance Ministers – Balcerowicz in Poland, Klaus in Czechoslovakia and Bokros in Hungary. In Poland Balcerowicz brought in a coherent and determinate team of economists and was vested with strong powers. In Czechoslovakia the move to radical fiscal reform occurred after Klaus and his team had consolidated their position within the government. In Hungary Bokros and Surányi were given full rein over economic policy and were backed by Prime Minister Horn. Conversely the critical role of change teams is also indicated by the fact that the Antall government's balking on fiscal reform coincided with the presence of a weak reform team.

From a comparative perspective, the situation at the outset of the transformation was rather favourable to committed reformers and offered them substantial 'technocratic windows of opportunity' (Nelson 1993, p. 455): economic reform was regarded broadly as a crucial issue, both in its own right and, given popular expectations of improving living standards, as a precondition for the consolidation of democracy. The public was very receptive to bold economic measures. Furthermore, the institutional vacuum at the beginning of the transformation implied extraordinary opportunities to shape administrative structures and to fill key economic positions.

Change teams continued to play an important role during the post-communist fiscal crisis. As the comparative analysis showed, the position of reformers was a key determinant of the fate of fiscal reform after the shock. Strong reformers proved vital for keeping reforms on track in both Czechoslovakia and Poland. A number of situational factors again increased the potential leeway of reformers and favoured the delegation of authority: pressing fiscal problems and the need for quick fixes strengthened the case for unconstrained executive action. At the same time the inability of the nascent, overloaded parliaments to formulate policies and to react to short-term pressures favoured self-restraint. As a consequence, determined change teams that were uncontested within cabinet enjoyed vast opportunities to continue reforms.

Since the end of the post-communist fiscal crisis, the position of reformers within governments has remained important. At the same time, however, it has become more difficult for reformers to shape economic reform. For one thing, the increasing institutionalization of policy-making in the course of transformation has constrained their room to manoeuvre. For another, the weakening reform pressures have clearly reduced the readiness to delegate far-reaching competencies to finance ministers. In a way, the 'heroic' days of reformers in the post-communist transition countries have ended.

Executive authority

According to the majority view within the PEPR literature, strong executive authority is crucial for a successful continuation and, to a lesser extent, the initiation of reform. As Section 2.5 documented in detail, frequent elections, multiparty coalitions, fragile parliamentary majorities, political instability and conflicts between presidents and governments are widely held to be inimical to the consolidation of reforms. Interestingly, the post-communist experience has led some observers to question this mainstream view. In a seminal article,

Joel Hellman (1998) has argued that electoral and coalitional pressures are in fact correlated positively with the extent of reform because political systems with more veto points and players are less likely to be captured by rent-seekers interested in partial reforms. Comparing Hungary and the Czech Republic, David Stark and László Bruszt (1998) have tried to show that constraints on executive authority can help to make economic policy more coherent.

As has been indicated above, this study's comparative analysis of post-communist fiscal reform in Hungary, Poland and the Czech Republic lends itself to a qualified confirmation of the mainstream view. On the one hand, it finds a limited role of executive authority during early transformation, on the other, it suggests that the importance of executive authority has grown in the course of the transformation. These findings are in line with the received view that executive authority is more important for the initiation than for the consolidation of reforms and matters more under 'normal' than other 'extraordinary' conditions.

As the comparative analysis of the initiation of fiscal reform at the outset of transformation showed, executive authority did not play a major role in getting reforms started at the outset of the transformation. In Poland and Czechoslovakia broad-based governments that faced heavy institutional constraints succeeded in launching far-reaching reforms. This suggests that executive authority is of only secondary importance for the initiation of reforms, subordinate to a variety of factors including broad acknowledgement of the need for reform, the government's possession of a strong mandate and policy coherence guaranteed by a strong change team. In such a situation a more inclusive government with a broader political base is even likely to benefit from a stronger mandate and thus may be in a better position to embark on reforms.

Conversely, executive authority becomes more critical for a successful initiation of reforms if the conditions mentioned above are not extant, that is, if the need for reform is controversial and if the government does not enjoy a strong mandate. In this study's sample this is borne out by the adoption of the Bokros Package in Hungary. As argued in Chapter 5, the Hungarian experience suggests that strong executive authority comprises a necessary precondition for the launching of reforms in the absence of an acute crisis and strong mandates.

The three country studies are more ambivalent concerning the role of executive authority in the consolidation of reforms. Strong executive authority did not prove to be of critical importance for the continuation of fiscal reform during the fiscal crisis. Reformers in Czechoslovakia and, with some qualifications, Poland managed to push through substantial austerity measures and to continue reforms despite severe constraints on executive authority. These findings indicate that a strong executive authority does not represent a necessary condition for the continuation of reform. They suggest that a clever reform design can help overcome even severe constraints on executive authority. The findings also suggest that crises not only may be crucial in getting reforms started but under certain conditions may help to keep reforms on track. The Polish case even suggests that in times of crisis a fragmented parliament and frequent changes in government may be a blessing in disguise. When incapable of acting on its own, a highly fragmented parliament may be more willing to delegate authority than a less fragmented one. Likewise a high government turnover can facilitate the adoption of austerity measures by allowing governments to fault predecessors and to claim the 'benefit of the doubt.'

The findings on the continuation of fiscal reform after the post-communist fiscal crisis are more in line with the received wisdom. As shown in the country chapters, executive authority has become a major determinant of reform. In all three countries electoral pressures, fragile parliamentary majorities and weak Prime Ministers have become major obstacles to fiscal reform.

Fiscal reform in new democracies

As Section 2.6 noted, most of the available analyses of economic reform in the West and the South arrive at the pessimistic conclusion that new democracies are likely to face peculiar obstacles to the initiation and continuation of reform. The post-communist experience strongly challenges this received wisdom. As for the East European transition countries, there is a strong positive correlation between the degree of democratization and the pace of economic reform: those countries in the region that have seen as successful consolidation of democracy have also been the front runners in economic reform; those countries where democratization has been limited have also been characterized by a low level of economic reform (Fish 1998, pp. 75-7; Hellman 1998, pp. 230-31; de Melo et al. 1996, pp. 419-21; Dethier et al. 1999; EBRD 1999; p. 113).

Since this book has covered three cases of successful democratization, it cannot control for the impact of regime change on fiscal reform. However, the analysis of fiscal reform in Hungary, Poland and the Czech Republic has at least shown that in the three countries under analysis the transition to democracy did not prevent the adoption of far-reaching tax and expenditure reforms. Moreover the finding that popular mandates played a crucial role in launching reforms suggests that democratization, in fact, was conducive to reform.

Government ideology

The role of government ideology has been another evergreen in the PEPR literature (cf. Section 2.7). In line with the evidence for the West and the South, the case studies in this book do not reveal any significant correlation between government ideology and the likelihood or direction of fiscal reform. In the countries under analysis, fiscal reform has been promoted by governments of rather different origins. In Poland the Balcerowicz Programme represented a case of 'labour-backed adjustment' (Levitsky and Way 1998) and was executed by a government with strong ties to a union movement. In the Czechoslovak case fiscal prudence was a major tenet of Klaus's liberal-conservative, ODS-led government, yet the massive fiscal adjustment from 1990 to 1992 was enacted by a broad-based government with social-liberal leanings. The conservative Antall government in Hungary postponed major reforms, whereas the socialist Horn government launched radical reforms.

The limited relevance of partisan ideology also extends to expenditure and revenue reform. A good case in point is the recent wave of pension reforms in Eastern Europe (Orenstein 2000; Müller 2003, Part III). Contrary to what one might expect, the socialist governments of Hungary and Poland passed 'neo-liberal' pension reforms that went beyond the measures undertaken by the liberal-conservative Klaus government in the Czech Republic. Governments in Hungary, Poland and the Czech Republic all have sought to increase the relative weight of indirect taxation and to reduce corporate income tax rates. As a matter of fact, it was Hungary's MSZP-led government that opened the recent wave of tax competition in the region by reducing Hungary's corporate income tax rate to 18 per cent in 1997.

These findings can be interpreted in two ways. On the one hand they corroborate the argument made in Chapter 1 that there has been a relatively broad professional consensus on the need for, and the direction of, post-communist fiscal reform. On the other hand the low salience of government ideology testifies to the characteristics of the post-communist party systems (Kitschelt et al. 1999). Especially in Hungary and Poland the left-right divide is still shaped strongly by cultural–ideological issues, so that parties on the right have not necessarily subscribed to more liberal policies than parties on the left.

Reform design

The political feasibility of reforms also hinges on their design (cf. Section 2.8). The sequencing and the composition of reforms influence the distribution of costs and benefits; the style of reforms shapes how discontent with reforms can be articulated. The case studies can be interpreted in various ways. On one level, a comparison of Hungarian, Polish and Czech fiscal reform supports the case for starting boldly (see also Åslund et al. 1996). The cautious continuation of fiscal reform in Hungary in 1990 did not help to make reforms more popular and to smooth their consolidation, but resulted in their retardation. In the end, Hungary did not escape the need for radical measures, while the bold initial reforms in Poland and Czechoslovakia, contrary to contemporary fears, did not undermine the continuation of reform.

These countries' 'experience' with post-communist fiscal reform also indicates that compensation can be instrumental in getting reforms adopted. In the Czechoslovak case a rather coherent social policy, the partial compensation of subsidy cuts by universal transfer payments and the mass privatization scheme contributed to the relative overall popularity of economic reform and increased the readiness of the population to accept draconian cuts in public spending during the early years of transformation. The same can be said about the 'consensual' and 'corporatist' elements of Czechoslovak transformation (Orenstein 1994, 1996; Rutland 1993). In Poland, by contrast, the 'technocratic' style of reforms and incoherent social policies may have reduced the acceptance of cuts in public sector wages and government spending (Orenstein 1996; Przeworski 1993).

The Hungarian case, however, illustrates the ambiguities of social pacts and highlights how the longing for such pacts can hinder the passage of reforms if a government lacks a clear strategy. In 1992 the Antall government's decision to enter into negotiations over Kupa's adjustment package brought little more than a dilution of the original reform proposals. In 1994 the Horn government's attempt to forge a pact with the trade unions likewise contributed to the delay of reforms. In both cases negotiations suffered from the fact that governments were divided over the course of economic policy. This allowed unions to capitalize on rifts within government and to adopt more 'obstructionist' positions.

International organizations

International organizations are the final potential determinant of fiscal reform investigated by the PEPR literature. As Section 2.9 noted, the available evidence indicates that international organizations are normally too weak to unilaterally impose reforms yet may help both to initiate reforms and to keep them on track, provided that there is some degree of domestic commitment to reform.

The examination of post-communist fiscal reform in Hungary, Poland and the Czech Republic documents the strong involvement of international organizations in the region. This applies particularly to the IMF and the EU.[1]

All three countries in the sample negotiated agreements with the IMF at the outset of the transformation. The initial stabilization programmes in Poland and Czechoslovakia were accompanied by agreements with the Fund. In Hungary a provisional agreement, concluded by the outgoing Németh government, was replaced by a three-year Extended Fund Facility programme in February 1991. This first generation of agreements was followed by a series of programmes. The last agreements with the IMF expired in March 1994 in the Czech Republic, in April 1996 in Poland and in February 1998 in Hungary. The IMF's economic philosophy found expression in the prominent position given to fiscal reform in all of these programmes. Moreover technical assistance by the IMF helped reform fiscal institutions and the tax system.

The overall impact of the IMF on the initiation and consolidation of fiscal reform is more difficult to assess. One distinguishing trait of post-communist economic reform was the 'self-imposed' nature of the initial reform programmes (Bruno 1993, p. 204, n. 4; Greskovits 1998, Chapter 4). Early reforms were clearly 'domestically owned,' at least in Central Eastern Europe.[2] Both in Poland and in Czechoslovakia the bold 1990 and 1991 reform programmes were essentially home-grown and did not reflect IMF pressure. The IMF helped design the programmes but was not the driving force behind them. Radical reforms were not imposed from outside but above all expressed the economic and political considerations of the local reformers (Bönker et al. 2002, pp. 4-12). In fact, in some instances the Fund argued for more caution and questioned the political feasibility of reforms.

The IMF's influence grew after the initiation of reform. Popular sentiments notwithstanding, all governments in the sample were keen on external assistance and the IMF's seal of approval. Aware of the economic and political 'value' of IMF agreements, governments were at pains not to fall out of compliance with the IMF. Of course this did not prevent some slippage. In the Hungarian case both the 1991 and the 1993 agreements were suspended because the government violated the programme criteria. The 1991 agreement in Poland suffered a similar fate. Despite these violations and some haggling, however, none of the governments dared turn its back on the Fund.

Illustrations of the 'disciplining' effects of the IMF abound. IMF conditionality was invoked in all countries in order to justify fiscal restraint and unpopular measures. While governments used this strategy in public justifications, reformers relied on it within government. In Poland all governments from Bielecki to Pawlak heavily alluded to IMF pressures when justifying their policies. This is most visible in governments that were elected on more populist platforms. In Poland both the conservative Olszewski and the post-communist Pawlak government struggled to reconcile their campaign promises with adherence to IMF demands after assuming office. In Hungary the conservative government's attempts at adjustment in the second half of 1993 were also motivated by the prospect of an economically and politically beneficial agreement with the IMF. The IMF's influence was greatest in Poland, where the Fund's role in foreign debt reduction increased the rewards of compliance.

The Hungarian reforms in 1995/96 also illustrate the impact of the IMF. Unlike other reform episodes in this sample, the Hungarian reforms were not embedded in an agreement with the Fund. However, the move to reform was supported by the IMF's insistence on fiscal restraint. The incoming Horn government was keen to hammer out an agreement with the IMF after assuming office. The IMF's reluctance, caused in part by the bad experience surrounding the 1993 agreement with the conservative government, raised the pressure on Hungary and helped convince Prime Minister Horn of the necessity of more radical measures (Lengyel 1995, pp. 44-5). After the start of reforms the IMF's tough stance likewise helped ensure the continuation of reforms. Despite the progress made in 1995, the Fund waited until March 1996 before it eventually endorsed an agreement. This delay strengthened the position of those reformers within government who had called for further adjustment and warned against a relaxation of reform efforts.

The EU has served as a second external anchor in Hungary, Poland and the Czech Republic. Given the strong desire to join the Union, EU provisions have been important focal points in designing new institutions. Not only have legal agreements with the EU established formal reform obligations, but the mere prospect of EU membership has provided a strong incentive to engage in reform, since delays might have provided the EU with further arguments to slow down the association process (Berglöf and Roland 1997; Fischer et al. 1998; Bönker 2006a).

The impact of the EU can be seen nicely in the field of tax reform (Bönker 2003b, pp. 523-5). During early transformation, Czechoslovakia, Hungary and Poland refrained from experiments and instead adopted tax systems broadly in line with EU standards. This far-reaching orientation towards the EU was partly brought about by advisers from the EU. However, it also reflected a pattern of 'anticipatory adaptation' (Haggard et al. 1993, p. 180). Reformers not only saw the EU as a source of inspiration and a model to emulate, but they also hoped to facilitate EU accession by introducing tax systems similar to those in the EU. As David Newbery (1995, p. 2) has observed:

> It might appear that the detailed design of an entirely new tax system would be a challenging task, but in practice the choice was fairly tightly circumscribed by the desire of these countries to join the European Union eventually.

The evidence is more ambivalent with regard to fiscal deficits. On the one hand, the Maastricht criteria became an important guideline for fiscal policy as early as in the second half of the 1990s. Since then medium-term fiscal programmes in the Czech Republic, Hungary and Poland have emphasized the commitment to meet the debt and deficit targets of the Maastricht Treaty. Finance ministers in the three countries have time and again justified fiscal reform as a precondition for a quick introduction of the Euro. The orientation toward the Maastricht criteria has given rise to some curious manifestations. For instance, Poland enshrined the Maastricht debt criterion in its 1997 constitution.

However, the more recent developments in fiscal policy also testify to the limits of the EU's 'disciplining' effect (see also Dyson 2006). As Chapter 6 showed, the Czech Republic, Hungary and Poland belong to those new member states that violate the provisions of the Stability and Growth Pact and have postponed Euro-area entry several times. The effect of the Stability and Growth Pact has been limited by the lack of sanctions and its current renegotiation by the old member states. Moreover, neither investors nor voters so far have perceived the postponement of Euro-entry as a major problem.

7.4   THE FADING PECULIARITIES OF POST-COMMUNIST FISCAL REFORM

Unlike most of the literature on post-communist economic reform, this study has sought to place post-communist fiscal reform in a broader perspective by using an analytical framework developed for the OECD and the developing countries. This is not to deny that post-communist fiscal reform has differed from fiscal reform in the West and the South. Quite to the contrary, the use of a broad and comparative analytical framework represents the best method of identifying rather than merely postulating the peculiarities of different country groups.

Three peculiarities have distinguished post-communist fiscal reform from other episodes of fiscal reform (cf. Section 3.4). First, the move towards fiscal reform was not driven primarily by fiscal problems but was essentially a by-product of the transition to capitalism. The substantial fiscal deficits that prevailed in some transition countries at the outset of the transformation underlined the case for fiscal reform but should not be mistaken for the ultimate reason for reforms. Second, post-communist fiscal reform has been characterized by an extremely ambitious reform agenda, which has combined tough fiscal restraint, comprehensive expenditure and revenue reforms and the overhaul of fiscal institutions. Third, post-communist fiscal reform has been embedded in a broader process of transformation that has left no sphere of society untouched. Representing only one element of the overall transition to capitalism and democracy, fiscal reform has coincided with sweeping economic and political changes.

As the case studies recall, these features have made post-communist fiscal reform a highly dramatic process. In contrast to most other cases of fiscal reform, strong fiscal pressures emerged or continued after the successful start of reforms. Due to the transformational recession and the problems associated with instituting a new tax system, all transition countries faced substantial fiscal tensions during the early phases of transformation. The high and out-of-control budget deficits that occurred in most of the countries were merely the most visible expression of this 'secondary fiscal crisis' (Dąbrowski 1997, p. 9). Post-communist fiscal reform also was characterized by a substantial decline in real government spending. Given the drop in GDP after the start of the transformation, government expenditures in real terms fell even in countries that experienced an increase in the share of expenditures in GDP. Declining public sector wages, eroding social transfers and a deteriorating public infrastructure represented major components of the 'social costs' of transformation.

Contrary to initial concerns but consistent with more general analyses of post-communist economic reform (Wiesenthal 1997; Bunce 1998; Greskovits 1998), this book's analysis suggests that the peculiar conditions of post-communist fiscal reform have increased the political feasibility of reforms. This applies particularly to those transition countries in which non-communist parties won the first elections, the state did not disintegrate and the 'pull' of the EU was felt strongly. In these countries, the peculiarities of post-communist fiscal reform opened huge and long-lasting 'windows of opportunity' for the launching of reforms.

- At the outset of the transformation, the aspired transition to capitalism almost automatically put fiscal reform on the reform agenda. After the start of reforms, escalating fiscal tensions helped maintain the desire for fiscal reform by underscoring the need for the overhaul of taxes and expenditures.
- The new democratic governments typically enjoyed rather strong mandates and benefited from significant honeymoon effects after 40 years of communist rule. In contrast to earlier cases of democratization, economic reform was a crucial part of the new governments' mandates. The transition to democracy was viewed as being closely intertwined with the move toward a market economy. This made it possible to balance economic 'losses' against the political 'gains' associated with democratization and the end of Soviet dominance. Similarly, fiscal

reform was regarded as part of a broader 'package' of economic reforms and as a necessary step on the way to an idealized market economy. This linkage allowed fiscal reformers to capitalize on the 'strong initial groundswell of popular support for radical economic reforms' (Haggard and Kaufman 1995, p. 374).

- Economic reformers benefited from the demobilization of the opposition and a weak civil society (Elster et al. 1998, pp. 11-17). Communism left the transition countries with an 'associational wasteland' (Offe) characterized by a weak organisation of interests and popular acquiescence (Greskovits 1998, Chapter 5; Schmitter and Karl 1994, pp. 179-80; Wiesenthal 1997, pp. 107-11). Free from fears of coups by the military or the old elites, the new democratic governments found themselves in a relatively secure position and enjoyed more leeway to adopt 'costly' reforms than their counterparts in Latin America or Southern Europe.
- The strong involvement of the IMF and the far-reaching orientation toward the EU have served as important 'external anchors.' The IMF and the EU have provided strong incentives for initiating and consolidating reform, financial and technical assistance and a sense of direction.

These peculiarities help explain why post-communist fiscal reform faced so little protest and resistance and has been a qualified success rather than a qualified failure. Despite the severe transformational recession and ubiquitous constraints on executive authority, Hungary, Poland and the Czech Republic have, by and large, succeeded in the unlikely adoption of far-reaching tax and expenditure reforms.

The case studies also demonstrate a certain 'normalization' of fiscal reform. This applies to the agenda and context of fiscal reform. With the initial fiscal tensions overcome and a new tax system in place, the reform agenda in the advanced transition countries has become more akin to the one in Western countries. As in the West, tax reform is no longer concerned with the creation of a new tax system but rather with the elimination of distortions within the tax system. On the expenditure side, the reform of pensions and health care now represents the main challenge. In the case of pensions Hungary and Poland may even be one step ahead of many traditional OECD countries.

The political context of fiscal reform also has changed with the consolidation of the new institutions and the rise of interest group politics. The 'extraordinary' conditions that characterized fiscal reform during early transformation have progressively faded away. As the case studies illustrated, the initial 'window of opportunity' is no longer open. Instead the continuation of fiscal reform in Central and Eastern Europe is governed increasingly by 'normal' political constraints. Hungary, Poland and the Czech Republic are encountering more and more of the obstacles to reform that are known all too well in Western countries. This convergence of problems represents a powerful testimony to the progress that these countries have made since 1989 in the transition from communism.

NOTES

1. Compared to the IMF and the EU, other international organizations have played a minor role in fiscal reform. The major exception may be the World Bank, which has been a key player in the recent wave of pension reform in Eastern Europe (cf. Müller 1999). For the general engagement of international financial organizations in the transition countries, see Dąbrowski 1998; Zecchini 1995.
2. For this notion, see Johnson and Wasty 1993; Killick 1998, Chapter 4 and the remarks in Section 2.9 above.

References

Abed, George T. and Hamid R. Davoodi (2000), 'Corruption, Structural Reforms, and Economic Performance in the Transition Economies', IMF, Working Paper WP/00/132, Washington, D.C.

Adam, Christopher S. and David L. Bevan (2005), 'Fiscal Deficits and Growth in Developing Countries', *Journal of Public Economics*, **89** (4), pp. 571-597.

Aghevli, Bijan B., Eduardo Borensztein and Tessa van der Willigen (1992), 'Stabilization and Structural Reform in the Czech and Slovak Federal Republic: First Stage', IMF, Occasional Paper No. 92, Washington, D.C.

Alam, Asa and Mark Sundberg (2002), 'A Decade of Fiscal Transition', World Bank, Policy Research Working Paper No. 2835, Washington, D.C.

Alesina, Alberto and Silvia Ardagna (1998), 'Tales of Fiscal Adjustment', *Economic Policy*, **27**, pp. 489-545.

Alesina, Alberto and Allan Drazen (1991), 'Why Are Stabilizations Delayed?', *American Economic Review*, **81** (5), pp. 1170-1188.

Alesina, Alberto and Roberto Perotti (1995a), 'Fiscal Expansions and Adjustments in OECD Countries', *Economic Policy*, **21**, pp. 207-248.

Alesina, Alberto and Roberto Perotti (1995b), 'The Political Economy of Budget Deficits', *IMF Staff Papers*, **42** (1), pp. 1-31.

Alesina, Alberto and Roberto Perotti (1997), 'Fiscal Adjustment in OECD Countries: Composition and Macroeconomic Effects', *IMF Staff Papers*, **44** (2), pp. 210-248.

Alesina, Alberto and Roberto Perotti (1999), 'Budget Deficits and Budget Institutions', in James M. Poterba, Jürgen von Hagen (eds), *Fiscal Institutions and Fiscal Performance*, Chicago and London: University of Chicago Press, pp. 13-36.

Alesina, Alberto and Guido Tabellini (1990), 'A Positive Theory of Fiscal Deficits and Government Debt', *Review of Economic Studies*, **57**, pp. 403-414.

Alesina, Alberto, Ricardo Hausmann, Rudolf Hommes and Ernesto Stein (1996), 'Budget Institutions and Fiscal Performance in Latin America', NBER, Working Paper No. 5586, Cambridge, Mass.

Alesina, Alberto, Nouriel Roubini and Gerald D. Cohen (1997), *Political Cycles and the Macroeconomy*, Cambridge, Mass. and London: MIT Press.

Alesina, Alberto, Roberto Perotti and José Tavares (1998), 'The Political Economy of Fiscal Adjustments', *Brookings Paper on Economic Activity* (1), pp. 197-248.

Allan, Bill (1994), 'Toward a Framework for a Budget Law for Economies in Transition', IMF, Working Paper WP/94/149, Washington, D.C.

Ambrus-Lakatos, Lorand and Mark E. Schaffer (eds) (1997), *Fiscal Policy in Transition. Forum Report of the Economic Policy Initiative No. 3*, London: CEPR, New York: Institute for EastWest Studies.

Amsden, Alice H., Jacek Kochanowicz and Lance Taylor (1994), *The Market Meets Its Match. Restructuring the Economies of Eastern Europe*, Cambridge, Mass. and London: Harvard University Press.

Andersson, Krister (1991), 'Taxation and the Cost of Capital in Hungary and Poland', *IMF Staff Papers*, **38** (2), pp. 327-355.

Andic, Suphan (1994), 'Organizational Dimensions of Public Finance in Transition Economies: An Assessment of the Recent Literature', in Salvatore Schiavo-Campo (ed.), *Insitutional Change and the Public Sector in Transitional Economies*, Washington, D.C.: World Bank, pp. 53-96.

Annett, Anthony (2002), 'Politics, Government Size, and Fiscal Adjustment in Industrial Countries', IMF, Working Paper WP/02/162, Washington, D.C.

Arato, Andrew (1994), 'Elections, Coalitions and Constitutionalism in Hungary', *East European Constitution Review*, **3** (3/4), pp. 26-32.

Åslund, Anders (2002), *Building Capitalism: The Transformation of the Former Soviet Bloc*, Cambridge: Cambridge University Press.

Åslund, Anders, Peter Boone and Simon Johnson (1996), 'How to Stabilize: Lessons from Post-communist Countries', *Brookings Paper on Economic Activity* (1), pp. 217-313.

Bahry, Donna (1983), 'The USSR and Eastern Europe II', in Charles L. Taylor (ed.), *Why Governments Grow. Measuring Public Sector Size*, Beverly Hills, London and New Delhi: Sage, pp. 117-135.

Balcerowicz, Leszek (1994a), 'Poland', in John Williamson (ed.), *The Political Economy of Policy Reform*, Washington, D.C.: Institute for International Economics, pp. 153-177.

Balcerowicz, Leszek (1994b), 'Understanding Postcommunist Transitions', *Journal of Democracy*, **5** (4), pp. 75-89.

Barany, Zoltan (1995), 'Socialist-Liberal Government Stumbles Through Its First Year', *Transition*, **1** (13), pp. 64-69.

Barro, Robert (1979), 'On the Determination of the Public Debt', *Journal of Political Economy*, **87** (5), pp. 940-971.

Barro, Robert (1996), 'Democracy and Growth', *Journal of Economic Growth*, **1** (1), pp. 1-27.

Bartlett, David L. (1997), *The Political Economy of Dual Transformations: Market Reform and Democratization in Hungary*, Ann Arbor: University of Michigan Press.

Bates, Robert H. (1989), 'A Political Scientist Looks at Tax Reform', in Malcolm Gillis (ed.), *Tax Reform in Developing Countries*, Durham and London: Duke University Press, pp. 473-491.

Bates, Robert H. and Anne O. Krueger (eds) (1993a), *Political and Economic Interactions in Economic Policy Reform: Evidence from Eight Countries*, Oxford and Cambridge, UK: Blackwell.

Bates, Robert H. and Anne O. Krueger (1993b), 'Generalizations Arising from the Country Studies', in Robert H. Bates and Anne O. Krueger (eds), *Political and Economic Interactions in Economic Policy Reform. Evidence from Eight Countries*, Oxford and Cambridge, UK: Blackwell, pp. 444-472.

Batt, Judy (1991), *East Central Europe from Reform to Transformation*, London: Pinter/ Royal Institue of International Affairs.

Begg, David (1991), 'Economic Reform in Czechoslovakia: Should We Believe in Santa Klaus?', *Economic Policy*, **13**, pp. 245-286.

Begg, David (1998), 'Pegging Out: Lessons from the Czech Exchange Rate Crisis', *Journal of Comparative Economics*, **26** (4), pp. 669-690.

Begg, David and Charles Wyplosz (2000), 'How Big a Government? Transition Economy Forecasts Based on OECD History', Birkbeck College, Discussion Paper No. 10/2000, London.

Begg, David, Barry Eichengreen, László Halpern, Jürgen von Hagen and Charles Wyplosz (2002), 'Sustainable Regimes of Capital Movements in Accession Countries', CEPR, Policy Paper No. 10, London.

Belka, Marek (1997), 'Poland 1997: How to Avoid Crash-Landing', *Emergo*, **4** (4), pp. 74-77.

Bennett, Adam, Maria Carkovic and Louis Dicks-Mireaux (1995), 'Record of Fiscal Adjustment', in Susan Schadler (ed.), IMF Conditionality: Experience Under Stand-By and Extended Arrangements. Part II: Background Papers, IMF, Occasional Paper No. 129, Washington, D.C.: IMF, pp. 6-35.

Berend, Ivan T. (1990), *The Hungarian Economic Reforms 1953-1988*, Cambridge: Cambridge University Press.

Berglöf, Erik and Gérard Roland (1997), 'The EU as an 'Outside Anchor' for Transition Reforms', SITE, Working Paper No. 132, Stockholm.

Bergsten, C. Fred and John Williamson (1994), 'Introduction', in John Williamson (ed.), *The Political Economy of Policy Reform*, Washington, D.C.: Institute for International Economics, pp. 3-7.

Biglaiser, Glen (2002), *Guardians of the Nation? Economists, Generals, and Economic Reform in Latin America*, Notre Dame and London: University of Notre Dame Press.

Bird, Graham (1998), 'The Effectiveness of Conditionality and the Political Economy of Policy Reform: Is It Simply a Matter of Political Will?', *Journal of Policy Reform*, **3** (1), pp. 89-113.

Birkland, Thomas A. (1997), *After Disaster. Agenda Setting, Public Policy, and Focusing Events*, Washington, D.C.: Georgetown University Press.

Birman, Igor (1981), *Secret Incomes of the Soviet State Budget*, The Hague, Boston and London: Martinus Nijhoff.

Birman, Igor (1990), 'The Budget Gap, Excess Money and Reform', *Communist Economies*, **2** (1), pp. 25-45.

Bjork, James (1995), 'The Uses of Conditionality: Poland and the IMF', *East European Quarterly*, **29** (1), pp. 89-124.

Blanchard, Olivier, Rüdiger Dornbusch and Paul Krugman (1991), *Reform in Eastern Europe*, Cambridge, Mass. and London: MIT Press.

Blazyca, George and Ryszard Rapacki (1996), 'Continuity and Change in Polish Economic Policy: The Impact of the 1993 Elections', *Europe-Asia Studies*, **48** (1), pp. 85-100.

Blejer, Mario I. and Fabrizio Coricelli (1995), *The Making of Economic Reform in Eastern Europe: Conversations with Leading Reformers in Poland, Hungary and the Czech Republic*, Aldershot, UK and Brookfield, US: Edward Elgar.

Bokros, Lajos (1998), 'The Unfinished Agenda', in Lajos Bokros and Jean-Jacques Dethier (eds), *Public Finance Reform during the Transition: The Experience of Hungary*, Washington, D.C.: World Bank, pp. 535-568.

Bolkowiak, Izabela (1993), 'Fiscal Policy in Poland 1990-1992', Institute of Finance, Working Paper No. 32, Warsaw.

Boltho, Andrea (1994), 'Why Do Countries Change Their Fiscal Policies? Western Europe in the 1980s', *Journal of International and Comparative Economics*, **3** (2), pp. 77-99.

Bönker, Frank (1994), 'External Determinants of the Patterns and Outcomes of East European Transitions', *Emergo*, **1** (1), pp. 34-54.

Bönker, Frank (1995), 'The Dog That Did Not Bark? Politische Restriktionen und ökonomische Reformen in den Visegrád-Ländern', in Hellmut Wollmann, Helmut Wiesenthal and Frank Bönker (eds), *Transformation sozialistischer Gesellschaften: Am Ende des Anfangs*, Opladen: Westdeutscher Verlag, pp. 180-206.

Bönker, Frank (2001a), 'Initiating and Consolidating Economic Reform: A Comparative Analysis of Fiscal Reform in Hungary, Poland and the Czech Republic, 1989-1999', in Jürgen Beyer, Jan Wielgohs and Helmut Wiesenthal (eds), *Successful Transitions: Political Factors of Socio-Economic Progress in Postsocialist Countries*, Baden-Baden: Nomos, pp. 120-138.

Bönker, Frank (2001b), 'Staatliche Reformfähigkeit in der Transformation: Finanzpolitik in Polen, Tschechien und Ungarn nach 1989', in Eckhard Schröter (ed.), *Empirische Policy- und Verwaltungsforschung: Lokale, nationale und internationale Perspektiven*, Opladen: Leske + Budrich, pp. 167-180.

Bönker, Frank (2003a), 'Staatseinnahmen und staatliche Handlungsfähigkeit: Das Beispiel der osteuropäischen Transformationsländer', in Petra Bendel, Aurel Croissant and Friedbert W. Rüb (eds), *Demokratie und Staatlichkeit: Systemwechsel zwischen Staatsreform und Staatskollaps*, Opladen: Leske + Budrich, pp. 81-98.

Bönker, Frank (2003b), 'Steuerpolitische Aspekte der EU-Osterweiterung', *Vierteljahreshefte zur Wirtschaftsforschung*, **72** (4), pp. 522-534.

Bönker, Frank (2006a), 'EU-Beitritt und ökonomische Transformation in Osteuropa', in Timm Beichelt, Božena Choluj, Gerald Rowe and Hans-Jürgen Wagener (eds), *Europa-Studien: Eine Einführung*, Wiesbaden: VS, pp. 399-413.

Bönker, Frank (2006b), 'From Pace-Setter to Laggard: The Political Economy of Negotiating Fit in the Czech Republic', in Kenneth Dyson (ed.), *Enlarging the Euro-Zone: The Euro and the Transformation of East-Central Europe*, Oxford: Oxford University Press, pp. 160-176.

Bönker, Frank, Klaus Müller and Andreas Pickel (2002), 'Cross-Disciplinary Approaches to Postcommunist Transformation: Context and Agenda', in Frank Bönker, Klaus Müller and Andreas Pickel (eds), *Postcommunist Transformation and the Social Sciences: Cross-Disciplinary Approaches*, Lanham, MD et al.: Rowman & Littlefield, pp. 1-37.

Boote, Anthony R. and János Somogyi (1991), 'Economic Reform in Hungary Since 1968', IMF, Occasional Paper No. 83, Washington, D.C.

Borrelli, Stephen A. and Terry J. Royed (1995), 'Government 'Strength' and Budget Deficits in Advanced Democracies', *European Journal of Political Research*, **28** (2), pp. 225-260.

Brady, Henry E. and David Collier (eds) (2004), *Rethinking Social Inquiry: Diverse Tools, Shared Standards*, Lanham, MD et al.: Rowman & Littlefield.

Brender, Adi and Allan Drazen (2005), 'Political Budget Cycles in New versus Established Democracies', *Journal of Monetary Economics*, **52** (7), pp. 1271-1295.

Bresser Pereira, Luiz Carlos (1993), 'Economic Reforms and Economic Growth: Efficiency and Politics in Latin America', in Luiz Carlos Bresser Pereira, José María Maravall, Adam Przeworski, *Economic Reforms in New Democracies. A Social-Democratic Approach*, Cambridge, UK: Cambridge University Press, pp. 15-76.

Brook, Anne-Marie and Willi Leibfritz (2005), 'Slovakia's Introduction of a Flat Tax as Part of Wider Economic Reforms', OECD, Economics Department, Working Paper No. 448, Paris.

Brunetti, Aymo (1997), 'Political Variables in Cross-Country Growth Analysis', *Journal of Economic Surveys*, **11** (2), pp. 163-190.

Bruno, Michael (1993), *Crisis, Stabilization, and Economic Reform. Therapy by Consensus*, Oxford: Clarendon Press.

Bruno, Michael and William Easterly (1996), 'Inflation's Children: Tales of Crisis That Beget Reforms', *American Economic Review*, **86** (2), pp. 213-217.

Brusis, Martin and Vesselin Dimitrov (2001), 'Executive Configuration and Fiscal Performance in Post-Communist Central and Eastern Europe', *Journal of European Public Policy*, **8** (6), pp. 888-910.

Bulow, Jeremy and Paul Klemperer (1999), 'The Generalized War of Attrition', *American Economic Review*, **89** (1), pp. 175-189.

Bunce, Valerie (1998), 'Regional Differences in Democratization: The East Versus the South?', *Post-Soviet Affairs*, **14** (3), pp. 187-211.

Burgess, Robin and Nicholas Stern (1993), 'Taxation and Development', *Journal of Economic Literature*, **31** (2), pp. 762-830.

Caiden, Naomi (1993), 'The Roads to Transformation: Budgeting Issues in the Czech and Slovak Federal Republic 1989-1992', *Public Budgeting and Finance*, **13**, pp. 57-71.

Campbell, John L. (1992), 'The Fiscal Crisis of Post-Communist States', *Telos*, **93**, pp. 89-110.

Campbell, John L. (1994), 'Transformations of Post-Communist Fiscal Systems', in John L. Campbell and Stanisław Owsiak (eds), *Fiscal Reforms in Post-Communist Countries*, Cracow: Cracow Academy of Economics, pp. 11-53.

Campbell, John L. (1995a), 'State Building and Postcommunist Budget Deficits', *American Behavioral Scientist*, **38** (5), pp. 760-787.

Campbell, John L. (1995b), 'Reflections on Fiscal Crisis of Post-Communist States', in Jerzy Hausner, Bob Jessop and Klaus Nielsen (eds), *Strategic Choice and Path-Dependency in Post-Socialism: Institutional Dynamics in the Transformation Process*, Aldershot, UK and Brookfield, US: Edward Elgar, pp. 84-112.

Campbell, John L. (1996), 'An Institutional Analysis of Fiscal Reform in Postcommunist Europe', *Theory and Society*, **25** (1), pp. 45-84.

Campbell, John (2001), 'Convergence or Divergence? Globalization, Neoliberalism and Fiscal Policy in Postcommunist Europe', in Jürgen Beyer, Jan Wielgohs and Helmut Wiesenthal (eds), *Successful Transitions: Political Factors of Socio-Economic Progress in Postsocialist Countries*, Baden-Baden: Nomos, pp. 95-119.

Campbell, John L. and Stanisław Owsiak (eds) (1994), *Fiscal Reforms in Post-Communist Countries*, Cracow: Cracow Academy of Economics.

Carlsen, Fredrik (1997), 'Counterfiscal Policies and Partisan Politics: Evidence from Industrialized Countries', *Applied Economics*, **29** (2), pp. 145-151.

Casanegra de Jantscher, Milka, Carlos Silvani and Charles L. Vehorn (1992), 'Modernizing Tax Administration', in Vito Tanzi (ed.), *Fiscal Policies in Economies in Transition*, Washington, D.C.: IMF, pp. 120-141.

Castles, Francis G. (1986), 'Whatever Happened to the Communist Welfare State?', *Studies in Comparative Communism*, 29 (3/4), pp. 213-226.

Chadha, Bankim and Fabrizio Coricelli (1997), 'Fiscal Constraints and the Speed of Transition', *Journal of Development Economics*, 52, pp. 221-249.

Chand, Sheetal and Henri R. Lorie (1992), 'Fiscal Policy', in Vito Tanzi (ed.), *Fiscal Policies in Economies in Transition*, Washington, D.C.: IMF, pp. 11-36.

Cheasty, Adrienne (1992), 'Financing Fiscal Deficits', in Vito Tanzi (ed.), *Fiscal Policies in Economies in Transition*, Washington, D.C.: IMF, pp. 37-66.

Chu, Ke-Young and Robert Holzmann (1992), 'Public Expenditure: Policy Aspects', in Vito Tanzi (ed.), *Fiscal Policies in Economies in Transition*, Washington, D.C.: IMF, pp. 254-267.

Clark, William R. and Mark Hallerberg (2000), 'Mobile Capital, Domestic Institutions, and Electorally Induced Monetary and Fiscal Policy', *American Political Science Review*, 94 (2), pp. 323-346.

Cnossen, Sijbren (1992), 'Key Questions in Considering a Value-Added Tax for Central and Eastern European Countries', *IMF Staff Papers*, 39 (2), pp. 211-255.

Collier, David (1993), 'The Comparative Method', in Ada W. Finifter (ed.), *Political Science: The State of the Discipline II*, Washington, D.C.: APSA, pp. 105-119.

Cook, Linda J. and Mitchell A. Orenstein (1999), 'The Return of the Left and Its Impact on the Welfare State in Poland, Hungary, and Russia', in Linda J. Cook, Mitchell A. Orenstein and Marilyn Rueschemeyer (eds), *Left Parties and Social Policy in Postcommunist Europe*, Boulder, CO: Westview, pp. 47-108.

Corrales, Javier (1998), 'Do Economic Crises Contribute to Economic Reform? Argentina and Venuezuela in the 1990s', *Political Science Quarterly*, 112 (4), pp. 617-644.

Corsetti, Giancarlo and Nouriel Roubini (1992), 'Tax Smoothing Discretion versus Balanced Budget Rules in the Presence of Politically Motivated Fiscal Deficits: The Design of Optimal Fiscal Rules for Europe After 1992', CEPR, Discussion Paper No. 682, London.

Cottarelli, Carlo (1998), 'Macroeconomic and Structural Adjustment During 1995-97: An Overview', in idem (ed.), Hungary: Economic Policies for Sustainable Growth, IMF, Occasional Paper No. 159, Washington, D.C., pp. 3-18.

Csaba, László (1992), 'Macroeconomic Policy in Hungary: Poetry versus Reality', *Soviet Studies*, 44 (6), pp. 947-964.

Csaba, László (1995), 'Hungary and the IMF: The Experience of a Cordial Discord', *Journal of Comparative Economics*, 20 (2), pp. 211-234.

Csillag, István (1995), 'Privatization and the New Government', in Csaba Gombár, Elemér Hankiss, László Lengyel, Györgyi Várnai (eds), *Question Marks: The Hungarian Government 1994-1995*, Budapest: Korridor, pp. 305-330.

Cukierman, Alex and Mariano Tommasi (1998), 'When Does It Take a Nixon to Go to China?', *American Economic Review*, 88 (1), pp. 180-197.

Cusack, Thomas R. (1999), 'Partisan Politics and Fiscal Policy', *Comparative Political Studies*, 32 (4), pp. 464-486.

Czech Government and Czech National Bank (2003), The Czech Republic's Euro-area Accession Strategy, Prague.

Dąbrowski, Marek (1992), 'The Polish Stabilization, 1990-1991', *Journal of International and Comparative Economics*, **1** (4), pp. 295-324.

Dąbrowski, Marek (1997), 'Dynamics of Fiscal Developments During Transition', in Lorand Ambrus-Lakatos and Mark E. Schaffer (eds), *Fiscal Policy in Transition. Forum Report of the Economic Policy Initiative No. 3*, London: CEPR, New York: Institute for EastWest Studies, pp. 3-15.

Dąbrowski, Marek (1998), 'Western Aid Conditionality and the Post-Communist Transition', *Journal of Policy Reform*, **3** (2), pp. 169-193.

Dąbrowski, Marek (2000), 'Macroeconomic and Fiscal Challenges During the EU Accession Process: An Overview', in Marek Dąbrowski, Jacek Rostowski (eds), *The Eastern Enlargement of the EU*, Boston, Dordrecht and London: Kluwer, pp. 1-33.

Dąbrowski, Marek, Malgorzata Antczak and Michał Gorzelak (2005), 'Fiscal Challenges Facing the EU New Member States', CASE, Studies & Analyses, No. 295, Warsaw.

Davies, R.W. (1958), *The Development of the Soviet Budgetary System*, Cambridge: Cambridge University Press.

de Crombrugghe, Alain (1994), 'The Polish Government Budget Stabilization and Sustainability', in Kálmán Mizsei (ed.), *Developing Public Finance in Emerging Market Economies*, Prague et al.: Institute for EastWest Studies, pp. 63-128.

de Crombrugghe, Alain (1997), 'Wage and Pension Pressure on the Polish Budget', CEPR, Discussion Paper No. 1767, London.

de Crombrugghe, Alain and David Lipton (1994), 'The Government Budget and the Economic Transformation of Poland', in Olivier J. Blanchard, Kenneth A. Froot and Jeffrey D. Sachs (eds), *The Transition in Eastern Europe. Vol. 2: Restructuring*, Chicago and London: University of Chicago Press, pp. 111-133.

de Haan, Jakob and Jan-Egbert Sturm (1994), 'Political and Institutional Determinants of Fiscal Policy in the European Union', *Public Choice*, **80** (1/2), pp. 157-172.

de Haan, Jakob and Jan-Egbert Sturm (1997), 'Political and Economic Determinants of OECD Budget Deficits and Government Expenditures: A Reinvestigation', *European Journal of Political Economy*, **13** (4), pp. 739-750.

de Haan, Jakob, Jan-Egbert Sturm and Geert Beekhuis (1997): The Weak Government Thesis: A Survey and New Evidence, Mimeo, Groningen.

de Melo, Martha, Cevdet Denizer and Alan Gelb (1996), 'Patterns of Transition from Plan to Market', *World Bank Economic Review*, **10** (3), pp. 397-424.

Deacon, Bob and Michelle Hulse (1997), 'The Making of Post-communist Social Policy: The Role of International Agencies', *Journal of Social Policy*, **26** (1), pp. 43-62.

Dethier, Jean-Jacques and Witold Orlowski (1998), 'Long Term Effects of Fiscal Adjustment', in Lajos Bokros and Jean-Jacques Dethier (eds), *Public Finance Reform during the Transition: The Experience of Hungary*, Washington, D.C.: World Bank, pp. 95-125.

Dethier, Jean-Jacques and Tamar Shapiro (1998), 'Constitutional Rights and the Reform of Social Entitlements', in Lajos Bokros and Jean-Jacques Dethier (eds), *Public Finance Reform during the Transition: The Experience of Hungary*, Washington, D.C.: World Bank, pp. 447-475.

Dethier, Jean-Jacques, Hafez Ghanem and Edda Zoli (1999), 'Does Democracy Facilitate the Economic Transition: An Empirical Study of Central and Eastern Europe and the Former Soviet Union', World Bank, Policy Research Working Paper No. 2194, Washington, D.C.

Diamond, Larry (1995), 'Democracy and Economic Reform: Tensions, Compatibilities, and Strategies for Reconciliation', in Edward P. Lazear (ed.), *Economic Transition in Eastern Europe and Russia*, Stanford/CA: Hoover Institution Press, pp. 107-158.

Dimitrov, Vesselin (2006), 'EMU and Fiscal Policies in East Central Europe', in Kenneth Dyson (ed.), *Enlarging the Euro-Zone: The Euro and the Transformation of East-Central Europe*, Oxford: Oxford University Press, forthcoming.

Dixit, Avinash (1996), *The Making of Economic Policy: A Transaction-Cost Politics Perspective*, Cambridge, Mass. and London: MIT Press.

Dollar, David and Jakob Svensson (2000), 'What Explains the Success or Failure of Structural Adjustment Programs?', *Economic Journal*, **110**, pp. 894-917.

Dominguez, Jorge I. (1997), 'Technopols. Ideas and Leaders in Freeing Politics and Markets in Latin America in the 1990s', in idem (ed.), *Technopols. Freeing Politics and Markets in Latin America in the 1990s*, University Park, PA: Pennsylvania State University Press, pp. 1-48.

Drábek, Zdenek (1995), 'IMF and IBRD Policies in the Former Czechoslovakia', *Journal of Comparative Economics*, **20** (2), pp. 235-264.

Drábek, Zdenek, Kamil Janacek and Zdenek Tůma (1994), 'Inflation in the Czech and Slovak Republics, 1985-1991', *Journal of Comparative Economics*, **18**, pp. 146-174.

Drazen, Allan (1996), 'The Political Economy of Delayed Reform', *Journal of Policy Reform*, **1** (1), pp. 25-46.

Drazen, Allan (2000), *Political Economy in Macroeconomics*, Princeton, N.J.: Princeton University Press.

Drazen, Allan and William Easterly (2001), 'Do Crises Induce Reform? Simple Empirical Tests of Conventional Wisdom', *Economics and Politics*, **13** (2), pp. 129-157.

Drazen, Allan and Vittorio Grilli (1993), 'The Benefit of Crises for Economic Reforms', *American Economic Review*, **83** (3), pp. 598-607.

Dyba, Karel and Jan Svejnar (1994), 'Stabilization and Transition in Czechoslovakia', in Olivier J. Blanchard, Kenneth A. Froot and Jeffrey D. Sachs (eds), *The Transition in Eastern Europe. Vol. 1: Country Studies*, Chicago and London: University of Chicago Press, pp. 93-122.

Dyson, Kenneth (2006), 'Domestic Transformation, Strategic Options and 'Soft' Power in Euro Area Accession', in Kenneth Dyson (ed.), *Enlarging the Euro-Zone: The Euro and the Transformation of East-Central Europe*, Oxford: Oxford University Press, forthcoming.

Earle, John S., Scott G. Gehlback, Zusana Saková, Večerník and Jiří Večerník (1997), 'Mass Privatization, Distributive Politics, and Popular Support for Reform in the Czech Republic', SITE, Working Paper No. 121, Stockholm.

Easterly, William (1996), 'When is Stabilization Expansionary? Evidence from High Inflation', *Economic Policy*, **22**, pp. 67-107.

Easterly, William and Sergio Rebelo (1993), 'Fiscal Policy and Economic Growth: An Empirical Investigation', *Journal of Monetary Economics*, **32**, pp. 417-458.

Eatwell, John, Michael Ellman, Mats Karlsson, D. Mario Nuti and Judith Shapiro (1995), *Transformation and Integration. Shaping the Future of Central and Eastern Europe*, London: Institute for Public Policy Research.

Ebbinghaus, Bernhard and Anke Hassel (2000), 'Striking Deals: The Role of Concertation in the Reform of the Welfare State', *Journal of European Public Policy*, **7** (1), pp. 44-62.

EBRD (1994), *Transition Report*, London.

EBRD (1999), *Ten Years of Transition. Transition Report 1999*, London.

Edin, Per-Anders and Henry Ohlsson (1991), 'Political Determinants of Budget Deficits: Coalition Effects versus Minority Effects', *European Economic Review*, **35**, pp. 1597-1603.

Edwards, Sebastian (1995), *Crisis and Reform in Latin America. From Despair to Hope*, New York: Oxford University Press.

Edwards, Sebastian and Guido Tabellini (1991a), 'Explaining Fiscal Policies and Inflation in Developing Countries', *Journal of International Money and Finance*, **10**, pp. 16-48.

Edwards, Sebastian and Guido Tabellini (1991b), 'Political Instability, Political Weakness and Inflation: An Empirical Analysis', NBER, Working Paper No. 3721, Cambridge, Mass.

Ekiert, Grzegorz and Jan Kubik (1998), 'Contentious Politics in New Democracies: East Germany, Hungary, Poland, and Slovakia, 1989-93', *World Politics*, **50** (4), pp. 547-581.

Elster, Jon (1995), 'Transition, Constitution-Making and Separation in Czechoslovakia', *Archives Européennes de Sociologie*, **36** (1), pp. 105-134.

Elster, Jon, Claus Offe and Ulrich K. Preuß (with Frank Bönker, Ulrike Götting and Friedbert W. Rüb) (1998), *Institutional Design in Post-communist Societies: Rebuilding the Ship at Sea*, Cambridge, UK: Cambridge University Press.

Ethier, Diane (1997), *Economic Adjustment in New Democracies: Lessons from Southern Europe*, Basingstoke and London: Macmillan.

Fakin, Barbara and Alain de Crombrugghe (1995), 'Patterns of Government Expenditure and Taxation in Transition vs. OECD Economies', Leuven Institute for Central and East European Studies, Working Paper 46/1995, Leuven.

Felkai, Roland (1996), *Die Reform des ungarischen Steuersystems. Ausgestaltung der Besteuerung bei Einführung der Marktwirtschaft*, Wiesbaden: Gabler/DUV.

Fernandez, Raquel and Dani Rodrik (1991), 'Resistance to Reform: Status Quo Bias in the Pressure of Individual-Specific Uncertainty', *American Economic Review*, **81** (5), pp. 1146-1155.

Fischer, Stanley and Alan Gelb (1991), 'The Process of Socialist Economic Transformation', *Journal of Economic Perspectives*, **5** (4), pp. 91-105.

Fischer, Stanley, Ratna Sahay and Carlos A. Végh (1998), 'How Far is Eastern Europe from Brussels?', IMF, Working Paper WP/98/53, Washington, D.C.

Fish, Steven M. (1998), 'The Determinants of Economic Reform in the Post-Communist World', *East European Politics and Societes*, **12** (1), pp. 31-78.

Franzese, Robert J. (2002), *Macroeconomic Policies of Developed Democracies*, Cambridge, UK: Cambridge University Press.

Fruchtmann, Jakob and Heiko Pleines (2002), *Wirtschaftskulturelle Faktoren in der russischen Steuergesetzgebung und Steuerpraxis*, Münster: Lit.

Funck, Bernard (ed.) (2002), 'Expenditure Policies Toward EU Accession', World Bank, Technical Paper No. 533, Washington, D.C.

Gabal, Ivan (ed.) (1996), *The 1990 Election to the Czechoslovakian Federal Assembly. Analyses, Documents and Data*, Berlin edition sigma.

Gandhi, Ved P. and Dubravko Mihaljek (1992), 'Scope for Reform of Socialist Tax Systems', in Vito Tanzi (ed.), *Fiscal Policies in Economies in Transition*, Washington, D.C.: IMF, pp. 142-165.

Ganghof, Steffen (1999), 'Steuerwettbewerb und Vetospieler: Stimmt die These der blockierten Anpassung?', *Politische Vierteljahresschrift*, **40** (3), pp. 458-472.

Gasiorowski, Mark J. (2000), 'Democracy and Macroeconomic Performance in Underdeveloped Countries. An Empirical Analysis', *Comparative Political Studies*, **33** (3), pp. 319-349.

Gavin, Michael and Ricardo Hausmann (1998), 'Fiscal Performance in Latin America: What Need to be Explained?', in Kichiro Fukasaku and Ricardo Hausmann (eds), *Democracy, Decentralisation and Deficits in Latin America*, Paris: OECD, pp. 33-64.

Geddes, Barbara (1994), *Politician's Dilemma. Building State Capacity in Latin America*, Berkeley, Los Angeles and London: University of California Press.

Gedeon, Peter (1995), 'Hungary: Social Policy in Transition', *East European Politics and Societies*, **9** (3), pp. 433-458.

Gergely, István (1988), 'Die Steuerreform in der Volksrepublik Ungarn', *Finanzarchiv*, **46** (1), pp. 98-113.

Giavazzi, Francesco and Marco Pagano (1990), 'Can Severe Fiscal Contractions Be Expansionary? Tales of Two Small European Countries', *NBER Macroeconomics Annual*, **5**, pp. 75-111.

Gleich, Holger (2003), 'Budget Institutions and Fiscal Performance in Central and Eastern European Countries', European Central Bank, Working Paper No. 215, Frankfurt, M.

Goetz, Klaus H. and Hellmut Wollmann (2001), 'Governmentalizing Central Executives in Post-Communist Europe: a Four-Country Comparison', *Journal of European Public Policy*, **8** (6), pp. 864-887.

Gomułka, Stanisław (1990), 'Reform and Budgetary Policies in Poland, 1989-90', *European Economy*, **43**, pp. 127-137.

Gomułka, Stanisław (1992), 'Polish Economic Reform, 1990-1991: Principles, Policies and Outcomes', *Cambridge Journal of Economics*, **16** (3), pp. 355-372.

Gomułka, Stanisław (1993), 'Poland: Glass Half Full', in Richard Portes (ed.), *Economic Transformation in Central Europe. A Progress Report*, London: CEPR, pp. 187-210.

Gomułka, Stanisław (1994), 'Budget Deficit and Inflation in Transition Economies', in Vit Bárta and C.M. Schneider (eds), *Stabilization Policies at Crossroads?*, Laxenburg: IIAS, pp. 45-69.

Gomułka, Stanisław (1995), 'The IMF-Supported Programs of Poland and Russia, 1990-1994: Principles, Errors, and Results', *Journal of Comparative Economics*, **20** (3), pp. 316-346.

Gordon, Roger H. (1994), 'Fiscal Policy During the Transition in Eastern Europe', in Kenneth A. Froot Olivier J. Blanchard and Jeffrey D. Sachs (eds), *The Transition in Eastern Europe, Vol. 2: Restructuring*, Chicago and London: University of Chicago Press, pp. 37-66.

Götting, Ulrike (1998), *Transformation der Wohlfahrtsstaaten in Mittel- und Osteuropa. Eine Zwischenbilanz*, Opladen: Leske + Budrich.

Gourevitch, Peter (1986), *Politics in Hard Times. Comparative Responses to International Economic Crises*, Ithaca, N.Y. and London: Cornell University Press.

Graham, Carol (1994), *Safety Nets, Politics, and the Poor: Transitions to Market Economies*, Washington, D.C.: Brookings.

Gray, Cheryl W. (1991), 'Tax Systems in the Reforming Socialist Economies of Europe', *Communist Economies and Economic Transformation*, **3** (1), pp. 63-79.

Greskovits, Béla (1998), *The Political Economy of Protest and Patience. East European and Latin American Transformations Compared*, Budapest: CEU Press.

Greskovits, Béla (1999), 'Consolidating Economic Reforms: the Hungarian Experience with Lessons for Poland', CASE, CASE-CEU Working Paper No. 31, Warsaw and Budapest.

Greskovits, Béla (2000), 'Hungary's Post-communist Development in Comparative Perspective', in Werner Baer and Joseph L. Love (eds), *Liberalization and its Consequences: A Comparative Perspective on Latin America and Eastern Europe*, Cheltenham, UK and Lyme, US: Edward Elgar, pp. 126-149.

Greskovits, Béla (2001), 'Brothers-in-Arms or Rival in Politics? Top Politicians and Top Policy Makers in the Hungarian Transformation', in János Kornai, Stephan Haggard and Robert R. Kaufman (eds), *Reforming the State: Fiscal and Welfare Reform in Post-Socialist Countries*, Cambridge, UK: Cambridge University Press, pp. 111-141.

Greskovits, Béla (2006), 'The First Shall Be the Last? Hungary's Road to EMU', in Kenneth Dyson (ed.), *Enlarging the Euro-Zone: The Euro and the Transformation of East-Central Europe*, Oxford: Oxford University Press, forthcoming.

Grilli, Vittorio, Donata Masciandaro and Guido Tabellini (1991), 'Political and Monetary Institutions and Public Financial Policies in the Industrial Countries', *Economic Policy*, **13**, pp. 342-392.

Grindle, Merilee S. and John W. Thomas (1991), *Public Choices and Policy Change. The Political Economy of Reform in Developing Countries*, Baltimore and London: Johns Hopkins University Press.

Gupta, Sanjeev, Benedict Clements, Emanuele Baldacci and Carlos Mulas-Granados (2004), 'The Persistence of Fiscal Adjustments in Developing Countries', *Applied Economic Letters*, **11** (4), pp. 209-212.

Gyulavári, Antal and Judit Neményi (1996), 'Fiscal Policy in Hungary under Transition', CASE, Studies & Analyses No. 64, Warsaw.

Haase, Herwig E. (1980), *Hauptsteuern im sozialistischen Wirtschaftssystem*, Berlin Duncker & Humblot.

Haggard, Stephan (2000), 'Interests, Institutions, and Policy Reform', in Anne O. Krueger (ed.), *Economic Policy Reform: The Second Stage*, Chicago, IL and London: University of Chicago Press, pp. 21-57.

Haggard, Stephan and Robert R. Kaufman (1989), 'Economic Adjustment in New Democracies', in Joan M. Nelson (ed.), *Fragile Coalitions. The Politics of Economic Adjustment*, New Brunswick and London: Transaction Books, pp. 57-77.

Haggard, Stephan and Robert R. Kaufman (eds) (1992), *The Politics of Economic Adjustment*, Princeton, N.J.: Princeton University Press.

Haggard, Stephan and Robert R. Kaufman (1995), *The Political Economy of Democratic Transitions*, Princeton, N.J.: Princeton University Press.

Haggard, Stephan and Steven B. Webb (1993), 'What Do We Know About the Political Economy of Policy Reform?', *World Bank Research Observer*, **8** (2), pp. 143-168.

Haggard, Stephan, Marc A. Levy, Andrew Moravcsik and Kalypso Nicolaidis (1993), 'Integrating the Two Halves of Europe: Theories of Interests, Bargaining, and Institutions', in Robert O. Keohane, Joseph S. Nye and Stanley Hoffmann (eds), *After the Cold War. International Institutions and State Strategies in Europe, 1989-1991*, Cambridge, UK and London: Harvard University Press, pp. 173-195.

Haggard, Stephan, Jean-Dominique Lafay and Christian Morrisson (1995), *The Political Feasibility of Adjustment in Developing Countries*, Paris: OECD.

Haggard, Stephan, Robert R. Kaufman and Matthew S. Shugart (2001), 'Politics, Institutions, and Macroeconomic Adjustment: Hungarian Fiscal Policy Making in Comparative Perspective', in János Kornai, Stephan Haggard and Robert R. Kaufman (eds), *Reforming the State: Fiscal and Welfare Reform in Post-Socialist Countries*, Cambridge, UK: Cambridge University Press, pp. 75-110.

Hahm, Sung Deuk (1996), 'The Political Economy of Deficit Spending: A Cross Comparison of Industrialized Democracies, 1955-90', *Environment and Planning C: Government and Policy*, **14**, pp. 227-250.

Hahm, Sung Deuk, Mark S. Kamlet and David C. Mowery (1996), 'The Political Economy of Deficit Spending in Nine Industrialized Parliamentary Democracies. The Role of Fiscal Institutions', *Comparative Political Studies*, **29** (1), pp. 52-77.

Hall, Peter A. (1997), 'The Role of Interests, Institutions, and Ideas in the Comparative Political Economy of the Industrialized Nations', in Mark Irving Lichbach and Alan S. Zuckerman (eds), *Comparative Politics: Rationality, Culture, and Structure*, Cambridge, UK: Cambridge University Press, pp. 174-207.

Hall, Peter A. (2003), 'Aligning Ontology and Methodology in Comparative Research', in James Mahoney and Dietrich Rueschemeyer (eds), *Comparative Historical Research*, Cambridge, UK: Cambridge University Press, pp. 373-404.

Hallerberg, Mark (2004), *Domestic Budgets in a United Europe*, Ithaca, NY. and London: Cornell University Press.

Hallerberg, Mark and Scott Basinger (1998), 'Internationalization and Changes in Tax Policy in OECD Countries: The Importance of Domestic Veto Players', *Comparative Political Studies*, **31** (3), pp. 321-352.

Hallerberg, Mark and Scott Basinger (1999), 'Globalization and Tax Reform: An Updated Case for the Importance of Veto Players', *Politische Vierteljahresschrift*, **40** (4), pp. 618-627.

Hallerberg, Mark and Jürgen von Hagen (1999), 'Electoral Institutions, Cabinet Negotiations, and Budget Deficits in the European Union', in James M. Poterba and Jürgen von Hagen (eds), *Fiscal Institutions and Fiscal Performance*, Chicago, IL and London: University of Chicago Press, pp. 209-232.

Hallerberg, Mark, Lucio Vinhas de Souza and William Roberts Clark (2002a), 'Political Business Cycles in EU Accession Countries', *European Union Politics*, **3** (2), pp. 231-250.

Hallerberg, Mark, Lúcio Vinhas de Souza and William Roberts Clark (2002b), 'Political Business Cycles in the EU Accession Countries', in Ronald H. Linden (ed.), *Norms and Nannies: The Impact of International Organizations on the Central and East European States*, Lanham, MD et al.: Rowman & Littlefield, pp. 341-368.

Ham, John C., Jan Svejnar and Katherine Terrell (1998), 'Unemployment and the Social Safety Net During Transitions to a Market Economy: Evidence from the Czech and Slovak Republics', *American Economic Review*, **88** (5), pp. 1117-1142.

Hanley, Seán (2004), ' A Nation of Sceptics? The Czech EU Accession Referendum of 13-14 June 2003', *West European Politics*, **27** (4), pp. 691-715.

Harberger, Arnold C. (1993), 'Secrets of Success: A Handful of Heroes', *American Economic Review*, **83** (2), pp. 343-350.

Hartwig, Karl-Hans and Iris Wellesen (1991), 'Reformen der staatlichen Finanzwirtschaft: Zu den neuen Funktionen staatlicher Haushaltspolitik', in Karl-Hans Hartwig and H. Jörg Thieme (eds), *Transformationsprozesse in sozialistischen.Wirtschaftssystemen. Ursachen, Konzepte, Instrumente*, Berlin et al: Springer, pp. 331-355.

Hausner, Jerzy (2001), 'Security Through Diversity: Conditions for Successful Reform of the Pension System in Poland', in János Kornai, Stephan Haggard and Robert R. Kaufman (eds), *Reforming the State: Fiscal and Welfare Reform in Post-Socialist Countries*, Cambridge, UK: Cambridge University Press, pp. 210-234.

Havel, Jiří, Jan Klacek, Jiří Kosta and Zdislav Sulc (1998), 'Economics and System Change in Czechoslovakia, 1945-92', in Hans-Jürgen Wagener (ed.), *Economic Thought in Communist and Post-Communist Europe*, London and New York: Routledge, pp. 213-263.

Heady, Christopher, Najma Rajah and Stephen Smith (1994), 'Tax Reform and Economic Transition in the Czech Republic', *Fiscal Studies*, **15** (1), pp. 64-80.

Heady, Christopher and Stephen Smith (1995), 'Tax and Benefit Reform in the Czech and Slovak Republics', in David M.G. Newbery (ed.), *Tax and Benefit Reform in Central and Eastern Europe*, London: CEPR, pp. 19-48.

Hedtkamp, Günter (1970), 'Volumen und Struktur der öffentlichen Ausgaben in Abhängigkeit vom Wirtschaftssystem', in Erich Boettcher (ed.), *Beiträge zum Vergleich von Wirtschaftssystemen*, Berlin Duncker & Humblot, pp. 219-245.

Heller, Peter S. and Jack Diamond (1990), 'International Comparisons of Government Expenditure Revisited: The Developing Countries, 1975-86', IMF, Occasional Paper No. 69, Washington, D.C.

Hellman, Joel S. (1998), 'Winners Take All: The Politics of Partial Reform in Postcommunist Transitions', *World Politics*, **50** (2), pp. 203-234.

Hetényi, István (1994), 'Public Finances in the Early 1990s', in Csaba Gombár, Elemér Hankiss, László Lengyel and Györgyi Várnai (eds), *Balance: The Hungarian Government 1990-1994*, Budapest: Korridor, pp. 182-211.

Hewitt, Daniel and Dubravko Mihaljek (1992), 'Government Budget and Accounting Systems', in Vito Tanzi (ed.), *Fiscal Policies in Economies in Transition*, Washington, D.C.: IMF, pp. 330-349.

Hirschman, Albert O. (1963), *Journeys Towards Progress. Studies of Economic Policy-Making in Latin America*, New York: Twentieth Century Fund.

Holmes, Stephen (1995), 'The Politics of Economics in the Czech Republic', *East European Constitutional Review*, **4** (2), pp. 52-55.

Holmes, Stephen (1996), 'Cultural Legacies or State Collapse? Probing the Postcommunist Dilemma', in Michael Mandelbaum (ed.), *Postcommunism: Four Perspectives*, New York: Council on Foreign Relations, pp. 22-76.

Holzman, Franklyn D. (1955), *Soviet Taxation. The Fiscal and Monetary Problems of a Planned Economy*, Cambridge, Mass.: Harvard University Press.

Holzmann, Robert (1991), 'Budgetary Subsidies in Central and Eastern European Economies in Transition', *Economic Systems*, **15** (2), pp. 149-176.

Holzmann, Robert (1992a), 'Die Neugestaltung des staatlichen Budgetwesens: Notwendigkeit und Erfahrungen in mittel- und osteuropäischen Ländern im Übergang', in Bernhard Gahlen, Helmut Hesse and Hans-Jürgen Ramser (eds), *Von der Plan- zur Marktwirtschaft*, Tübingen: Mohr, pp. 175-210.

Holzmann, Robert (1992b), 'Tax Reform in Countries in Transition: Central Policy Issues', *Public Finances/Finances Publiques*, **47** (S), pp. 233-255.

Hood, Christopher (1994), *Explaining Economic Policy Reversals*, Buckingham, Bristol: Open University Press.

Hussain, Athar and Nicholas Stern (1993), 'The Role of the State, Ownership and Taxation in Transitional Economics', *Economics of Transition*, **1** (1), pp. 61-87.

Hutchings, Raymond (1983), *The Soviet Budget*, Albany: State University of New York Press.

IMF (1995), 'Eastern Europe – Factors Underlying the Weakening Performance of Tax Revenues', *Economic Systems*, **19** (2), pp. 101-124.

IMF (2000), 'Republic of Poland: Staff Report for the 1999 Article IV Consultation', IMF, Staff Country Report No. 00/45, Washington, D.C.

Ivanova, Anna, Michael Keen and Alexander Klemm (2005), 'The Russian Flat Tax Reform', IMF, Working Paper No. 05/16, Washington.

Jessop, Bob (1993), 'Reflections on the Financial Crisis of the Postsocialist State', *International Journal of Political Economy*, **23** (2), pp. 9-34.

John, Christoph (1998), *Steuerpolitik im Transformationsprozeß: Eine ökonomische Analyse der ungarischen Güterbesteuerung*, München: ifo.

Johnson, John H. and Sulaiman S. Wasty (1993), 'Borrower Ownership of Adjustment Programs and the Political Economy of Reform', World Bank, Discussion Paper No. 199, Washington, D.C.

Johnson, Simon and Marzena Kowalska (1994), 'Poland: The Political Economy of Shock Therapy', in Stephan Haggard and Steven Webb (eds), *Voting for Reform: Democracy, Political Liberalization, and Economic Adjustment*, Oxford and New York: Oxford University Press, pp. 185-241.

Juchler, Jakob (1994), *Osteuropa im Umbruch. Politische, wirtschaftliche und gesellschaftliche Entwicklungen 1989-1993. Gesamtüberblick und Fallstudien*, Zürich: Seismo.

Kahler, Miles (1990), 'Orthodoxy and its Alternatives: Explaining Approaches to Stabilization and Adjustment', in Joan Nelson (ed.), *Economic Crisis and Policy Choice: The Politics of Adjustment in the Third World*, Princeton, N. J.: Princeton University Press, pp. 33-61.

Karl, Terry Lynn and Philippe C. Schmitter (1995), 'From an Iron Curtain to a Paper Curtain Grounding Transitologists or Students of Postcommunism?', *Slavic Review*, **54** (4), pp. 965-978.

Keeler, John T.S. (1993), 'Opening the Window for Reform. Mandates, Crises, and Extraordinary Policy-Making', *Comparative Political Studies*, **25** (4), pp. 433-486.

Keen, Michael and John King (2002), 'The Croatian Profit Tax: An ACE in Practice', *Fiscal Studies*, **23** (3), pp. 401-418.

Killick, Tony (with Ramandi Gunatilaka and Ana Marr) (1998), *Aid and the Political Economy of Policy Change*, London and New York: Routledge.

King, Charles (2000), 'Post-Postcommunism: Transition, Comparison, and the End of 'Eastern Europe'', *World Politics*, **53** (1), pp. 143-172.

King, Gary, Robert O. Keohane and Sidney Verby (1994), *Designing Social Inquiry. Scientific Inference in Qualitative Research*, Princeton, N.J.: Princeton University Press.

Kingdon, John W. (1995), *Agendas, Alternatives, and Public Policies*, 2nd. New York: HarperCollins.

Kiss, Gábor P. and György Szapáry (2000), 'Fiscal Adjustment in the Transition Process: Hungary, 1990-1999', *Post-Soviet Geography and Economics*, **41** (4), pp. 233-264.

Kitschelt, Herbert (2001), 'Constitutional Design and Postcommunist Economic Reform', in Jürgen Beyer, Jan Wielgohs and Helmut Wiesenthal (eds), *Successful Transitions: Political Factors of Socio-Economic Progress in Postsocialist Countries*, Baden-Baden: Nomos, pp. 40-63.

Kitschelt, Herbert (2003), 'Accounting for Postcommunist Regime Diversity: What Counts as a Good Cause?', in Grzegorz Ekiert and Stephen E. Hanson (eds), *Capitalism and Democracy in Central and Eastern Europe: Assessing the Legacy of Communist Rule*, Cambridge, UK: Cambridge University Press, pp. 49-88.

Kitschelt, Herbert (2004), 'Historische Pfadabhängigkeit oder Strategiewahl? Zur politischen Ökonomie postkommunistischer Wirtschaftsreform', in Jürgen Beyer and Petra Stykow (eds), *Gesellschaft mit beschränkter Hoffnung? Die ungewisse Aussichtslosigkeit rationaler Politik*, Wiesbaden: VS, pp. 87-115.

Kitschelt, Herbert, Zdenka Manfeldová, Radosław Markowski and Gábor Tóka (1999), *Post-Communist Party Systems: Competition, Representation, and Inter-Party Competition*, Cambridge, UK: Cambridge University Press.

Kočárník, Ivan (1992), 'The Problems of Fiscal Management in the CSFR in a Time of Transition', CERGE, Working Paper No. 14, Prague.

Kołodko, Grzegorz W. (1992), 'From Output Collapse to Sustainable Growth in Transition Economies: Fiscal Implications', IMF, Mimeo, Washington, D.C.

Kołodko, Grzegorz and D. Mario Nuti (1997), 'The Polish Alternative. Old Myths, Hard Facts and New Strategies in the Successful Transformation of the Polish Economy', UNU/WIDER, Research for Action 33, Helsinki.

Koltay, Jeno (1993), 'Tax Reform in Hungary', in Istvan Szekely, David M.G. Newbery (eds), *Hungary: An Economy in Transition*, Cambridge, UK: Cambridge University Press, pp. 249-270.

Kondratowicz, Andrzej and Marek Okolski (1993), 'The Polish Economy on the Eve of the Solidarity Take-over', in Henryk Kierzkowski, Marek Okolski and Stanisław Wellisz (eds), *Stabilization and Structural Adjustment in Poland*, London and New York: Routledge, pp. 7-28.

Kopits, George (1991), 'Fiscal Reforms in the European Economies in Transition', in Paul Marer and Salvatore Zecchini (eds), *The Transition to a Market Economy, Vol. 2: Special Issues*, Paris: OECD, pp. 359-388.

Kornai, János (1990), *The Road to a Free Economy. Shifting from a Socialist System: The Example of Hungary*, New York and London: Norton.

Kornai, János (1992a), 'The Postsocialist Transition and the State: Reflections in the Light of Hungarian Fiscal Problems', *American Economic Review*, **82** (2), pp. 1-21.

Kornai, János (1992b), *The Socialist System: The Political Economy of Communism*, Princeton, N.J.: Princeton University Press.

Kornai, János (1994), 'Transformational Recession: The Main Causes', *Journal of Comparative Economics*, **19** (1), pp. 39-63.

Kornai, János (1996), 'Paying the Bill for Goulash Communism: Hungarian Development and Macro-Stabilization in a Political Economy Perspective', *Social Research*, **63** (4), pp. 943-1040. Reprinted in idem, *Struggle and Hope: Essays on Stabilization and Reform in a Post-Socialist Economy*, Cheltenham, UK and Lyme, US: Edward Elgar 1997, pp. 121-179.

Kornai, János (1997), 'Adjustment without Recession: A Case Study of Hungarian Stabilization', in Salvatore Zecchini (ed.), *Lessons from the Economic Transition. Central and Eastern Europe in the 1990s*, Dordrecht, Boston and London: Kluwer and OECD, pp. 123-151.

Kosta, Jiří (1997), 'Die ökonomische Transformationsstrategie Tschechiens im Vergleich zur Slowakei, Ungarn und Polen', WZB, Discussion Paper FS II 97-602, Berlin.

Kregel, Jan, Egon Matzner and Gernot Grabher (eds) (1992), *The Market Shock: An Agenda for Socio-Economic Reconstruction of Central and Eastern Europe*, Vienna: Austrian Academy of Sciences, Research Unit for Socio-Economics.

Kroupa, Ales and Tomás Kostelecky (1996), 'Party Organization and Structure at National and Local Level in the Czech Republic Since 1989', in Paul G. Lewis (ed.), *Party Structure and Organization in East-Central Europe*, Cheltenham, UK and Brookfield, US: Edward Elgar, pp. 89-119.

Krueger, Anne O. (1993), *Political Economy of Policy Reform in Developing Countries*, Cambridge, Mass. And London: MIT Press.

Kupka, Martin, Zdenek Tůma and Jozef Zieleniec (1993), 'Czecho-Slovak Survey', in Jan Winiecki and Andrzej Kondratowicz (eds), *The Macroeconomics of Transition. Developments in East Central Europe*, London and New York: Routledge, pp. 43-61.

Kurtán, Sándor (1994), 'Politische Stabilität und Konfliktregulierung durch Parteien in Ungarn', in Dieter Segert (ed.), *Konfliktregulierung durch Parteien und politische Stabilität in Ostmitteleuropa*, Frankfurt, M. et al.: Lang, pp. 115-129.

Lang, Joachim (1993), *Entwurf eines Steuergesetzbuchs*, Bonn: Bundesministerium der Finanzen.

Lang, Joachim (1999), 'The Concept of a Tax Code', in Manfred Rose (ed.), *Tax Reform for Countries in Transition to Market Economies*, Stuttgart: Lucius & Lucius, pp. 185-195.

Laski, Kazimierz (1993), 'Fiscal Policy and Effective Demand During Transformation', WIIW, Research Report No. 189, Vienna.

Laski, Kazimierz and Amit Bhaduri (1997), 'Lessons To Be Drawn from Main Mistakes in the Transition Strategy', in Salvatore Zecchini (ed.), *Lessons from the Economic Transition. Central and Eastern Europe in the 1990s*, Dordrecht, Boston and London: Kluwer and OECD, pp. 103-121.

Laski, Kazimierz and Leon Podkaminer (1995), 'Issues in Fiscal Policy, Inflation and Public Debt', WIIW, Research Report No. 223, Vienna.

Lengyel, László (1991), 'Nineteen ninety-one', in Sándor Kurtán, Péter Sándor, László Vass (eds), *Magyarország Politikai Évkönyve (Hungarian Political Yearbook) 1991*, Budapest: Demokrácia Kutatások Magyar Központja Alapítvány, pp. 35-45.

Lengyel, László (1995), 'The Mousetrap', in Csaba Gombár, Elemér Hankiss, László Lengyel and Györgyi Várnai (eds), *Question Marks: The Hungarian Government 1994-1995*, Budapest: Korridor, pp. 13-51.

Lenin, Vladimir I. (1965), *Collected Works, Vol. 27: February-July 1918*, Moscow: Progress Publishers.

Levitsky, Steven, Lucan A. Way (1998), 'Between a Shock and a Hard Place: The Dynamics of Labor-Backed Adjustment in Poland and Argentina', *Comparative Politics*, **30** (2), pp. 171-192.

Lichnovská, Marie, Dana Dluhosová and Eva Kociánová (1994), 'Transformations of Post-Communist Fiscal System in the Czech Republic', in John L. Campbell and Stanisław Owsiak (eds), *Fiscal Reforms in Post-Communist Countries*, Cracow: Cracow Academy of Economics, pp. 121-143.

Lindauer, David L. and Ann D. Velenchik (1992), 'Government Spending in Developing Countries: Trends, Causes, and Consequences', *World Bank Research Observer*, **7** (1), pp. 59-78.

Lindenberg, Marc and Shantayanan Devarajan (1993), 'Prescribing Strong Medicine. Revisiting the Myths about Structural Adjustment, Democracy, and Economic Performance in Developing Countries', *Comparative Politics*, **25** (2), pp. 169-182.

Linz, Juan J. and Alfred Stepan (1996), *Problems of Democratic Transition and Consolidation. Southern Europe, South America, and Post-Communist Europe*, Baltimore and London: Johns Hopkins University Press.

Lipton, David and Jeffrey Sachs (1990), 'Creating a Market Economy in Eastern Europe: The Case of Poland', *Brookings Papers on Economic Activity*, (1), pp. 75-147.

Little, Ian M.D., Richard N. Cooper, W. Max Corden and Sarath Rajapatirana (1993), *Boom, Crisis, and Adjustment. The Macroeconomic Experience of Developing Countries*, New York: Oxford University Press.

Lora, Eduardo (2000), 'What Makes Reforms Likely? Timing and Sequencing of Structural Reforms in Latin America', Inter-American Development Bank, Research Department, Working Paper No. 424, Washington, D.C.

Lorie, Henrie (2003), 'Priorities for Further Fiscal Reforms in the Commonwealth of Independent States', IMF, Working Paper WP 03/209, Washington, D.C.

Lutz, Mark S. and Thomas H. Krueger (1995), 'Developments and Challenges in Hungary', in Biswajit Banerjee et al., 'Road Maps of the Transition. The Baltics, the Czech Republic, Hungary and Russia', IMF, Occasional Paper No. 127, Washington, D.C., pp. 36-52.

Mackenzie, G.A., David W.H. Orsmond and Philip R. Gerson (1997), 'The Composition of Fiscal Adjustment and Growth. Lessons from Fiscal Reforms in Eight Countries', IMF, Occasional Paper No. 149, Washington, D.C.

Maggs, Peter B. (1979), 'Characteristics of Soviet Tax and Budgetary Law', in Donald G. Barry, F.J.M. Feldbrugge, George Ginsburgs and Peter M. Maggs (eds), *Soviet Law After Stalin III*, Alphen aan den Rijn and Germantown, MD: Sijthoff & Noordhoff, pp. 93-121.

Maravall, José María (1993), 'Politics and Policy: Economic Reforms in Southern Europe', in Luiz Carlos Bresser Pereira, José María Maravall and Adam Przeworski, *Economic Reforms in New Democracies. A Social-Democratic Approach*, Cambridge, UK: Cambridge University Press, pp. 77-131.

Maravall, José María (1994), 'The Myth of Authoritarian Advantage', *Journal of Democracy*, **5** (4), pp. 17-31.

Maravall, José María (1997), *Regimes, Politics and Markets. Democratization and Economic Change in Southern and Eastern Europe*, Oxford and New York: Oxford University Press.

Marer, Paul (1999), 'Economic Transformation, 1990-1998', in Aurel Braun, and Zoltan Barany (eds), *Dilemmas of Transition: The Hungarian Experience*, Lanham, MD et al.: Rowman & Littlefield, pp. 157-201.

Martin, Peter (1990), '"Scenario for Economic Reform" Adopted', *Report on Eastern Europe*, **1** (42), pp. 5-8.

Martin, Peter (1991), 'The 1991 Budget: Hard Times Ahead', *Report on Eastern Europe*, **2** (9), pp. 12-16.

Martinelli, César and Mariano Tommasi (1997), 'Sequencing of Economic Reforms in the Presence of Political Constraints', *Economics and Politics*, **9** (2), pp. 115-131.

McDermott, C. John and Robert F. Wescott (1996), 'An Empirical Analysis of Fiscal Adjustments', *IMF Staff Papers*, **43** (4), pp. 725-753.

McKinnon, Ronald I. (1993), *The Order of Economic Liberalization. Financial Control in the Transition to a Market Economy*, 2nd ed. Baltimore and London: Johns Hopkins University Press.

McLure, Charles E. (1992), 'A Simpler Consumption-Based Alternative to the Income Tax for Socialist Economies in Transition', *World Bank Research Observer*, **7** (2), pp. 221-237.

McLure, Charles, et al. (1995), *Tax Policy in Central Europe*, San Francisco: International Center for Economic Growth.

Michta, Andrew A. (1997), 'Democratic Consolidation in Poland after 1989', in Karen Dawisha and Bruce Parrott (eds), *Democratization and Authoritarianism in Postcommunist Societies, Vol. 1: The Consolidation of Democracy in East-Central Europe*, Cambridge, UK: Cambridge University Press, pp. 66-108.

Milesi-Ferretti, Gian Maria (1997), 'Fiscal Rules and Budget Process', CEPR, Discussion Paper No. 1664, London.

Ministry of Finance (2003), 'Budgetary Outlook, 2003-2006: Concept of Public Budget Reforms', Prague.

Mizsei, Kálmán (ed.) (1994), *Developing Public Finance in Emerging Market Economies*, Prague et al.: Institute for EastWest Studies.

Mizsei, Kálmán and Jacek Rostowski (1994), 'Fiscal Crises During Economic Transition in East Central Europe: An Overview', in Kálmán Mizsei (ed.), *Developing Public Finance in Emerging Market Economies*, Prague et al.: Institute for EastWest Studies, pp. 1-17.

Morales, Juan Antonio (1996), 'Economic Policy after the Transition to Democracy: A Synthesis', in Juan Antonio Morales and Gary McMahon (eds), *Economic Policy and the Transition to Democracy. The Latin American Experiment*, Basingstoke and London: Macmillan, pp. 1-29.

Müller, Katharina (1999), *The Political Economy of Pension Reform in Central-Eastern Europe*, Cheltenham, UK and Lyme, US: Edward Elgar.

Müller, Katharina (2003), *Privatising Old-Age Security: Latin America and Eastern Europe Compared*, Cheltenham, UK and Lyme, US: Edward Elgar.

Munich, Daniel and Vit Sorm (1996), 'The Czech Republic as a Low-Unemployment Oasis', *Transition*, **2** (13), pp. 21-25.

Muraközy, L. (1989), 'What Is the Hungarian Budget Like?', *Acta Oeconomica*, **41** (1/2), pp. 212-236.

Musgrave, Richard A. (1969), *Fiscal Systems*, New Haven/London: Yale University Press.

Musgrave, Robert (1991), 'Tax Policy for the Transition', in OECD (ed.), *The Role of Tax Reform in Central and Eastern European Countries*, Paris: OECD, pp. 35-40.

Mutén, Leif (1992), 'Income Tax Reform', in Vito Tanzi (ed.), *Fiscal Policies in Economies in Transition*, Washington, D.C.: IMF, pp. 166-187.

Myant, Martin (1989), *The Czechoslovak Economy 1948-1988: The Battle for Economic Reform*, Cambridge, UK: Cambridge University Press.

Myant, Martin (1993), *Transforming Socialist Economies. The Case of Poland and Czechoslovakia*, Aldershot, UK and Brookfield, US: Edward Elgar.

Myant, Martin (2003), *The Rise and Fall of Czech Capitalism: Economic Development in the Czech Republic since 1989*, Cheltenham, UK and Lyme, US: Edward Elgar.

NBH (1990), *Annual Report*, Budapest.

NBH (1991), *Annual Report*, Budapest.

NBH (1992), *Annual Report*, Budapest.

Nelson, Joan M. (ed.) (1990), *Economic Crisis and Policy Choice: The Politics of Adjustment in the Third World*, Princeton, N. J.: Princeton University Press.

Nelson, Joan M. (1993), 'The Politics of Economic Transformation. Is Third World Experience Relevant in Eastern Europe?', *World Politics*, **45** (3), pp. 433-463.

Nelson, Joan M. (1997), 'Social Costs, Social-Sector Reforms, and Politics in Post-Communist Transformations', in idem, Charles Tilly and Lee Walker (eds), *Transforming Post-Communist Political Economies*, Washington, D.C.: National Academy Press, pp. 247-271.

Nelson, Joan M. (2001), 'The Politics of Pension and Health-Care Reforms in Hungary and Poland', in János Kornai, Stephan Haggard and Robert R. Kaufman (eds), *Reforming the State: Fiscal and Welfare Reform in Post-Socialist Countries*, Cambridge, UK: Cambridge University Press, pp. 235-266.

Nelson, Joan et al. (1989), *Fragile Coalitions: The Politics of Economic Adjustment*, New Brunswick and Oxford: Transaction Books.

Newbery, David M.G. (1991), 'An Analysis of the Hungarian Tax Reform', CEPR, Discussion Paper No. 558, London.

Newbery, David M.G. (1995), 'Tax and Benefit Reform in Central and Eastern Europe', in David M.G. Newbery (ed.), *Tax and Benefit Reform in Central and Eastern Europe*, London: CEPR, pp. 1-18.

Newcity, Michael A. (1986), *Taxation in the Soviet Union*, New York, Westport and London: Praeger.

Nove, Alec (1977), *The Soviet Economic System*, London: Allen & Unwin.

Oberhauser, Alois (1993), 'Public Finance and the Transformation Process to Market Economies in the Countries of Eastern Europe', in Takashi Matsugi and Alois Oberhauser (eds), *Adjustments of Economics and Enterprise in a Changing World*, Berlin: Duncker & Humblot, pp. 33-44.

Obrman, Jan and Jiří Pehe (1990), 'Difficult Power-sharing Talks', *Report on Eastern Europe*, **1** (49), pp. 5-9.

OECD (1991a), *Czech and Slovak Federal Republic: Economic Survey*, Paris.

OECD (1991b), *Hungary: Economic Survey*, Paris.

OECD (1992), *Poland: Economic Survey*, Paris.

OECD (ed.) (1993), *Hungary: Economic Survey*, Paris.

OECD (1994), *Poland: Economic Survey*, Paris.

OECD (1995), *Hungary: Economic Survey*, Paris.

OECD (1996), *The Czech Republic: Economic Survey*, Paris.

OECD (1997), *Hungary: Economic Survey*, Paris.

OECD (1998), *Poland: Economic Survey*, Paris.

OECD (1999), *Hungary: Economic Survey*, Paris.

OECD (2000a), *Poland: Economic Survey*, Paris.

OECD (2000b), *Hungary: Economic Survey*, Paris.

OECD (2004), *Hungary: Economic Survey*, Paris.

OECD (2005a), *Hungary: Economic Survey*, Paris.

OECD (2005b), *Czech Republic: Economic Survey*, Paris.

Ofer, Gur (1989), 'Budget Deficit, Market Disequilibrium and Soviet Economic Reforms', *Soviet Economy*, **5** (2), pp. 107-161.

Offe, Claus (1991), 'Capitalism by Democratic Design? Democratic Theory Facing the Triple Transition in East Central Europe', *Social Research*, **58** (4), pp. 865-892.

Offe, Claus (1996), *Varieties of Transition: The East European and East German Experience*, Cambridge, UK: Polity Press.

Okolicsanyi, Karoly (1991), 'The Antall Government's First Budget', *Report on Eastern Europe*, **2** (5), pp. 15-19.

Okolicsanyi, Karoly (1992), 'The Hungarian Budget Deficit', *RFE/RL Research Report*, **1** (29), pp. 53-55.

Okolicsanyi, Karoly (1993), 'Hungary's Budget Deficit', *RFE/RL Research Report*, **2** (37), pp. 42-45.

Olson, David M. (1996), 'The Czech Senate: From Constitutional Inducement to Electoral Challenge', *East European Constitutional Review*, **5** (4), pp. 47-50.

Olson, David M. (1997), 'Democratization and Political Participation: the Experience of the Czech Republic', in Karen Dawisha and Bruce Parrot (eds), *Democratization and Authoritarianism in Postcommunist Societies, Vol. 1: The Consolidation of Democracy in East-Central Europe*, Cambridge, UK: Cambridge University Press, pp. 150-196.

Olson, Mancur (1965), *The Logic of Collective Action: Public Goods and the Theory of Groups*, Cambridge, Mass. and London: Harvard University Press.

Orenstein, Mitchell (1994), 'The Political Success of Neo-Liberalism in the Czech Republic', CERGE, Working Paper No. 68, Prague.

Orenstein, Mitchell (1996), 'The Failures of Neo-Liberal Social Policy', *Transition*, **2** (13), pp. 16-20.

Orenstein, Mitchell (1998), 'Václav Klaus: Revolutionary and Parliamentarian', *East European Politics and Societies*, **7** (1), pp. 46-55.

Orenstein, Mitchell (2000), 'How Politics and Institutions Affect Pension Reform in Three Postcommunist Countries', World Bank, Policy Research Working Paper No. 2310, Washington, D.C.

Orosz, Éva, Guy Ellena and Melitta Jakab (1998), 'Reforming the Health Care System: The Unfinished Agenda', in Lajos Bokros and Jean-Jacques Dethier (eds), *Public Finance Reform during the Transition: The Experience of Hungary*, Washington, D.C.: World Bank, pp. 211-253.

Owens, Jeffrey (1991), 'Financing Public Expenditure: The Role of Tax Reform and the Design of Tax Systems', in Paul Marer and Salvatore Zecchini (eds), *The Transition to a Market Economy, Vol. 2: Special Issues*, Paris: OECD, pp. 317-358.

Owsiak, Stanisław (1994), 'Transformations of Fiscal Systems in Post-Communist Countries: The Polish Case', in John L. Campbell and Stanisław Owsiak (eds), *Fiscal Reforms in Post-Communist Countries*, Craców: Craców Academy of Economics, pp. 241-269.

Padovano, Fabio (1991), 'The Budget Deficit in the Soviet Economic System: Origins and Perspectives', *Economia delle scelte pubbliche*, **9** (1), pp. 41-56.

Pamp, Oliver (2004), 'Partisan Preferences and Political Institutions: Explaining Fiscal Retrenchment in the European Union', FU Berlin, Ezoneplus Working Paper No. 24, Berlin.

Pataki, Judith (1993), 'Hungarian Government Signs Social Contract with Unions', *RFE/RL Research Report*, **2** (5), pp. 42-45.

Pehe, Jiří (1996), 'Elections Result in Surprise Stalemate', *Transition*, **2** (13), 36f.

Pehe, Jiří (1997), 'Czechs Fall From Their Ivory Tower', *Transitions*, **4** (3), pp. 22-27.

Perotti, Roberto (1996), 'Fiscal Consolidation in Europe: Composition Matters', *American Economic Review*, **86** (2), pp. 105-110.

Perotti, Roberto (1998), 'The Political Economy of Fiscal Consolidations', *Scandinavian Journal of Economics*, **100** (1), pp. 367-394.

Perotti, Roberto, Rolf Strauch and Jürgen von Hagen (1997), 'Sustainability of Public Finances', CEPR, Discussion Paper No. 1781, London.

Persson, Torsten and Lars E.O. Svensson (1989), 'Why a Stubborn Conservative Would Run a Deficit: Policy with Time-Inconsistent Preferences', *Quarterly Journal of Economics*, **104** (2), pp. 325-346.

Persson, Torsten and Guido Tabellini (2000), *Political Economics: Explaining Economic Policy*, Cambridge, Mass. and London: MIT Press.

Persson, Torsten and Guido Tabellini (2004), 'Constitutions and Economic Policy', *Journal of Economic Perspectives*, **18** (1), pp. 75-98.

Peters, B. Guy (1991), *The Politics of Taxation. A Comparative Perspective*, Cambridge, Mass. and Oxford: Blackwell.

Petri, Martin, Günther Taube and Aleh Tsyvinski (2002), 'Energy Sector Quasi-Fiscal Activities in the Countries of the Former Soviet Union', IMF, WP/02/60, Washington, D.C.

Pierson, Paul (1994), *Dismantling the Welfare State? Reagan, Thatcher, and the Politics of Retrenchment*, Cambridge, UK: Cambridge University Press.

Pierson, Paul (2000), 'Increasing Returns, Path Dependence, and the Study of Politics', *American Political Science Review*, **94** (2), pp. 251-267.

Pirttilä, Jukka (2001), 'Fiscal Policy and Structural Reforms in Transition Economies', *Economics of Transition*, **9** (1), pp. 29-52.

Pitlik, Hans and Steffen Wirth (2003), 'Do Crises Promote the Extent of Economic Liberalization? An Empirical Test', *European Journal of Political Economy*, **19** (3), pp. 565-581.

Pitruzzello, Salvatore (1997), 'Social Policy and the Implementation of the Maastricht Fiscal Convergence Criteria: The Italian and French Attempts at Welfare and Pension Reforms', *Social Research*, **64** (4), pp. 1590-1642.

Premchand, A. and L. Garamfalvi (1992), 'Government Budget and Accounting Systems', in Vito Tanzi (ed.), *Fiscal Policies in Economies in Transition*, Washington, D.C.: IMF, pp. 268-290.

Pryor, Frederic L. (1968), *Public Expenditures in Communist and Capitalist Nations*, London: Allen and Unwin.

Przeworski, Adam (1991), *Democracy and the Market. Political and Economic Reforms in Eastern Europe and Latin America*, Cambridge, UK: Cambridge University Press.

Przeworski, Adam (1993), 'Economic Reforms, Public Opinion, and Political Institutions: Poland in the Eastern European Perspective', in Luiz Carlos Bresser Pereira, José María Maravall and Adam Przeworski (eds), *Economic Reforms in New Democracies. A Social-Democratic Approach*, Cambridge, UK: Cambridge University Press, pp. 132-198.

Przeworski, Adam (1996), 'Public Support for Economic Reform in Poland', *Comparative Political Studies*, **29** (5), pp. 520-543.

Przeworski, Adam and Fernando Limongi (1993), 'Political Regimes and Economic Growth', *Journal of Economic Perspectives*, **7** (3), pp. 51-69.

Przeworski, Adam, et al. (1995), *Sustainable Democracy*, Cambridge, UK: Cambridge University Press.

Raiser, Martin (1994), 'Ein tschechisches Wunder? Zur Rolle politikinduzierter Anreizstrukturen im Transformationsprozeß', Institut für Weltwirtschaft, Kieler Diskussionsbeitrag Nr. 233, Kiel.

Ram, Rati (1987), 'Wagner's Hypothesis in Time-Series and Cross-Section Perspectives: Evidence from 'Real' Data for 115 Countries', *Review of Economics and Statistics*, **69** (2), pp. 194-204.

Ranis, Gustav and Syed Akhtar Mahmood (1992), *The Political Economy of Development Policy Change*, Cambridge, Mass. and Oxford: Blackwell.

Remmer, Karen L. (1990), 'Democracy and Economic Crisis: The Latin American Experience', *World Politics*, **42** (3), pp. 315-335.

Remmer, Karen L. (1993), 'The Political Economy of Elections in Latin America, 1980-1991', *American Political Science Review*, **87** (2), pp. 393-407.

Rhodes, Martin (2002), 'Why EMU Is – or May Be – Good for European Welfare States', in Kenneth Dyson (ed.), *European States and the Euro: Europeanization, Variation, and Convergence*, Oxford: Oxford University Press, pp. 305-333.

Roberts, Andrew (2003), 'Demythologising the Czech Opposition Agreement', *Europe-Asia Studies*, **55** (8), pp. 1273-1303.

Rodrik, Dani (1989), 'Promises, Promises: Credible Policy Reform Via Signalling', *Economic Journal*, **99** (3), pp. 756-772.

Rodrik, Dani (1993), 'The Positive Economics of Policy Reform', *American Economic Review*, **83** (2), pp. 356-361.

Rodrik, Dani (1994), 'Comment', in John Williamson (ed.), *The Political Economy of Policy Reform*, Washington, D.C.: Institute for International Economics, pp. 212-215.

Rodrik, Dani (1996), 'Understanding Economic Policy Reform', *Journal of Economic Literature*, **34** (1), pp. 9-41.

Roland, Gérard (2000), *Transition and Economics: Politics, Markets, and Firms*, Cambridge, Mass. and London: MIT Press.

Roland, Gérard (2002), 'The Political Economy of Transition', *Journal of Economic Perspectives*, **16** (1), pp. 29-50.

Rose, Amanda (1999a), 'Extraordinary Politics in the Polish Transition', *Communist and Post-Communist Studies*, **32** (2), 195-210.

Rose, Manfred (1999b), 'Recommendations on Taxing Income for Countries in Transition to Market Economies', in idem (ed.), *Tax Reform for Countries in Transition to Market Economies*, Stuttgart: Lucius & Lucius, pp. 23-62.

Rosenbaum, Eckehard F., Frank Bönker and Hans-Jürgen Wagener (2000), 'Privatization in Context: An Introduction', in Eckehard F. Rosenbaum, Frank Bönker and Hans-Jürgen Wagener (eds), *Privatization, Corporate Governance and the Emergence of Markets*, Basingstoke and London: Macmillan, pp. 1-13.

Ross, Fiona (1997), 'Cutting Public Expenditures in Advanced Industrial Democracies: The Importance of Avoiding Blame', *Governance*, **10** (2), pp. 175-200.

Roubini, Nouriel (1991), 'Economic and Political Determinants of Budget Deficits in Developing Countries', *Journal of International Money and Finance*, **10**, pp. S49-S72.

Roubini, Nouriel and Jeffrey Sachs (1989a), 'Political and Economic Determinants of Budget Deficits in the Industrial Countries', *European Economic Review*, **33**, pp. 903-938.

Roubini, Nouriel and Jeffrey Sachs (1989b), 'Government Spending and Budget Deficits in the Industrial Countries', *Economic Policy*, **8**, pp. 100-132.

Ruggiero, Edgardo (1998), 'Reform of Public Finances, 1994-1997', in Carlo Cottarelli et al., 'Economic Policies for Sustainable Growth', IMF, Occasional Paper No. 159, Washington, D.C.: IMF, pp. 31-47 .

Rutland, Peter (1993), 'Thatcherism, Czech-Style: Transition to Capitalism in the Czech Republic', *Telos*, **94**, pp. 103-129.

Sachs, Jeffrey D. (1993), *Poland's Jump to the Market Economy*, Cambridge/Mass. and London: MIT Press.

Sachs, Jeffrey (1994), 'Life in the Economic Emergency Room', in John Williamson (ed.), *The Political Economy of Policy Reform*, Washington, D.C.: Institute for International Economics, pp. 503-523.

Sachs, Jeffrey D. (1996), 'The Transition at Mid Decade', *American Economic Review*, **86** (2), pp. 128-133.

Sajó, András (1996), 'How the Rule of Law Killed Hungarian Welfare Reform', *East European Constitutional Review*, **5** (1), pp. 31-41.

Sakamoto, Takyuki (2001), 'Effects of Government Characteristics on Fiscal Deficits in 18 OECD Countries, 1961-1994', *Comparative Political Studies*, **34** (5), pp. 527-544.

Sandford, Cedric (1993), *Successful Tax Reforms: Lessons from an Analysis of Tax Reform in Six Countries*, Bath: Fiscal Publications.

Saxonberg, Steven (1999), 'Václav Klaus: The Rise and Fall and Re-emergence of a Charismatic Leader', *East European Politics and Societies*, **13** (2), pp. 391-418.

Schaffer, Mark E. (1992a), 'The Polish State-Owned Enterprise Sector and the Recession of 1990', *Comparative Economic Studies*, **34** (1), pp. 58-85.

Schaffer, Mark (1992b), 'The Enterprise Sector and Emergence of the Polish Fiscal Crisis 1990-91', World Bank, Country Economics Department, Transition and Macro-Adjustment Division, Research Paper No. 31, Washington, D.C.

Schaffer, Mark (1995), 'Government Subsidies to Enterprises in Central and Eastern Europe: Budgetary Subsidies and Tax Arrears', in David M.G. Newbery (ed.), *Tax and Benefit Reform in Central and Eastern Europe*, London: CEPR, pp. 115-144.

Schamis, Hector E. (2002), *Re-Forming the State: The Politics of Privatization in Latin America and Europe*, Ann Arbor: University of Michigan Press.

Scharpf, Fritz W. (1991), *Crisis and Choice in European Social Democracy*, Ithaca, N.Y. and London: Cornell University Press.

Schmitter, Philippe C. (1996), 'The Influence of the International Context Upon the Choice of National Institutions and Policies in Neo-Democracies', in Laurence Whitehead (ed.), *The International Dimension of Democratization. Europe and the Americas*, Oxford and New York: Oxford University Press, pp. 26-54.

Schmitter, Philippe C. and Terry Lynn Karl (1994), 'The Conceptual Travels of Transitologists and Considologists: How Far to the East Should They Attempt to Go?', *Slavic Review*, **53** (1), pp. 173-185.

Schroeder, Gertrude E. and John S. Pitzer (1983), 'The USSR and Eastern Europe I', in Charles L. Taylor (ed.), *Why Governments Grow. Measuring Public Sector Size*, Beverly Hills, London and New Delhi: Sage, pp. 97-116.

Schuknecht, Ludger (1996), 'Political Business Cycles and Fiscal Policies in Developing Coutries', *Kyklos*, **49** (2), pp. 155-170.

Schumpeter, Joseph A. (1918), 'The Crisis of the Tax State', in Richard Swedberg (ed.), *Joseph A. Schumpeter: The Economics and Sociology of Capitalism*, Princeton, N.J.: Princeton University Press 1991, pp. 99-140.

Schwartz, Gerd (1994), 'Public Finance', in Liam P. Ebrill et al., Poland: The Path to a Market Economy, IMF, Occasional Paper No. 113, Washington, D.C., pp. 7-22.

Semjén, András (1995), 'Tax Policies in Hungary', in Charles McLure et al., *Tax Policy in Central Europe*, San Francisco: International Center for Economic Growth, pp. 19-87.

Shi, Min and Jakob Svensson (2002a), 'Conditional Political Budget Cycles', CEPR, Discussion Paper No. 3352, London.

Shi, Min and Jakob Svensson (2002b), Political Budget Cycles in Developed and Developing Countries, Mimeo, Stockholm.

Shleifer, Andrei and Daniel Treisman (2000), *Without a Map: Political Tactics and Economic Reform in Russia*, Cambridge, Mass. and London, England: MIT Press.

Siermann, Clemens L.J. (1998), *Politics, Institutions and the Economic Performance of Nations*, Cheltenham, UK and Lyme, US: Edward Elgar.

Siermann, Clemens L.J. and Jakob de Haan (1993), 'On Sustainability and Political Determinants of Government Debt in Developing Countries', *International Review of Economics and Business*, **40** (1), pp. 81-92.

Sipos, Sándor and István G. Tóth (1998), 'Poverty Alleviation: Social Assistance and Family Benefits', in Lajos Bokros and Jean-Jacques Dethier (eds), *Public Finance Reform during the Transition: The Experience of Hungary*, Washington, D.C.: The World Bank, pp. 287-316.

Slay, Ben (1992), 'The Polish Economy: Between Recession and Recovery', *RFE/RL Research Report*, **1** (36), pp. 49-57.

Stallings, Barbara (1992), 'International Influence on Economic Policy: Debt, Stabilization, and Structural Reform', in Stephan Haggard and Robert R. Kaufman (eds), *The Politics of Economic Adjustment*, Princeton, N.J.: Princeton University Press, pp. 41-88.

Stark, David and László Bruszt (1998), *Postsocialist Pathways. Transforming Politics and Property in East Central Europe*, Cambridge: Cambridge University Press.

Stein, Ernesto, Ernesto Talvi and Alejandro Grisanti (1999), 'Institutional Arrangements and Fiscal Performance: The Latin American Experience', in James M. Poterba and Jürgen von Hagen (eds), *Fiscal Institutions and Fiscal Performance*, Chicago, IL and London: University of Chicago Press, pp. 103-133.

Štěpánek, Pavel, Milena Horcicova, Vera Kamenickova, Vera Uldrichova and Drahomira Vaskova (1995), 'Fiscal Policy in the Czech Republic under Transition', CASE, Studies & Analyses, No. 51, Warsaw.

Stepanyan, Vahram (2003), 'Reforming the Tax System: Experiences of the Baltics, Russia and Other Countries of the Former Soviet Union States', IMF, Working Paper WP 03/03, Washington, D.C.

Stokes, Susan C. (2001), *Mandates and Democracy: Neoliberalism by Surprise in Latin America*, Cambridge, UK: Cambridge University Press.

Stone, Randall W. (2002), *Lending Credibility: The International Monetary Fund and the Post-Communist Transition*, Princeton, N.J. and Oxford: Princeton University Press.

Straussman, Jeffrey D. (1993), 'Ideals and Reality in the Evolution of Fiscal Reform in Central and Eastern Europe', *Public Budgeting and Finance*, **16** (2), pp. 79-95.

Sturzenegger, Federico and Mariano Tommasi (eds) (1998), *The Political Economy of Reform*, Cambridge, Mass. and London: MIT Press.

Svejnar, Jan (1993), 'Czech and Slovak Federal Republic: A Solid Foundation', in Richard Portes (ed.), *Economic Transformation in Central Europe. A Progress Report*, London: CEPR, pp. 21-57.

Svitek, Ivan (1992a), 'The 1992 State Budgets in Czechoslovakia', *RFE/RL Research Report*, **1** (9), pp. 34-37.

Svitek, Ivan (1992b), 'The Czechoslovak Tax Reform of 1993', *RFE/RL Research Report*, **1** (24), pp. 38-41.

Szamuely, László and László Casba (1998), 'Economics and System Change in Hungary, 1945-96', in Hans-Jürgen Wagener (ed.), *Economic Thought in Communist and Post-Communist Europe*, London and New York: Routledge, pp. 158-212.

Szarvas, László (1995), 'Parties and Party Factions in the Hungarian Parliament', in Terry Cox and Andy Furlong (eds), *Hungary: The Politics of Transition*, London: Cass, pp. 120-136.

Szilagyi, Zsofia (1995), 'A Year of Economic Controversy', *Transition*, **1** (21), pp. 62-66.

Szilagyi, Zsofia (1996), 'Slowing the Pace of Economic Reform', *Transition*, **2** (20), pp. 40-44.

Tait, Alan (1991), 'Designing a VAT in Central and Eastern Europe', in OECD (ed.), *The Role of Tax Reform in Central and Eastern European Countries*, Paris: OECD, pp. 203-218.

Tait, Alan A. (1992), 'Introducing Value-Added Taxes', in Vito Tanzi (ed.), *Fiscal Policies in Economies in Transition*, Washington, D.C.: IMF, pp. 188-208.

Tanzi, Vito (1991a), 'Fiscal Issues in Economies in Transition', in Vittorio Corbo, Fabrizio Coricelli and Jan Bossak (eds), *Reforming Central and Eastern European Economies: Initial Results and Challenges*, Washington D.C.: World Bank, pp. 221-228.

Tanzi, Vito (1991b), 'Tax Reform and the Move to a Market Economy: Overview of the Issues', in OECD (ed.), *The Role of Tax Reform in Central and Eastern European Countries*, Paris: OECD, pp. 19-34.

Tanzi, Vito (1993a), 'Financial Markets and Public Finance in the Transformation Process', in idem (ed.), *Transition to Market. Studies in Fiscal Reform*, Wshington, D.C.: IMF, pp. 1-28.

Tanzi, Vito (1993b), 'The Budget Deficit in Transition', *IMF Staff Papers*, **40** (3), pp. 697-707.

Tanzi, Vito (1994), 'Reforming Public Finances in Economies in Transition', *International Tax and Public Finance*, **1** (2), pp. 149-163.

Tanzi, Vito (1996), 'Fiscal Developments: An Overview', *Moct-Most*, **6** (3), pp. 1-5.

Tanzi, Vito (1997), 'Economic Transformation and the Policies for Long-Term Growth', in Mario I. Blejer and Marko Skreb (eds), *Macroeconomic Stabilization in Transition Economies*, Cambridge, UK: Cambridge University Press, pp. 313-326.

Tanzi, Vito (1998), 'Essential Fiscal Institutions in Selected Economies in Transition', Collegium Budapest, Discussion Paper No. 53, Budapest.

Tanzi, Vito (2001), 'Creating Effective Tax Administrations: The Experience of Russia and Georgia', in János Kornai, Stephan Haggard and Robert R. Kaufman (eds), *Reforming the State: Fiscal and Welfare Reform in Post-Socialist Countries*, Cambridge, UK: Cambridge University Press, pp. 53-74.

Tanzi, Vito and George Tsibouris (2000), 'Fiscal Reform over Ten Years of Transition', IMF, Working Paper WP/00/113, Washington, D.C.

Tanzi, Vito and George Tsibouris (2001), 'Transition and the Changing Role of Government', in Oleh Havrylyshyn and Saleh M. Nsouli (eds), *A Decade of Transition: Achievements and Challenges*, Washington, D.C.: IMF, pp. 229-250.

Ter-Minassian, Teresa, Pedro P. Parente and Pedro Martinez-Mendez (1995), 'Setting up a Treasury in Economies in Transition', IMF, Working Paper WP/95/16, Washington, D.C.

Thirsk, Wayne R. (1993), 'Recent Experience With Tax Reform in Developing Countries', in Ricardo Faini and Jaime de Melo (eds), *Fiscal Issues in Adjustment in Developing Countries*, New York: St. Martin's, pp. 169-195.

Tóka, Gábor (ed.) (1995), *The 1990 Election to the Hungarian National Assembly*, Berlin edition sigma.

Tommasi, Mariano (2004), 'Crisis, Political Institutions, and Policy Reform: The Good, the Bad, and the Ugly', in Bertil Tungodden, Nicholas Stern and Ivar Kolstadt (eds), *Toward Pro-Poor Policies: Aid, Institutions, and Globalization*, Washington, D.C.: World Bank, pp. 135-164.

Tommasi, Mariano and Andrés Velasco (1996), 'Where Are We in the Political Economy of Reform?', *Journal of Policy Reform*, **1** (2), pp. 187-238.

Tornell, Aaron (1995), 'Are Economic Crises Necessary for Trade Liberalization and Fiscal Reform? The Mexican Experience', in Rüdiger Dornbusch and Sebastian Edwards (eds), *Reform, Recovery, and Growth. Latin America and the Middle East*, Chicago, IL and London: University of Chicago Press, pp. 53-73.

Toye, John (1994), 'Comment', in John Williamson (ed.), *The Political Economy of Policy Reform*, Washington, D.C.: Institute for International Economics, pp. 35-43.

Treisman, Daniel S. (1998), 'Fighting Inflation in a Transitional Regime. Russia's Anomalous Stabilization', *World Politics*, **50** (2), pp. 235-265.

Tsebelis, George (2002), *Veto Players: How Political Institutions Work*, Princeton, N.J.: Princeton University Press.

Tullock, Gordon (1959), 'Some Problems of Majority Voting', *Journal of Political Economy*, **67**, pp. 571-579.

Turnovec, Frantisek (1997), 'Votes, Seats and Power: 1996 Parliamentary Election in the Czech Republic', *Communist and Post-Communist Studies*, **30** (3), pp. 289-305.

van de Walle, Nicolas (1999), 'Economic Reform in a Democratizing Africa', *Comparative Politics*, **32** (1), pp. 21-41.

van der Willigen, Tessa (1994), 'Some Lessons from Fiscal Reform in Czechoslovakia: An Extended Comment on Kamenickova et al.', in Kálmán Mizsei (ed.), *Developing Public Finance in Emerging Market Economies*, Prague et al.: Institute for EastWest Studies, pp. 165-182.

Varga, György (1989), 'The Reform of Taxation in Hungary', in Roger Clarke (ed.), *Hungary: The Second Decade of Economic Reform: Perspectives on Eastern Europe*, Harlow: Longman, pp. 29-45.

Večerník, Jiří (1996), *Markets and People. The Czech Reform Experiment in a Comparative Perspective*, Aldershot et al.: Avebury.

Velasco, Andrés (1999), 'A Model of Endogenous Fiscal Deficits and Delayed Fiscal Reform', in James M. Poterba and Jürgen von Hagen (eds), *Fiscal Institutions and Fiscal Performance*, Chicago, IL and London: University of Chicago Press, pp. 37-57.

Velasco, Andrés (2000), 'Debts and Deficits with Fragmented Fiscal Policymaking', *Journal of Public Economics*, **76** (1), pp. 105-125.

Vinton, Louisa (1993), 'Political Brinkmanship: Polish Coalition Wins Budget Vote', *RFE/RL Research Report*, **2** (11), pp. 7-15.

Vinton, Louisa (1994), 'Power Shifts in Poland's Ruling Coalition', *RFE/RL Research Report*, **3** (11), pp. 5-14.

von Hagen, Jürgen (2005), 'Fiscal Policy Challenges for European Union Acceding Countries', in Susan Schadler (ed.), *Euro Adoption in Central and Eastern Europe: Opportunities and Challenges*, Washington, D.C.: IMF, pp. 75-87.

von Hagen, Jürgen and Ian Harden (1996), 'Budget Processes and Commitment to Fiscal Discipline', IMF, Working Paper WP/96/78, Washington, D.C.

Wagener, Hans-Jürgen (1997), 'Transformation als historisches Phänomen', *Jahrbuch für Wirtschaftsgeschichte*, (2), pp. 179-191.

Wagener, Hans-Jürgen (1999), 'Social Security: A Second Phase Transformation Phenomenon?', in Katharina Müller, Andreas Ryll and Hans-Jürgen Wagener (eds), *Transformation of Social Security: Pensions in Central-Eastern Europe*, Heidelberg: Physica, pp. 13-30.

Wagner, Franz W. and Ekkehard Wenger (1996), 'Theoretische Konzeption und legislative Transformation eines marktwirtschaftlichen Steuersystems in der Republik Kroatien', in Dieter Sadowski, Hans Czap and Hartmut Wächter (eds), *Regulierung und Unternehmenspolitik*, Wiesbaden: Gabler, pp. 399-418.

Wagschal, Uwe (1996), *Staatsverschuldung. Ursachen im internationalen Vergleich*, Opladen: Leske + Budrich.

Wagschal, Uwe (1999a), 'Blockieren Vetospieler Steuerreformen?', *Politische Vierteljahresschrift*, **40** (4), pp. 628-640.

Wagschal, Uwe (1999b), 'Schranken staatlicher Steuerungspolitik: Warum Steuerreformen scheitern können', in Andreas Busch and Thomas Plümper (eds), *Nationaler Staat und internationale Wirtschaft*, Baden-Baden: Nomos, pp. 223-247.

Wanless, P.T. (1985), *Taxation in Centrally Planned Economies*, London and Sydney: Croom Helm.

Waterbury, John (1992), 'The Heart of the Matter? Public Enterprise and the Adjustment Process', in Stephan Haggard and Robert R. Kaufman (eds), *The Politics of Economic Adjustment*, Princeton, N.J.: Princeton University Press, pp. 182-220.

Wellisz, Stanisław, Henryk Kierzkowski and Marek Okolski (1993), 'The Polish Economy 1989-1991', in Henryk Kierzkowski, Marek Okolski, and Stanisław Wellisz (eds), *Stabilization and Structural Adjustment in Poland*, London and New York: Routledge, pp. 29-63.

WERI (1992), *Poland: International Economic Report 1991/92*, Warsaw.

WERI (1993), *Poland: International Economic Report 1992/93*, Warsaw.

WERI (1994), *Poland: International Economic Report 1993/94*, Warsaw.

Weyland, Kurt (1998a), 'The Political Fate of Market Reform in Latin America, Africa, and Eastern Europe', *International Studies Quarterly*, **42** (4), pp. 645-674.

Weyland, Kurt (1998b), 'Swallowing the Bitter Pill: Sources of Popular Support for Neoliberal Reform in Latin America', *Comparative Political Studies*, **31** (5), pp. 539-568.

Whitehead, Laurence (1996), 'Three International Dimensions of Democratization', in idem (ed.), *The International Dimensions of Democratization. Europe and the Americas*, Oxford and New York: Oxford University Press, pp. 3-25.

Wiesenthal, Helmut (1997), 'The Crisis of Holistic Policy Approaches and the Project of Controlled System Transformation', in Andreas Pickel and Helmut Wiesenthal, *The Grand Experiment. Debating Shock Therapy, Transition Theory, and the East German Experience*, Boulder, Col.: Westview, pp. 91-113.

Williamson, John (1990), 'What Washington Means By Policy Reform', in idem (ed.), *Latin American Adjustment. How Much Has Happened?*, Washington, D.C.: Institute for International Economics, pp. 7-20.

Williamson, John (1994), 'In Search of a Manual for Technopols', in John Williamson (ed.), *The Political Economy of Policy Reform*, Washington, D.C.: Institute for International Economics, pp. 11-28.

Williamson, John and Stephan Haggard (1994), 'The Political Conditions for Economic Reform', in John Williamson (ed.), *The Political Economy of Policy Reform*, Washington, D.C.: Institute for International Economics, pp. 527-596.

World Bank (1991), *Czechoslovakia: Transition to a Market Economy*, Washington, D.C.

World Bank (1994), *Poland: Policies for Growth with Equity*, Washington, D.C.

World Bank (1995), *Hungary: Structural Reforms for Sustainable Growth*, Washington, D.C.

World Bank (1997), *The State in a Changing World. World Development Report 1997*, Washington, D.C.

World Bank (1999), *Hungary: On the Road to European Union*, Washington, D.C.

Zamrazilova, Eva (1994), 'Tax Reform', in J. Krovák (ed.), *Current Economics and Politics of (ex-) Czechoslovakia*, Commack, N.Y.: Nova Science Publishers, pp. 177-213.

Zecchini, Salvatore (1995), 'The Role of International Financial Institutions in the Transition Process', *Journal of Comparative Economics*, **20** (1), pp. 116-138.

Zubek, Radosław (2001), 'A Core in Check: The Transformation of the Polish Core Executive', *Journal of European Public Policy*, **8** (6), pp. 911-932.

Zubek, Radosław (2006), 'Poland: Patterns of Domestic Leadership and EMU Convergence', in Kenneth Dyson (ed.), *Enlarging the Euro-Zone: The Euro and the Transformation of East-Central Europe*, Oxford: Oxford University Press, forthcoming.

Index

accountability 22
accounting practices 134, 140–41
administrative capacity 20
Alesina, Alberto 27–8, 30
allocative and distributive goals 37, 38, 46
Antall, József 71–6, 98, 99, 148, 153, 156
Ardagna, Silvia 30
authoritarian governments 21, 26

Balcerowicz, Leszek 15, 60–61, 83, 116, 123–5, 148, 150–51, 152, 156
bankruptcy 100, 151
Barro, Robert 57
Basinger, Scott 23–4
Bauc, Jarosław 116, 125, 126
Békesi, László 107, 108, 109, 152
Belka, Marek 116, 118, 121–2, 127–8, 151
Bielecki, Jan 82, 85
'big bang', in reform sequencing 28, 50
Bokros, Lajos 108, 109–11, 130, 152
Borowski, Marek 116, 118–19
Brusis, Martin 149
Bruszt, László 154
budget deficits *see* fiscal deficits
budgetary procedure reform 50
budgets 19–20, 36, 37
Bulgaria 41, 42, 44, 45
Buzek, Jerzy 116, 126

Campbell, John L. 150
capitalism 53, 152, 160, 161
central banks 36, 39, 41, 46, 131, 132, 133, 145
change teams
    Czech Republic 138–9
    Czechoslovakia 63, 66, 92–3, 148,

149, 152, 153, 154
    as fiscal reform variable 18–20, 32
    Hungary 74, 148, 152
    Poland 59, 61, 83, 148, 149, 152, 153, 154
    and windows of opportunity 152, 153
    see also reformers
Cimoszewicz, Włodzimierz 116, 118, 120, 121
coalition governments
    Czech Republic 135–7, 138–41
    Czechoslovakia 63–70
    and fiscal reform 14, 22, 23, 24
    Hungary 97, 98, 107–11, 128–33, 150
    Poland 82–3, 115–28
collective action, as barrier to fiscal reform 13
communist economic reform 36, 37, 38, 46–7
communist economic systems 35–6
communist fiscal systems
    fiscal reform issues 47–51
    qualitative features 36–40
    quantitative comparison of
        expenditure and revenue patterns 40–46
communist tax reform, compared to OECD countries 36
compensation 29, 69, 157
consultation, with interest groups in reform design 29–30
corporate income tax 43, 51, 105, 119, 121, 125, 140, 156
crises
    Czechoslovakia 122
    and executive authority 155
    as fiscal reform variable 15–17, 32, 33, 151
    Hungary 71–2